Toronto Medieval Texts and Translations 4

ICON AND LOGOS

SOURCES IN EIGHTH-CENTURY ICONOCLASM

Iconoclasm is a major topic in the history of the Byzantine Empire; its imposition was a traumatic event, with results lasting over a hundred years. The documents included in this volume, arising from the controversy surrounding the lifting of the ban on icons (sacred images), are of major significance, but until the publication of this book no English translation of the conciliar texts, in their entirety, has been available to scholars working in the field who do not easily read eighth-century Byzantine Greek.

Along with an introduction to the history of the controversy and the theology of the icons, Daniel J. Sahas presents a translation of conciliar texts on the icon debate: the Sixth Session of the iconophile Council of Nicea (787), in which the Definition of the iconoclastic Council of Constantinople (754) was read and refuted, point by point, and the Definition of the Council of Nicea (which became the Seventh Ecumenical Council of the Christian Church). The translation is carefully annotated to make the texts as useful as possible to their many modern audiences: scholars and students of medieval history, church history, Christian doctrine and thought, Byzantine studies, Eastern Christianity, and the history of art.

DANIEL J. SAHAS is a member of the Department of Religious Studies at the University of Waterloo, Waterloo, Ontario; the author of *John of Damascus on Islam: The 'Heresy of the Ishmaelites'* (Leiden, 1972) and of a number of articles on Byzantine-Muslim relations; and a member of the Executive Committee, and representative of the Greek Orthodox Diocese of Canada at the General Board, of the Canadian Council of Churches.

'John, insultingly called by them "Mansur," . . . after he took up his own cross as well as that of Christ, and followed Him, . . . sounded his trumpet from the East in favour of Christ and of those who are Christ's.'   (357B–C)

St John of Damascus. Fresco by Frankos Katelanos, 1548. Monastery of Barlaam, Meteora, Greece. By courtesy of *Sobornost/Eastern Churches Review*

DANIEL J. SAHAS

Icon and Logos:
Sources in Eighth-Century
Iconoclasm

An annotated translation of
the Sixth Session of the Seventh Ecumenical Council (Nicea, 787),
containing the Definition of the Council of Constantinople (754)
and its refutation,
and the Definition of the Seventh Ecumenical Council

UNIVERSITY OF TORONTO PRESS
Toronto Buffalo London

© University of Toronto Press 1986
Toronto Buffalo London
Printed in Canada
ISBN 0-8020-5645-8

Canadian Cataloguing in Publication Data

Council of Nicaea (2nd : 787)
Icon and logos: sources in eighth-century
iconoclasm

Bibliography: p.
Includes index.
ISBN 0-8020-5645-8

1. Iconoclasm - History - Sources. 2. Icons -
Cult - Controversial literature. 3. Orthodox
Eastern Church and art - History - Sources.
I. Sahas, Daniel J. (Daniel John), 1940-
II. Title.

BR240.C68 1986   246'.53   C85-099750-X

This book has been published with the help of a grant from the Canadian Fed-
eration for the Humanities, using funds provided by the Social Sciences and
Humanities Research Council of Canada, and a grant from the Andrew W.
Mellon Foundation to the University of Toronto Press.

To my father and mother
as an expression of profound gratitude,
διά τό 'κατ' εἰκόνα'

Οὐ προσκυνῶ τῇ κτίσει παρά τόν κτίσαντα,
ἀλλά προσκυνῶ τόν κτίστην κτισθέντα τό κατ᾽ ἐμέ
καί εἰς κτίσιν ἀταπεινώτως καί ἀκαθαιρέτως κατεληλυθότα,
ἵνα τήν ἐμήν δοξάσῃ φύσιν
καί θείας κοινωνόν ἐπεργάσηται φύσεως

John of Damascus, *Against those who defame the holy icons*, Oration I:4

Contents

'Which of the divine Fathers has declared that the art of the painters is incompatible with this very crucial doctrine of our salvation, that is, the dispensation of Christ?' (241A)

Christ, *Hē Chōra tōn Zōnton* (The Place of the Living). Mosaic in the narthex over the entrance to the nave, before 1335. Monastery of Chora (Kariye Djami), Istanbul, Turkey. Photograph by the author

Preface

The history, the role, and the meaning of the icon in the Christian Church are little known and, as a result, much misunderstood. The student of the history of the Christian Church will not hear much during the course of his studies about the iconoclastic controversies of the eighth and ninth centuries, or about the Seventh Ecumenical Council. The student of the history of Christian thought will hear little about the theology of the icon and its organic connection with the Christological doctrine. The student of Christian art will hear even less about the theological connotations of Byzantine iconography and the forms it uses to articulate the dogma in colours. The student of the history of religions will perhaps never hear at all about some of the Jewish, Christian, and Islamic arguments in opposition to icon-making; or about the Jewish and Islamic influences on Christian iconoclasm; or about some of the intricate phenomenological and theological affinities between the Mu^{c}tazilite and the iconoclastic movements. For the student of church history the texts translated here are significant because they constitute part of the acts of a council of the Church acclaimed by the as yet undivided Christendom as Ecumenical (in recognition that this council expressed the faith of the Church in its fullness). These texts also contain the Definition of the iconoclastic Council of 754, in all probability in its authentic form.

Given the fact that an ecumenical council did not produce or invent doctrines of its own, and in a vacuum, but rather confirmed and defined *quod ubique, quod semper, quod ab omnibus creditum est,*[1] and, in doing so, reviewed and reaffirmed the definitions of previous ecumenical councils,

---

1 Vincent of Lerins, *Commonitorium, primum,* PL 50:640.

these texts constitute source materials for a concise view of the development and definition of Christian thought up to the last part of the eighth century. Even the student of the history of religions will find these texts useful since the theology and art of the icons raise fundamental questions about the nature of God, his attributes, and revelation, questions which are at the heart of monotheistic theology. For the student of the Orthodox Church these texts, and especially the material implied between the lines, offer a characteristic glimpse into the theological, spiritual, and cultural fabric of the Church. And as the icon constitutes the culmination of the Christological faith of the Church, with all its ramifications for the Trinitarian theology, and for the ecclesiology, anthropology, and soteriology of the Church, the icon itself is a characteristic way of discovering the spirit of Eastern Orthodoxy. From this point of view the attempt of a non-Orthodox scholar like Ernst Benz[2] to introduce his readers to the Orthodox Church through a chapter on the icons is successful and very perceptive. Finally, as the Orthodox Church is preparing for her Pan-Orthodox Council,[3] these texts provide a timely reminder of and a link with the Church's conciliar ecumenical tradition. One may wish that, as the Church of the past used colours, brushes, wax, boards, and walls – the humble elements of creation – to broaden and illuminate the mystery of the Incarnation, the contemporary Church may turn to the issues and the challenges of our present-day world – the temporal and frustrating consequences of a complex society – to state and elucidate the uniqueness of the mystical Body of Christ in space and time.

But the primary purpose of this book lies elsewhere. Iconoclastic texts have not survived. A reconstruction of the theses of the iconoclasts can be attempted primarily through the writings of those who defended the icons. The Acts of the Seventh Ecumenical Council (Nicea, 787) are the best source of information on the subject. In its Sixth Act, or Session (4 October 787), the participants heard what may be

---

2 Benz, *The Eastern Orthodox Church* (1963).
3 On this Pan-Orthodox Council see the following: Orthodox Centre of the Ecumenical Patriarchate, *Towards the Great Council. Introductory Reports of the Interorthodox Commission in Preparation for the Next Great and Holy Council of the Orthodox Church* (London, 1972); the special series *Synodika* of the Orthodox Centre of the Ecumenical Patriarchate (Chambésy-Geneva, 1976–); the special issue of *The Greek Orthodox Theological Review* 24(Summer/Fall 1979) and below, Introduction, n 203; Panagopoulos, 'The Orthodox Church Prepares for the Council'; Bria, 'L'Espoir du Grand Synode orthodoxe.'

considered the *Horos*, or Definition, of the iconoclastic Council of Constantinople (754) along with a refutation of each of its main points. They then proceeded to articulate in a new Definition the Church's theology of the icon. The three texts presented here in translation are from the edition of Giovanni Domenico Mansi.[4] These texts are significant in two important ways. First, granted that the Sixth Act contains the authentic version of the *Horos* of the iconoclastic Council of 754, this is the only substantial iconoclastic document we possess. Second, the juxtaposition of the arguments of the iconoclastic *Horos* and its Refutation, item by item, provides a concise summary of the theses of both sides of the argument. The fact that these are contemporary texts, vested with the authority of two general councils, one of which has been acclaimed Ecumenical, adds to the importance of the texts.

It is hoped that this translation will serve an additional purpose for members of the educated public, students, and scholars who are not able to use the source materials in this area in their original language. The notes attempt to make the reading of the texts more informative and to put them into context. An interest in the source materials on iconoclasm has been demonstrated by the publication of a small anthology entitled *Textus byzantinos ad iconomachiam pertinentes. In usum academicum*, edited by Herman Hennephof. However, this collection, in spite of its usefulness, is sketchy, the pertinent texts are inexcusably fragmented, and the selection betrays the sympathies of its editor in favour of the iconoclastic theology, thus rendering the claim of its subtitle, *In usum academicum*, meaningless. For example, although Hennephof has reproduced the entire text of the *Horos* of the iconoclastic Council of 754 (pp 61–78), he gives no examples from either the Refutation or the *Horos* of the Council of 787. This seems to be in agreement with Hennephof's own view that, although 'The Iconoclastic movement ... is generally considered a dark age in the history of Byzantium,' 'it might nevertheless be interesting to investigate the possibility that the darkness was due not to the Iconoclasts but to their opponents' (p vii).

Small portions of the texts presented in this book have appeared in translation in other collections and writings:
1 In the Select Library of the Nicene and Post-Nicene Fathers, vol XIV, 2nd series, pp 543–546.
2 Hefele in his work on the councils, *A History of the Councils of the Church*, vol V (1896), pp 309–315, gives in translation the main points

4 *Sacrorum Conciliorum nova et amplissima Collectio*, vol XIII (Florence, 1867).

of the *Horos* of the iconoclastic Council of 754, exclusively. This rendering is a paraphrase with a partial translation of the original. Hefele also gives in paraphrase the main points of the *Horos* of the Council of 787 (pp 373–376).

3 Mango, *The Art of the Byzantine Empire 312–1453. Sources and Documents*, has translated the following portions from the Sixth Act of the Council of 787 (based on Mansi's edition):
   (a) from the iconoclastic *Horos* (754): 240C, 241E, 244D, 245D, 248E, 256A, 257E–260A, 268B–C, 277C–E, 328C, 329D, 332B, and 332D (pp 165–168);
   (b) from the Refutation of the *Horos* by the Seventh Ecumenical Council (787): 252B–D (pp 172–173) and 356A–B (p 154).

4 Geischer's collection of texts, *Der byzantinische Bilderstreit. Texte zur Kirchen und Theologiegeschichte*, vol 9 (1968), has included sections from the *Horos* of the Council of 754, as well as the *Horos* of the Council of 815, but nothing from the Seventh Ecumenical Council of 787.

It is obvious that the second Council of Nicea (787) has often been ignored, although it is the council that most fully countered iconoclastic theology and promulgated a definition of the icons, and although this is the council that was acclaimed Ecumenical!

The scholarly literature on this subject, covering the history of iconoclasm, the theological issues of the debate at the time and later, the role of the icon in the spiritual experience of the Christian East, as well as the art of the icon and its interpretation – this is indeed an impressive and perhaps an unmanageable field for one person to study. I pretend no special expertise or originality on the subject but unabashedly repeat with John of Damascus: 'I will say nothing of my own.'[5]

The introduction aims at bringing together the various issues and noting some of the most important works on the subject for the sake of the student of the icon and of iconoclasm, and for the reader who wants to make fuller use of the particular texts offered here in translation. Books and articles are cited in the notes by author and short title alone. For full bibliographical data the reader should consult the Bibliography, pp 195–204. The Old Testament quotations are from the Septuagint version which the Christian East still uses and which the Seventh Ecumenical Council has quoted. The English version of the Septuagint is from *The Septuagint Version of the Old Testament with an English Translation* (Grand

5 Prologue to the *Fount of Knowledge*, Kotter, I, 53, line 60 (PG 94:525A).

Rapids, Mich., 1975), unless otherwise indicated. The New Testament quotations are from the *Revised Standard Version. An Ecumenical Edition* (New York, 1973), but the RSV rendering is at times highly questionable. In such instances I have given my own translation of the original with the corresponding rendering of the RSV for comparison. In the translation of the texts quotations from the Bible are printed in italic type.

References to patristic literature are generally, for reasons of convenience, to Migne's collection, *Patrologiae cursus completus. Series Latina* (abbreviated PL) and *Series Graeca* (abbreviated PG), although reference is made to critical editions whenever they are available. Matters of authenticity or authorship are not discussed or decided upon here. The use of and the information given about patristic texts in this context must in itself be of interest to historians of Christian literature and thought.

Bringing eighth-century Byzantine texts to a twentieth-century Western reader is an arduous task. When the text is a piece of Byzantine controversial literature, the product of a passionate era on a passionate issue, employing extravagant, derogatory, and at times highly intricate and sophisticated theological language, there is an additional burden for the translator. I have tried to maintain the style of the language of the original as much as possible. Often, however, I have had to break extremely long and complicated sentences into shorter units in order to make them manageable and comprehensible.

The reader must bear at times with harsh expressions, name-calling, and linguistic idiosyncracies which are persistently repeated throughout the arguments. Generally I have chosen the easiest words available in my vocabulary in order to make the reading smoother. Yet I know that I have not succeeded in all instances; often I have failed to display the passion and the forcefulness of expression of the composers of the texts. But what translation is not an adulteration of the original? Retelling a theological argument thirteen centuries later, translating it from one language, culture, and theological frame of mind to another, is a kind of reinterpretation of the original. This is a shortcoming of which I am fully aware and for which I accept responsibility. As a Chinese aphorism has it: 'To err by a hair's breadth is to miss by a thousand miles.' But another aphorism, 'A picture is worth a thousand words,' is also attributed to the Chinese. The two, I think, go together. Perhaps where the idea being translated – and for that matter any verbal communication – becomes too delicate or too precarious for one to put it into words, then an image can take its place and allow man to move ahead 'a thousand miles.' Isn't that precisely what the Christian East did when it employed the icon side by side with the written and the spoken word?

The idea and the encouragement for the translation of these texts on icons belongs to the late Professor Ford Lewis Battles, a well-known scholar and a translator of Calvin! A number of people, with their skills and talent, have contributed to the completion of this work, typing drafts and making corrections. I would like to acknowledge particularly the kind and able help of Bonnie Quecke, Kathy Chambré, and Linda Daniel. Prudence Tracy and Joan A. Bulger of the University of Toronto Press were extremely sensitive and meticulous in editing the book for the press. Thanks are also due to friends and staff at St Michael's College and at the Pontifical Institute of Mediaeval Studies in Toronto for the gracious way in which they made available to me their facilities and their excellent library collections. I am grateful to the Fathers and His Eminence Archbishop Damianos of Sinai for contributing to this book illustrations of some icons from the archives of the historic Monastery of St Catherine – a testimony to their unfailing commitment to and watchfulness of the past; and also to Father Theodore Koufos, a Byzantine iconographer from Toronto, for his contribution of some of his own works – a testimony that Byzantine iconography is a living tradition in North America today! A special acknowledgment is due to my colleague Professor John North of the Department of English at the University of Waterloo for reading the translation and for his diligent efforts to lead me through the intricacies of the English language and its idiom. Although, in faithfulness to the text and its character, I was unable to comply with all his suggestions, nevertheless because of his help the translation contains fewer awkward expressions than it would otherwise have done. However, as the icon is a subject that is not exhausted by terminological definitions and linguistic expressions, I would invite the reader, as he studies the texts, to start observing and acquiring the feeling of the Byzantine icon. Then, where a word has erred by a hair's breadth, one may gain a thousand words!

DANIEL J. SAHAS
Waterloo, Ontario
13 October 1985,
Sunday of the Fathers of the Seventh Ecumenical Council

'Remembrance of the holy Seventh Council of the three hundred-and-sixty-six holy Fathers.' Miniature from the *Menologion* of Basil II. Bibliotheca Apostolica Vaticana, Vat. gr. 1613, fol. 108. By courtesy of Foto Bibliotheca Vaticana

'The making of icons is not an invention of the painters but an accepted institution and tradition of the catholic Church; and that which excels in antiquity is worthy of respect.' (252B)

Graves of martyrs, paintings, and symbols in the catacomb of St Callistus, Rome. Photograph by the author

'That which the narrative declares in writing is the same as that which the icon does in colours.' (232C)

The birth of the Forerunner. Portable icon from the iconostasion of St John's Greek Orthodox Church, Scarborough, Ontario. Painted by Theodore Koufos, 1983

'In some venerable icons, and pointed to by the finger of the Forerunner, there is the drawing of a lamb, which has been received as the figure of grace, making what is for us the true Lamb – Christ our God . . .' (Eighty-Second Canon of the Sixth Ecumenical Council, 680/1: 220C–D)

St John the Forerunner. Portable icon from the iconostasion of St John's Greek Orthodox Church, Scarborough, Ontario. Painted by Theodore Koufos, 1983

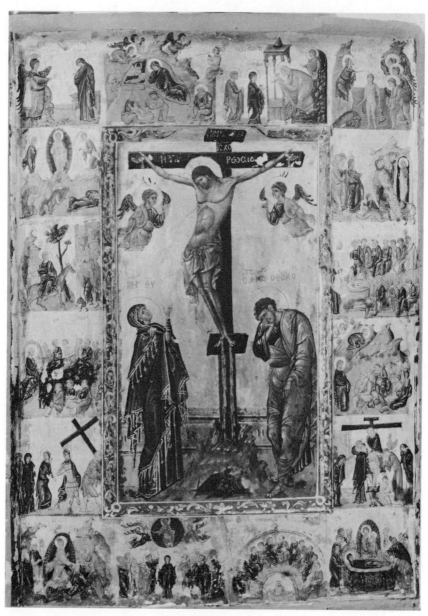

'They [the iconoclasts] ought to feel ashamed before the multitude of . . . all those who have been Christians since the gospel was first proclaimed, for rejecting and debasing the recounting of the gospel through painting.' (217c)

Crucifixion, surrounded by sixteen biblical scenes. Portable icon, twelfth century. By courtesy of St Catherine's monastery, Sinai

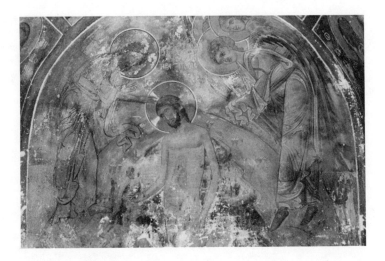

'. . . by making an icon of Christ in his human form one does not express the belief that this is a fourth person [in the Trinity], but rather confesses that God the Word became man truly, not in conjecture.' (344E)

The Baptism of Christ. Fresco, 1192. Church of the Virgin of Araka near Lagoudhera, Cyprus. Photograph by the author

'Great, therefore, is the magnitude of [man's] dignity since, although earth-born, he has been honoured with the icon of God.' (213E)

Resurrection. Mosaic, fourteenth century. Church of the Holy Apostles, Thessaloniki, Greece

'[Christ] did not say "Take; eat the icon of my body" . . . [but] *"This is my body which is broken for you"* . . . [and] *"This cup is the new covenant in my blood."* . . . Thus, nowhere did either the Lord, or the Apostles, or the Fathers call the bloodless sacrifice, offered through the priest, an "icon," but rather "this very body" and "this very blood".' (265A–B)

Top: Communion of the bread. (*Metādhosis*). *Bottom:* Communion of the cup (*He Metālepsis*). Frescoes, twelfth century. Ayios Neophytos hermitage (Englistra), Paphos, Cyprus. Photographs by the author

'Thus, the . . . sons of the adorned bride of Christ, . . . when through the sense of sight they see the venerable icon of Christ or of the holy Theotokos . . . or the icons of the angels and of all the saints, are sanctified, and they set their mind to the remembrance of them.'   (249D–E)

Theotokos with saints and angels. Encaustic icon, fifth century. By courtesy of St Catherine's monastery, Sinai

'. . . as by reading in books narratives about saints we are reminded of their zeal, so it is with the iconographic representations. Looking at their sufferings, we come to remember their bravery and their life inspired by God.'   (348C–D)

Detail of a calendar icon for the month of December. Portable icon, twelfth century. By courtesy of St Catherine's monastery, Sinai

'She [the Church] catches the one who has spent his life in luxury and who is dressed in soft clothes, . . . [and] she shows Basil the Great, and a crowd of ascetics and monks with emaciated bodies.'   (360D–E)

Athonite Fathers. Fresco from the exterior of the Church of Protaton, thirteenth century. Karyes, Mount Athos. Photograph by the author

'No one, of course, has thought to reproduce with colours his divinity, for *No One*, it says, · *has ever seen God*. He is uncircumscribable, invisible, and incomprehensible, although circumscribable according to his humanity.' (244A–B)

Deisis (Supplication). Mosaic, thirteenth century. St Sophia, Istanbul, Turkey. Photograph by the author

'The name "Christ" implies two natures, the one being visible and the other invisible. Thus this Christ, while visible to men by means of the curtain, that is his flesh, made the divine nature . . . manifest through signs.' (340D)

Iconostasion. Holy Trinity Greek Orthodox Church, Indianapolis, Indiana. Photograph by the author.

ICON AND LOGOS

'Thus, as when we receive the sound of the reading with our ears, we transmit it to our mind, so by looking with our eyes at the painted icons, we are enlightened in our mind. Through two things following each other, that is, by reading and also by seeing the reproduction of the painting, we learn the same thing, that is, how to recall what has taken place.' (220E)

Illuminated manuscript of the beginning of the Gospel according to Luke, with the icon of the Evangelist. Twelfth century. By courtesy of St Catherine's monastery, Sinai

Introduction

Today there is renewed interest in the study of the icon[1] as a result of a greater awareness of Eastern Christianity and its heritage, the rising profile of Orthodoxy in the West, and a reappreciation of its sources by the Orthodox people themselves.[2] With the growth of Byzantine studies the bibliography on the history, the art, and the theology of the icon has been constantly growing.[3] Exhibitions[4] are bringing the

1 See, for example, *Iconoclasm*; and also Kirschbaum, *Lexikon der christlichen Ikonographie*.
2 'He Orthodôxos Monê tou Deir-el-Harf, kêntron anaviôseos tes eikonographîas eis ton Lîvanon,' *Episkepsis*. 3 (1972) 8–9. See also Kalokyris, *The Essence of Orthodox Iconography*, which is directed primarily to Orthodox people in an effort to make them aware of the distinct character of Orthodox iconography. The writings and the iconographic work of Kontoglou and his school are a major source of self-awareness in Greece today.
3 See, for example, some recent illustrated collections and studies such as Beckwith, *Early Christian and Byzantine Art*; Gerhard, *The World of Icons*; the several works by André Grabar, *Byzantine Painting, Byzantium. From the Death of Theodosius to the Rise of Islam, Byzantium. Byzantine Art in the Middle Ages, L'Art paléochrétien et l'art byzantin, L'Art du Moyen Age en Occident*; Kitzinger, *The Art of Byzantium and the Mediaeval West*, and also his *Byzantine Art in the Making*; Onasch, *Russian Icons*; Papageorgiou, *Icons of Cyprus*; the several works of David Talbot Rice, *Byzantine Art, Art of the Byzantine Era, The Appreciation of Byzantine Art, Byzantine Painting. The Last Phase*; David and Tamara Talbot Rice, *Icons and Their Dating* (on the many studies of Byzantine art and iconography connected with the name of David Talbot Rice see Henderson, 'The Published Works of David Talbot Rice'; Tamara Talbot Rice, *Russian Icons*; Schiller, *Iconography of Christian Art*; Schug-Wille, *Art of the Byzantine World*; Walter, *Studies in Byzantine Iconography*, and also his *Art and Ritual of the Byzantine Church*; Weitzmann, *Icons from South Eastern Europe and Sinai*, and also his *The Icon. Holy Images Sixth to Fourteenth Century*; Weitzmann, Chatzidakis, and Radojcic, *Icons*; also Weitzmann, et al, *The Icon*.
4 *Masterpieces of Byzantine Art*, sponsored by the Edinburgh Festival Society in association with the Royal Scottish Museum and the Victoria and Albert Museum; *Byzantine Art*.

Byzantine icon to the modern viewer – although an Orthodox would be most reluctant to accept the notion that the icon disseminates all its dynamic in an exhibition hall divorced from its proper liturgical and iconographic context. Old icons and iconographies are being restored throughout the Orthodox world. Byzantine churches with icons are being reconstructed or renovated.[5] Old monasteries with an abundance of Byzantine icons are persistently visited by scholars and other interested people on account of their Byzantine treasures.[6] Even in communist Russia a massive campaign has been under way to recover whatever icons survived the destruction of the Bolshevik revolution, albeit for a different purpose, to preserve Russia's cultural past.[7]

It seems that in the late twentieth century we are more eager and better equipped to understand and appreciate the icon. In an age of rationalism and industrial domination there is an underlying quest for a language which includes symbolism and spiritual categories. Communication and language are becoming more and more allusive, condensed, multi-media, using symbolism, imagery, and figures of speech and form. The icon, without being sensational, without competing with any other medium of communication, but merely because of its antinomical nature and its otherworldliness, today has the chance to become a means of theological reflection and expression.[8] However, because

---

An European Art, ninth exhibition held under the auspices of the Council of Europe, esp. Part II, pp 227–290; 'Exhibition of Feast Day Icons,' London, November 1973–January 1974. On this subject see Eastern Churches Review 6 (1974) 90–91; Temple Gallery, Masterpieces of Byzantine and Russian Icon Painting. 12th–16th Century, and 'Icons at the Temple Gallery'; Bank, Byzantine Art in the Collection of Soviet Museums; Treasures from the Kremlin; Splendeur de Byzance.

5 For example, see Underwood, 'First Preliminary Report on the Restoration of the Frescoes in the Kariye Camii at Istanbul'; his major work The Kariye Djami; and his 'The Deisis Mosaic in the Kahrie Cami at Istanbul.' See also Belting, Mango, and Mouriki, The Mosaics and Frescoes of St. Mary Pammakaristos (Fethiye Camii) at Istanbul.

6 The monastery of St Catherine in Sinai is still one of the most significant of places because of its valuable collection of old icons. See Forsyth and Weitzmann, The Monastery of Saint Catherine at Mount Sinai; and also Weitzmann, The Monastery of St. Catherine at Mount Sinai. The Icons.

7 Soloukhin, Searching for Icons in Russia. On the theology of the icon and its place in Russian culture see Trubetskoi, Icons. Theology in Color. See also Novgorod Icons. 12th–17th Century.

8 Within the Orthodox Church, and especially in the monasteries, iconography is still an endeavour of spirituality. This tradition is now shared by non-Orthodox as well, as the example of John Walstead, a monk of the Episcopal Order of the Holy Cross (Mount Calvary Retreat House, California) and a mature Byzantine iconographer, indicates.

of the perfection of the art of the photograph, something which the icon is not, the icon is still bound to be seen condescendingly or with suspicion. Its understanding requires a certain degree of theological sensitivity and awareness, qualities which are not the priorities of today. The icon in its simplicity, humility, mysticism, antinomy, and metaphysical beauty contains ingredients which provoke an examination of Christianity in its essentials.

SOME THEOLOGICAL IMPLICATIONS OF THE ICON

The icon is not a form of visual and aesthetic *art* as such; it is, primarily, an expression of the theological experience and faith of the Church, and a statement of it. This is how it has been treated from the earliest days by the Church.[9] From its beginnings Christianity claimed 'catholicity,' that is, wholeness, and fostered comprehensiveness. It never lacked expression. Spontaneity and freedom were always characteristics of the Christian Church. Monasticism, for example, or symbolism, music, architecture, and worship must be seen as innovating and, in some cases, radical ways of articulating the Christian faith and ethos at the same time that they are articulated in words. All these expressions are indicative of the spirit of freedom which, according to the belief of the Christian community, has burst upon the world with the incarnation of the Word of God and his victory over death. That event ushered in the beginning of a 'new creation': 'Behold, everything is new,' exclaimed Paul.[10]

The icon cannot be understood apart from the wider cultural and theological context to which it belongs. This context includes the character of the early Christian community, the essential distinctiveness of Christian theology from other perceptions of God in terms of a dynamic monarchianism, the value that Christianity bestows on man and on the material creation, the distinct faith in the incarnation of God and man's redemption and participation in the divine life, the theology of the Church in terms of her soteriological nature and liturgical character – to mention only a few aspects of this context. Apart from this theological context, or independent of any aspect of it, the icon becomes another painting, and obscure, unintelligible, or naïve, for that matter. A familiarity with the essentials of Christian theology and a willingness to draw from and refer to them are prerequisites for under-

9 See Campenhausen, 'The Theological Problem of Images in the Early Church.'
10 2 Cor. 5:17.

standing the icon as a phenomenon. The reverse is also true. The icon allows one who has a theological and contemplative disposition to see the basic theological principles of Christianity in relief or, in fact, in colour. I have attempted to summarize some of these principles under four headings, drawing from the ideas found in our texts.[11]

1 / The icon is a demonstration of the Christian belief in the *personal* character of God. Although the essence of God is absolutely unique and as such transcendent, unknown, and incomprehensible, God in the Christian tradition is neither abstract nor detached from and unrelated to the human reality. He *relates* Himself to man and to the world. In the Old Testament He relates Himself *through* history, and He speaks *through* events, signs, commandments, and prophets, spokesmen of his covenant. In the New Testament God manifests Himself *in person*. His own Lôgos, that is his own creative-expressive being,[12] 'became flesh and dwelt among us; and we saw His glory, glory as of an only-begotten One from the Father, full of grace and truth.'[13] Thus, on account of the incarnation, which is the only theological justification of the icon, God becomes 'known.'[14] By depicting God the Word in so far as He became flesh, the icon confirms the Christian belief in the incarnation, as well as in the personal character of the

11 There are many studies on the theology of the icon. A few titles are mentioned here for their continuing interest: Pelican, *The Spirit of Eastern Christendom*, pp 91–133; Ouspensky, *Theology of the Icon*, esp pp 179–229; Ouspensky and Lossky, *The Meaning of Icons*; Evdokimoff, *L'Art de l'icône. Théologie de beauté*; Sendler, *L'Icône*; Trubetskoi, *Icons. Theology in Color*; Ware, 'The Theology of the Icon'; Barnard, 'The Theology of Images'; Cavarnos, *Orthodox Iconography*; Nellas, 'Théologie de l'image'; The whole of issue no. 88 of *Contacts*, 26 (1974), is dedicated to 'Approches d'une théologie de l'Icône'; see also Scouteris, 'Never as gods: Icons and Their Veneration'.

12 It is important to remember here that the Greek word *Lôgos*, which the author of the fourth gospel uses, means 'logic,' 'wisdom,' 'intellect,' *as well as* 'word,' 'utterance,' 'speech.' Thus the Word, through whom God created the world by uttering his will and command (see Gen. 1), this pre-eternal wisdom and power of his, in time takes up flesh and is born as a man. This is the gist of the Christian doctrine of the incarnation.

13 John 1:14.

14 John of Damascus prefaces his discussion of the holy Trinity with a chain of apophatic (or 'negative') adjectives stressing the unknowability of the essence of God, and concluding with the affirmation that this 'one God, one beginning without beginning ... uncircumscribable ... non-composite ... a power known by no measure whatever ... *is known* and worshipped in three perfect hypostases by one worship': *Expositio Fidei* [*An Accurate Exposition of the Orthodox Faith*], Kotter, *Die Schriften des Johannes von Damaskos*, II, 18–19 (PG 94:808–809).

Godhead: as 'Father' who originates, as 'Son' who is born and redeems, and as holy 'Spirit' who animates, directs, preserves, purifies and guards man's knowledge of God, 'in so far as it is accessible to the human nature.'[15]

2 / The icon is a consequence and a culmination of the Christological definition. The Christological faith found its final cosmic meaning in the Seventh Ecumenical Council.[16] If in Christ we have the pre-eternal Word of God in whom 'the whole fullness of deity dwells bodily,'[17] this means that in one and the same person we have the fullness of the divine and the human natures, 'without confusion, without change, without division, without separation.'[18] Thus the event of the icon proclaims the mystery of the incarnation and strikes the 'orthodox,'[19] that is the upright, faith of the Church, in a definite, 'colourful,' and apologetic way: first, against Docetism, as it depicts Christ as a *real* human person with all his human characteristics, and not in conjecture;[20] second, against Nestorianism, as it depicts Christ in a human form, although venerated in the one icon, not as a 'mere' (*psilôs*) human being, but as *one person*, hypostatically united with the divinity, two natures depictable in one person; third, against Monophysitism, as it depicts the human nature of Christ in flesh, united with but not swallowed or absorbed by the divine nature, which cannot be depicted.

3 / The icon is an affirmation of the dignity of the human nature. God the Word assumed up to Himself that which was 'fallen,' which, although stained and distorted, neither was destroyed nor vanished. Even after its fall human nature did not become abhorent, but remained precious in the eyes of God. With the fall man's characteristic 'according to the image' of God (*kat' eikôna*) was stained or darkened. That rendered man incapable of attaining the characteristic 'according to the likeness' of God for which he was created. It is this disabled human nature

15 St John Damascene (John of Damascus), *Barlaam and Ioasaph*, VIII, 60, in Loeb Classical Library (Cambridge, Mass: Harvard University Press, 1914; 1962), p 102.
16 Schmemann, *The Historical Road of Eastern Orthodoxy*, p 207.
17 Col. 2:9.
18 From the Definition of the Council of Chalcedon (451): in Mansi, *Sacrorum consiliorum nova et amplissima Collectio*, VII, 116f. Subsequent references to this collection will cite only the editor's name and the volume and page numbers.
19 *isôrropon*: see below, 208B and n 12.
20 John of Damascus, in another context, defines the icon (of a man) in terms of its cause, the real man himself: Kotter, I 67, lines 113–114 (PG 94:548).

that God the Word assumed up to Himself.[21] By its union with the divine, human nature was 're-created,' brought back to its course and restored to its primordial beauty,[22] and thus reconciled with God.[23] The icon affirms the ontological dignity of the human nature and its affiliation with God on account of the one person of Christ, in whom a new man was made 'in the place of the two.'[24] The icon is a pointer to the re-created, or actually transfigured, human nature by the means of its association with the divine in the person of Christ. Thus, holiness becomes not an abstract and alien category but a tangible and accessible goal for every human being who is willing to denounce the ways of fallen man and put on Christ, 'the new man, created after the likeness of God in true righteousness and holiness.'[25] Thence an icon is not only the icon of Christ vested in humanity but also the icon of ordinary men vested in the gown of holiness. The icon is a reminder of and a pointer to holiness. As such it is venerable, and the honour that one pays to the icon is conveyed to the prototype.[26]

4 / The icon points to the value of the material creation. With the incarnation of the Logos not only man but also the entire creation shares in the event of the re-creation. The new Adam is in no tension with the material creation. He sees matter not as an expression or a trap of evil but as an act of divine love and providence, and as an instrument of doing good. He is able to see the material creation without the fear and suspicion of fallen man. He is free from the fear of deception and able to see things in their simplicity and unity. Christianity and idolatry are seen by the Fathers of the Seventh Ecumenical Council as mutually exclusive. The icon is a manifestation of the faith that God 'liberated us from the cunning of the devil.'[27] 'Born anew ... to an inheritance

21 A very concise word which the following texts and the patristic literature in general use is *to prôslemma*, literally 'that which was assumed (by God the Word) in addition to that which He himself is' (below, 217A).

22 The text of the funeral service of the Orthodox Church speaks eloquently of man's stained glory: 'I am an icon of the unutterable glory of Yours, even though I bear the stains of my mistakes'; and of his quest to attain the likeness of God: 'bring me back to the state of your likeness, thus reforming my primordial beauty.'

23 See Eph. 2:16.

24 Eph. 2:15.

25 Eph. 4:24.

26 St Basil's phrase, 'the honour offered to the icon is conveyed to the prototype' (*On the Holy Trinity*, 18, 45), is standardly used to distinguish both an idol from an icon and the worship of God from the veneration or honour offered to an icon.

27 See below, 216A, 216C–E, and many other similar expressions. This particular phrasing may be intentional. As McHugh writes in 'The Demonology of Saint Ambrose,' 209:

which is imperishable, undefiled, and unfading,'[28] and preoccupied with holiness and an eschatological vision of the Kingdom, the new Adam sees and uses all forms of material substance (even though matter in itself is perishable, defilable, and fading) as a means of expressing and proclaiming sacred realities which are incorruptible and eternal. The new man employs the material creation in order to explore and manifest the divine mystery and glory.[29] Thus, the brush, the colour, the wood, the wax, the board, and the wall become instruments to proclaim the liberation of man and of all creation from the usurper and the pangs of death. A man who shares in the reality of the new creation shares also in the foretaste of the Kingdom of God, here and now. The Byzantine icon makes this point eloquently by depicting holy persons and scenes against a golden-plated or golden-painted background. Thus the icon serves as a window through which man gains a glimpse, carnal and figurative though it may be, of the Kingdom, and a sense of the divine bliss and incorruptibility of the life to come.

THE ICON AS A LITURGICAL ACT OF THE CHURCH

The Church is not a thing but a living reality. It is not an option either, but an article of the Christian faith. 'I believe in one, holy, catholic and apostolic Church,' proclaims the Nicene-Constantinopolitan Creed. The Church is the mystical Body of Christ[30] and his 'bride,'[31] 'the tent of God with men,'[32] the reality of a continuous interaction of the divine

'Orthodox Hebrew belief identified demons with pagan gods [Deut. 32,17; Ps. 105(106),36f]; Paul makes reference to the same concept (1 Cor. 10,20f.; see Apoc. 9,20). It is the purpose of the early apologists to strengthen such identification as a warning against idolatry; the argument appears in one form or another in Justin Martyr, Origen, Tertullian and Minucius Felix among others.' The reasoning of the Fathers of the Council of 787 is simple: if Christ is the true God, his coming abolished all false deities and demons and certainly their idols. Thus, it is impossible for a Christian to be an idolater. The one is mutually exclusive of the other. The claim, therefore, that the icon of Christ is an idol is absurd. See also Stuart, Ikons, pp 38–39.

28 1 Peter 1:3-4.
29 See Ware, 'The Value of the Material Creation,' esp. pp 163–164. According to Stuart: 'The Byzantine world-view stresses the concept of unity and total synthesis – to the Byzantine all things in the universe are related, and all the parts are interdependent on the whole. God cannot be separated from the universe nor matter from spirit' (Ikons, p 37). See also André Grabar, Les Voies de la création en iconographie chrétienne.
30 Eph. 1:23; Col. 1:24.
31 See also below, 229B–C.
32 Rev. 21:3.

with the human, of the invisible with the visible, of the spiritual with the material, of the eternal with the temporal, of the incorruptible with the corruptible. The Church as a Body is a living organism that functions. The Church, through the use of historical-material elements, prepares the historical-eschatological community for its transhistorical destiny.[33] This is the 'liturgy,' the function as such of the Church. In worship, the liturgy *par excellence* of the Church, not only speech but also movement, music, architecture, and colour – the entire material creation – have a part. The Orthodox worship activates and synthesizes all these elements, thus enabling the worshipper 'to participate actively with all his senses within a framework which encompasses form and content, painting and architecture, language, music and gestures.'[34]

In the Orthodox Church the icon is not seen as one of many instruments of religion. As Leonid Ouspensky has remarked: 'Since in its essence the icon, like the word, is a liturgical act, it never served religion but, like the word, has always been and is an integral part of religion, one of the instruments of the knowledge of God, one of the means of communion.'[35]

The icon is an act *of* the Church *for* the Church. Fotis Kontoglou, the foremost contemporary student and reviver of Byzantine iconography in Greece, writes:

The most venerable art of iconography in the Eastern Orthodox Church, is a holy and liturgical art, as all the arts of the Church that have a spiritual purpose. These holy arts do not aim only at decorating a church with paintings in order for it to be aesthetically attractive and pleasant to the worshippers, or in order to please their hearing with music, but rather in order to elevate them to the mystical world of faith through the spiritual ladder that has such steps like the reverend arts, hymnology, chanting, architecture, iconography and the rest of the arts.[36]

The icon blends with the word, as it does with the music, the incense,

---

33 See Schilling, *Contemporary Continental Theologians*, p 241, with reference to Nikos Nissiotis.
34 Stuart, *Ikons*, p 39.
35 Ouspensky, *The Meaning of Icons*, p. 33.
36 Kontoglou, *Ekphrasis*, I, xv. Belting, 'An Image and Its Function in the Liturgy,' emphatically states that "there is no longer any need to argue for the existence of a link between art and liturgy. Nowadays everyone is aware of the use of art made by the Church, and, as a result, of its use in the liturgy' (p. 1).

the kneeling, the signing of the cross, the bowing of the head, the act of taking communion, and so on, so that the whole experience becomes a *leitourgîa* (liturgy). Thus, according to Patriarch Germanus of Constantinople (715-730), 'the most holy name of God is glorified through what is visible and invisible.'[37]

In Orthodox worship the Church also manifests its full dimension as a 'communion of saints.' In this realization the icon plays a significant role. While ontologically all men of all ages, baptized in the name of Christ, in his death and resurrection, share with Him and among themselves in the Kingdom, this incomprehensible reality becomes also a visible experience. The celebrant clergy and the congregation are surrounded by the icons of Christ and a representative chorus of saints. The Eucharist – the 'reasonable and bloodless sacrifice' – is celebrated and offered, not only for 'those who receive the Gifts for the purification of their souls, for the remission of their sins, and for the fellowship of the Holy Spirit,' that is for the living participants, but 'also for those who have fallen asleep in the faith, forefathers, fathers, patriarchs, prophets, apostles, preachers, evangelists, martyrs, confessors, ascetics, and every righteous spirit in faith made perfect.'[38] Many of these 'righteous spirits' are not only mentioned and commemorated with words but actually viewed in iconic representations. From their immaterial state, through the means of matter, they reach the 'militant' or marching Church with which they form one Body. The icon makes the notion of the 'communion of saints' not only a statement of belief but a visual experience as well.

Although the proper place for an icon is the church, this is not exclusively so. The icon also has a place at home, 'the house church,' another place of prayer. Icons which are to be found in an Orthodox home have first been brought to the church for a period of time, usually for forty days. The popular expression for an icon which has been blessed in the Church is that 'it has been part of the liturgy (*eleitourgêthe*). As such an icon is treasured and venerated, not as a piece of art decorating a wall, but as a religious object of sacred value enhancing prayer. Popular piety, especially, holds an icon in great respect and reverence. When Vladimir Soloukhin, a young Russian collector of icons from the

---

37 *Letter to Thomas of Claudiopolis* (ca 724), in Mansi, 13:121E. See also Galavaris, *The Icon in the Life of the Church*.
38 The divine liturgy of St John Chrysostom. See below, 252B-C. See also André Grabar, *Martyrium*.

Department of Cultural Affairs of the Communist Party, was negotiating with a middle-aged woman for the icon the 'Virgin of Kazan,' he was faced with a popular, although definite, idea of what an icon is, as the following exchange indicates:

'... how do I know who'd get hold of it? You'd only make fun of it, anyway, you and your friends.'

'... But we couldn't Aunt Dunya – the very opposite! Everyone would admire it as a beautiful picture, a great work of Russian art!'

'There you are, who says icons are there to be admired? Prayers are what they're for – you pray to them and you keep a light burning in front of them. Is an icon some sort of naked girl, that you want to admire it?'[39]

Icons inside an Orthodox church are not like pictures, each one framed separately from the other, decorative pieces of art hung in a certain way to serve the aesthetic requirements of a particular wall.[40] Icons are painted in 'cycles,' with a continuous coherent meaning, in a particular form and order, and in relationship to each other.[41] They and their position serve to 'articulate' and accentuate the word of the Scriptures and the theology of the Church. They serve as a means of spiritual elevation and an instrument of instruction, not only for the illiterate,[42] but even for the literate ones who want, however, to penetrate beyond the realm of the word and of reason. John of Damascus, the celebrated defender of icons, himself an accomplished theologian and writer, writes in a disposition of prayer:

Of course, as far as You are concerned, being lofty and immaterial, and having become One who is beyond merely a body, sort of fleshless, you despise everything visible. However, myself, remaining a man and having a body that I am subject to, I have the desire to communicate physically and see the things that are holy. Condescend, therefore, to my humble sentiment, You who are the High One, so that You may keep your height.[43]

39 Soloukhin, *Searching*, p 161.
40 Sherrard, 'The Art of the Icon,' p 58.
41 See Kontoglou, *Ekphrasis*, I, 75-411.
42 John of Damascus calls the icons 'books for those who are illiterate, endless heralds of the veneration of saints, that instruct those who look at them with a soundless voice and sanctify the sight': Kotter, III, 151. A similar argument was also used by earlier defenders of the icons, such as Hypatius of Ephesus. Baynes, 'The Icons before Iconoclasm.' p 228.
43 Kotter, III, 148, lines 27–31.

As the word became a means of instruction through hearing, so did the icon through vision. St Basil, himself a powerful orator, in his encomium to Barlaam the martyr, calls upon the Christian painter to iconograph the glory of the martyr, for the iconographer would be able to express the glory of the martyr in colour better than he himself in words.[44] As a matter of fact, there is ample evidence that oratorical skills and eloquence on the one hand and iconography on the other developed in parallel lines and influenced each other.[45] The Byzantine Church integrated all forms of communication as means of instruction, as sacred arts, and as expressions of theology and worship. Taking all these into consideration, 'an icon divorced from its framework ceases to be an icon. An icon divorced from a place and act of worship is a contradiction in terms.'[46]

THE WORD AND THE ICON

What offended the opponents of icons in the eighth century, and what continues to offend many Christians today, is what they perceive to be a prohibition against icons and the absence of any specific justification of them in the Bible. In this respect the iconoclasts of the eighth century were the literalists, and the forerunners of the *sola Scriptura* of the Protestant Reformation. What is at stake here is the right perception of the notion of the Word of God in Christianity, as well as of the essence of the Christian tradition. The Logos- or Word-theology of Christianity is most eloquently articulated at the beginning of the fourth gospel. According to John the Word of God in Christianity is not a book. What Christianity believes and where it bases its faith is in the Word of God made flesh.[47] According to Ignatius of Antioch, Christ is the 'Word derived from silence,'[48] that is from the unfathomable mystery of God's own essence. The Bible and its canon, the earliest record of the Church's experience of God the Word in flesh, is the product of the mystical Body of Christ, that is of the Church, and the expression of her theological self-understanding, and not the other way around. Christ, the incarnate Word of God, was always and from the

---

44 In Mansi, 13:80C (PG 94:1360C–D).
45 Maguire, *Art and Eloquence in Byzantium*, and 'The Iconography of Symeon.' See also Cutler, *Transfigurations*.
46 Sherrard, 'The Art of the Icon,' p 58.
47 John 1:14.
48 *Magnesians*, VIII, 2.

beginning the central person of reference, by word of mouth, by action, and by the very life of the Church, prior to and after the composition of the Christian Scripture. The Word of God is lived rather than talked about, celebrated and re-enacted in worship rather than prescribed and confined, expressed in confessions of faith and symbols rather than scholasticized. In the ancient liturgies, celebrated in Byzantium at the time of iconoclasm and celebrated until today in the Orthodox Church, the Scripture is chanted, preached, but also elaborately and prominently shown, processed, venerated, and even elaborately decorated. The content of the Scripture is not found exclusively in its pages. It has also saturated the hymnology of the Orthodox Church to the extent that even the illiterate know a substantial portion of the Scripture through hymns and prayers. It has also been made into church services and translated into symbols and, even more, into icons. It is interesting that the word for Scripture in Greek (*Graphê*) means both 'writing' and 'painting'; in the Greek Orthodox mind there is no separation, no division, between these two forms of communication, let alone abrogation of each other. Thus, that which writing conveys through reading, the icon conveys and enhances through the sense of sight.[49] The icon is a narrative in shapes and forms through the medium of colours. Indeed, the icon is traditionally called *histôresis* (which means both written narrative and painting), iconography is called *historîa* (history or narrative), and the iconographer *historiogrâphos* (painter of narratives) or *historistês* (narrator).[50] The icon and the word are in no tension with each other. The icon serves as a reminder of and as a commentary upon the Scriptures and has always been an integral part of the liturgical, didactic, and missionary ministry of the Church. The iconographer is a hagiographer, a painter, and a minister of sacred art, 'another priest and preacher,' according to Kontoglou.[51] It is not simply artistic talent

---

49 See below, 220E, 232C, and elsewhere. The illustration of the Scriptures and of other writings is an early practice. See, for example, the excellent works of Galavaris, *The Illustrations of the Prefaces in Byzantine Gospels*, and *The Illustrations of the Liturgical Homilies of Gregory Nazianzenus*; Huber, *Image et message*; Nelson, *The Iconography of Preface and Miniature in the Byzantine Gospel Book*; Spatharakis, *Corpus of Dated Illuminated Greek Manuscripts*; Walter, 'Liturgy and the Illustration of Gregory of Nazianzen's Homilies,' esp. pp 190–192; Weitzmann, et al, *The Place of Book Illumination in Byzantine Art*; Weitzmann, *Byzantine Liturgical Psalters and Gospels*.

50 Kontoglou, *Ekphrasis*, I, 416. See also below, 232B. The word *schêma* (scheme) also, used in rhetoric, means both a figure of rhetoric and a pose of painting. Maguire, *Art and Eloquence in Byzantium*, p 9.

51 Kontoglou, *Ekphrasis*, I, xv. Most of the iconographers were members of the monastic community. The perception of iconography as a 'priestly' ministry and as a sacred art

but, more than that, personal spirituality, profound knowledge of the Church's life and tradition, and commitment to her essential function that are the prerequisite qualifications of an iconographer.[52]

Byzantine iconography is a liturgical art with theological meaning and purpose. Its style is simple, unassuming, and otherworldly. Its purpose is not to attract the attention of the viewer but to lift up the spirit of the worshipper from the corruptible world to that of the incorruptibility of the Kingdom of God, and to feed the faithful with spiritual visions and hearings.[53] John of Damascus expressed this feeling in simple language: 'I saw the human shape of God and my soul found its salvation.'[54] The Byzantine icon is not a specimen of aesthetic art but an expression of spirituality. For the iconographer everything becomes an instrument of spirituality, even the tools, the colours, the walls, the brushes, and the boards in their crude material form. The beauty of the liturgical art of iconography is not carnal or aesthetic. In the icon the flesh has been crucified, 'along with the passions and its desires.'[55] Here, exactly, lies the essential difference between Byzantine iconography and the religious painting of the Renaissance. The Byzantine icon is lean and fasting; it is a statement of faith and of a certain ethos that expresses what is rich in poverty, humility, contrition,

(*hagiographia*) is also demonstrated by the special spiritual preparation to which the iconographer subjected himself. One undertook extensive reading, prayer, and fasting before painting an icon. See French, *The Eastern Orthodox Church*, p 130. Kontoglou writes about 'Those early hagiographs' who even 'changed their underwear in order to be clean inside and outside and (who) while working they were chanting, so that their work may be done sanctimoniously and their mind might not be left to wander in worldly concerns' (*Ekphrasis*, ɪ, xvii). See also Stuart, *Ikons*, p 49, n 1.

52 Manuals for a Byzantine iconographer are few and scarce. In such manuals a substantial section is devoted to the theology of the icon, the painting of icons, and the meaning of the different icons and symbols. One of the most complete of these manuals is the *Hermeneîa tes zographikês têchnes*, a compilation of notes and instructions from earlier hagiographers composed by the monk Dionysios of Fourna in 1730; there is an English translation by Hetherington, *The Painter's Manual of Dionysios of Fourna*. Kontoglou in his two-volume work *Ekphrasis* has attempted to rectify certain misconceptions of Dionysios and to clarify technical matters, thus producing a work which is as unmistakenly theological as it is technical. Two informative books on Byzantine iconography, its characteristics and techniques, are Stuart's *Ikons* and Taylor's shorter *Icon Painting*.

53 See the disposition of the iconographer in the analysis of some themes by Cutler, *Transfigurations*, pp 53–110.

54 *Against those who defame the holy icons*, ɪ, 22 (PG 94:1256; Kotter, ɪɪɪ, 111, lines 4–5).

55 Gal. 5:24.

with a disposition to the quest for sanctity. 'As the gospel and the Old Testament,' writes Kontoglou, 'are synoptic and concise, so is the Orthodox iconography simple, without excessive decorations and exhibitions.'[56] The icon, according to St Gregory of Nyssa, 'knows how to be a silent scripture that speaks from the wall.'[57]

The theology and the making of icons have gone through a long process of maturation and refinement. What is offered here is a bird's-eye view of the background currents, events, persons, circumstances, and issues during the first phase (726–787) of the iconoclastic controversies, leading up to the particular texts translated in this volume.[58]

JUDAISM AND BYZANTINE ICONOCLASM

There is an antecedent for the opposition towards icons, statues, and human representations for religious purposes in the Jewish tradition, which the Christian Church took seriously, as the Law and the religious experience of Israel are 'the teacher leading to Christ.'[59] It is this attitude towards the Jewish religious experience that justifies, for the Christian, the notions of the Church as the 'New Israel' and her constitution as the 'New Covenant' or 'New Testament.' Jews and some Christians throughout the centuries have read Exodus 20:4 ('You shall not make for yourself a graven image, or any likeness of anything that is in heaven above, or that is in the earth beneath, or that is in the water under the earth') and its reiterations[60] as an unconditional prohibition of

---

56 Kontoglou, *Ekphrasis*, I, xvii. For a discussion of the spiritual dimension of the icon see Stuart, *Ikons*, pp 21–39.
57 PG 46:737C–740A.
58 The bibliography on iconoclasm is too extensive and too diversified to be mastered by any one person. For a review of the era, with more bibliography, consult Brehier, *La Querelle des images VIIIe–IXe siècles*, and his 'La Querelle des images jusqu'au Concile iconoclaste de 754'; Martin, *A History of the Iconoclastic Controversy*; Ostrogorsky, *Studien zur Geschichte des byzantinischen Bilderstreites*; Anastos, 'Iconoclasm and Imperial Rule 717–842'; and the appropriate chapters in such general but respected works as Ostrogorsky, *History of the Byzantine State*, pp 130–186; Vasiliev, *History of the Byzantine Empire*, pp 234–299; Jenkins, *Byzantium. The Imperial Centuries*, pp 74–89; as well as some studies with a particular focus or point of view, such as Brown 'A Dark Age Crisis'; Ladner, 'Origin and Significance of the Byzantine Iconoclastic Controversy'; André Grabar, *L'Iconoclasme byzantin*.
59 Gal. 3:24.
60 Exod. 20:34, 34:17; Lev. 19:4, 26:1; Deut. 4:15–19, 5:8, 27:15.

icons,[61] although in reality this injunction did not prohibit even Judaism itself from developing images, symbols, and artefacts for its religious expression, as the Hebrew Bible[62] and Jewish tradition indicate.[63] Indeed even Christian apologists of the icons prior to the iconoclasm of the eighth century defended the icons on the basis of the text of the Hebrew

61 At this moment it is essential to resort once more to the etymological meaning of the key words of this subject. An icon is neither an 'image' nor an 'idol' nor a 'picture.' 'Image' (from *imago*) implies a depiction out of one's imagination; an image compared to an icon is a *desideratum*, not a statement. An 'idol' (from *eîdolon*) is the reflection of an object, its illusion or its distortion, depending on the reflective qualities of the medium. To the Greek Fathers an idol, or a three-dimensional artefact, is the representation of something that does not really exist; the term applies for example to the representation of a deity of the ancient Greek religion. This is one of the reasons why the Christian East rejected statues in favour of two-dimensional icons. It is interesting that Pope Adrian in his letter to the Council of Nicea (787) uses prominently the words of Stephen, Bishop of Basra, who makes a distinction between a statue and an icon (Mansi, 12:1067D–E. See also Nicodemos Hagioretes, *Pedâlion*, p 314. 'Picture' is a depiction or reproduction of externals as an artist today, or a camera, sees them. It is a selective representation of characteristics from a particular angle, under a particular light, and in the particular way one chooses to see them. A picture tells us something of the appearance of an object or of a person, not its true nature. 'Icon' is the noun from the perfect tense (*êoika*) of the Greek verb *eîko* ('to be like'); even the grammatical detail is significant, in that it suggests that the likeness is an already accomplished fact. It is quite interesting that the Septuagint translates Gen. 1:26 as 'Let us make man according to our *icon* (*Kat' eikôna*) and according to our likeness.' The implication of this rendering is that the characteristics or qualities of God in man are definite, real, unchangeable, not potential. However, the same Septuagint translates Exod. 20:4 as 'Thou shall not make thyself an *idol*' (*eîdolon*). 'Icon' implies a real prototype. An icon does not exist apart from its prototype. That is why 'the honour to the icon is transferred to the prototype,' according to St Basil, a key notion in the defence of the icons. Second, the icon is not identical to the prototype. That is why the veneration of the icon does not compromise the worship of God. (Compare in the texts below the distinction between *latreîa* (worship) and *timetikê proskŷnesis* (veneration of honour). Third, an icon, properly speaking, is not of a thing but of a person, that is, of a being that has qualities of relationship, with inner qualities relating to the viewer and inducing him to emulate them. That is why an icon is an icon of a *holy* person. (The word 'icon' cannot be used for the depiction of any being; that would be a picture.) Thus the veneration is offered not to the representation itself but to what the 'icon' represents, that is to the 'grace and truth,' as the Council *in Trullo* (692) phrased it: Schmemann, *The Historical Road*, p.203. See also Ladner, 'The Concept of the Image'; and Müller, 'The Theological Significance of a Critical Attitude in Hagiography.'
62 See 2 Kings 13; Gutmann, ed, *No Graven Images*. See also Gutmann's 'Deuteronomy: Religious Reformation or Iconoclastic Revolution?'; Frey, 'La Question des images chez les Juifs.'
63 See Kraeling, *Excavations at Dura-Europos*.

Scriptures, which they were reading typologically and in the spirit of the New Testament.[64]

To what extent Judaism actually influenced Byzantine iconoclasm is difficult to state with precision. Certainly the emergence of several Judaeo-Christian sects from the earliest times of Christianity[65] and the subsequent continuous interaction between Jews and Christians within the Byzantine Empire[66] had a profound effect on the Christian use of icons, especially in areas where the Jewish presence was noticeable, or among Christians of Jewish background or with Jewish leanings. At any rate, the Seventh Ecumenical Council characterized those who destroyed icons as 'godless Jews and enemies of the truth'[67] and made repeated references to iconoclastic acts initiated by Jews.[68]

ISLAM AND BYZANTINE ICONOCLASM

Opposition to the icons also arose from Islam,[69] with which Byzantium came into contact from the beginning. In solidarity with Judaism on this matter, Islam rejected images and representations of humans as idols,[70] a distinction which the Qur'ân did not make.[71] In Islam an image is understood as equivalent to and consubstantial with the prototype.[72] Thus, if it is only Allah who creates and fashions man, 'what ye make?'[73]

---

64 See Barnard, *The Graeco-Roman and Oriental Background of the Iconoclastic Controversy*, esp. ch. 3, 'The Jews and Iconoclasm,' pp 34–50.

65 See, for example, Epiphanius, *Panarion*, heresies, 18(38), 19(39), 20(40), PG 41:653ff.

66 See Starr, *The Jews in the Byzantine Empire*.

67 Mansi, 13:41E.

68 Mansi, 13:24E–32A.

69 From the extensive bibliography on the subject I should like to mention Barnard, 'Byzantium and Islam,' and the appropriate chapter in his *The Graeco-Roman and Oriental Background*, pp 10–33; Becker, *Vom Werden und Wesen der islamischen Welt*, I, 432–449; Oleg Grabar, 'Islam and Iconoclasm'; Grunebaum, 'Byzantine Iconoclasm and the Influence of the Islamic Environment.'

70 The corresponding literature on Islam is equally extensive; see Creswell, 'The Lawfulness of Painting in Early Islam'; Farès, *Philosophie et Jurisprudence illustrés par les Arabes*; Hodgson, 'Islam and Image.'

71 6:74; 21:51; 25:3. The Qur'ân contains no direct prohibition of icons. Vasiliev, *History of the Byzantine Empire*, I, 255, has erroneously assumed that the Muslims were guided against the images by the words of surah 5:90/92. In this passage the reference is clearly to idols.

72 An equation which the iconoclast Emperor Constantine V made later between Christ and the icon of Christ. See below, 261E–264C.

73 37:96.

In Islam the painting of a human image is perceived as compromising the absolute unity (*tawhid*) of God, who is 'The Creator, the Shaper out of naught, the fashioner' (*musawwir*).[74] This view was reinforced by reference to traditional incidents in Muhammad's life[75] and to other Hadith stories.[76] The human artist who in defiance of God's commandment has painted images of humans will be called on the Day of Judgment to instil life into them,[77] obviously in order that his folly become apparent. The early history of the Umayyad Caliphate contains various iconoclastic incidents,[78] culminating in the issuing of an official decree by which Caliph Yazid II (720–724) ordered the destruction of all icons found in the Christian churches under his dominion.[79] Theophanes the Chronographer (d 818) places the date of this decree in 724, the year of Yazid's death.[80]

Three years later, according to Theophanes, the Byzantine Emperor Leo III The Isaurian (717–741) issued his own iconoclastic decree condemning the veneration of icons as idolatrous, and promising to convene an ecumenical council to seal his decision.[81] Leo's cultural background and the proximity in time of these two iconoclastic edicts, one Muslim and one Christian, have, and justifiably so, raised the question of whether Islam has influenced the Byzantine iconoclasm.[82]

---

74 59:24.
75 Guillaume, *The Life of Muhammad*, p 552.
76 See Guillaume, *The Traditions of Islam*, pp 128–129.
77 See the article 'Sura' in the *Shorter Encyclopaedia of Islam*, ed H.A.R. Gibb and J.H. Kramers (Ithaca, 1965), p 554.
78 Theophanes, *Chronographia*, ed de Boor, I, 342, lines 22–28.
79 Ibid, I, 401–402.
80 On the authenticity of this decree see Becker, *Von Werden und Wesen der islamischen Welt*, I, 446. See also the report of the Armenian historian G. Ghevond (late eighth century) in Nersessian, 'Image Worship in Armenia and Its Opponents,' 73.
81 See below, pp 24–30.
82 Vasiliev, 'The Iconoclastic Edict of the Caliph Yazid II'; Diehl, 'Leo III and His Isaurian Dynasty'; Jeffery, 'Ghevond's Text of the Correspondence between 'Umar I and Leo III.' Gero maintains that this correspondence is an Armenian composition of the eleventh to thirteenth centuries: 'Notes on Byzantine Iconoclasm,' Some modern Muslims pride themselves on the conjecture that it was Islam that contributed to iconoclasm and actually influenced Leo III. Karâmat ꜤAlî Jawnpûrî (d 1873), a ShiꜤa Muslim from Pakistan, in his major work *MaꜤâkhiz al-Ꜥulûm*, translated into English by ꜤUbaydî and Amîr ꜤAlî (Calcutta, 1867) blames Martin Luther 'for lack of historical honesty in supressing the evidence of the Islamic contribution to iconoclasm and the actual Islamic influence on Leo the Isaurian.' See Ahmad, *Islamic Modernism in India and Pakistan*, p 22. Another Pakistani Muslim, Ameer Ali (d 1928), regrets the defeat of

For Theophanes, Leo's decree was an act by a 'Saracene-minded,' 'most miserable' emperor, 'like his Arab teachers.'[83] Leontius Sabaites calls Leo's successor, the iconoclast Emperor Constantine V, a 'second Mahomet, burner of images and enemy of the saints.'[84] The Fathers of the Seventh Ecumenical Council also called the iconoclasts 'Arab wolves who pretentiously wore a skin of sheep.'[85]

The Paulicians have also been cited as another influence on Byzantine iconoclasm.[86] However, one has to remember that Leo III and his son and successor, Constantine V, turned against all three groups, Jews, Muslims, and Paulicians, with equal vehemence. It must also be borne in mind that, while few icons, including mosaics, symbols, and other religious artefacts, survived in the immediate area of the Byzantine capital, icons were preserved in other lands which, during the century and a half when the iconoclastic controversies raged, were parts of the Muslim empire. In such lands the mosaics inside the churches 'were not even covered with plaster as was done later by the Turks in the churches of Constantinople and elsewhere in the Byzantine Empire.'[87] Thus, one must look for the internal and indigenous theological reasons which prompted Byzantine iconoclasm, primarily the inherent Christological character of the question and its progressive application and refinement. It was the political circumstances, the resemblance in the

---

the Arabs at the siege of Constantinople (717) for, among other reasons, this disrupted and left incomplete the iconoclastic movement! See his *The Spirit of Islam*, p 399. For an intriguing comparison between Mu^{c}tazilite and iconoclastic theology see Haddad, 'Iconoclasts and Mu^{c}tazila.'

83 De Boor, I, 405, line 14; I, 406, line 25.

84 Quoted by Hefele, *A History of the Councils of the Church*, V, 317. See also n 87.

85 Mansi, 13:401D.

86 Barnard, *The Graeco-Roman and Oriental Background*, pp 104–118.

87 Weitzmann, 'Introduction to the Mosaics and Monumental Paintings,' in Forsyth and Weitzmann, *The Monastery of Saint Catherine*, p 11. One of the best examples is, perhaps, the monastery of St Catherine itself. See also Weitzmann, *The Icon*, p 17. Other mosaics and icons which survived the fury of the iconoclastic controversy are to be found on the island of Cyprus, which was, temporarily at least, controlled by the Muslims. Leontius Sabaites, in his biography of St Stephen (725–794), nephew of John of Damascus, the staunchest defender of icons during the first phase of iconoclasm, states that Stephen counselled the monks who were fleeing the capital to establish themselves in the Eastern Patriarchates, which were under Muslim domination and, thus, outside the power of the iconoclast Emperor Constantine V the Copronyme: *Analecta Bollandiana*, I, 401, 447. On the *Vita Stephani Sabaitae* see Sahas, *John of Damascus on Islam*, p 48, nn 3, 4.

absolute character of their arguments, and the actions taken against the icons as an idol-worship by Jews, Muslims, and Paulicians that prompted the defenders of the icons to identify Byzantine iconoclasts with them, and call them *Christianocatêgoroi* ('offenders or accusers of the Christians') and enemies of the Christian state.

THE ICONS BEFORE ICONOCLASM

It is clear that opposition to icons did not come only as a result of Jewish or Muslim influence. Within the Christian community itself voices and actions of protest – some of them loud and violent – were raised before the iconoclasm. 'Placuit picturas in ecclesia esse non debere, non quod colitur et adoratur in parietibus depingatur,' proclaimed the local council of Elvira in Spain in the first decade of the fourth century, in its thirty-sixth Canon.[88] Although not in the same official way, similar protests and actions have been recorded in the East as well.[89] Various groups or individuals had taken a position against icons on the basis of their own particular theology.[90] In several instances during the sessions of the Seventh Ecumenical Council Patriarch Tarasius of Constantinople named the Hebrews, the Saracens, the Greeks, the Samaritans, the Manichaeans, the Marcionists, the Theopaschites, the Docetists or 'Fantasiasts,' and 'those who confused the two natures of Christ,' like Peter Gnapheus, Xenias of Hierapolis, and Severus, as predecessors of the eighth-century iconoclasts, and responsible for the iconoclasm.[91]

88 Mansi, 2:264A. About this controversial council see Hefele, *A History of the Christian Councils*, vol I: *To the close of the Council of Nicea A.D. 325*, pp 131–172. It is worth remembering that the Church of Spain in its rather rigorous defence against Nestorianism rendered itself puritanical on the icons and pietistic towards the Incarnation. It may not be accidental that both the introduction of the *filioque* clause into the Nicene-Constantinopolitan Creed and the notion of the *immaculata in utero*, which developed into the *immaculata conceptio* doctrine of the Roman Church, have their origin in the Church of Spain.

89 For references to sources and secondary material see Baynes, 'The Icons before Iconoclasm,' pp 226–239; Kitzinger, 'The Cult of Images in the Age before Iconoclasm,' esp. pp 129–134, and his 'On Some Icons of the Seventh Century,' esp. pp 138–144; Finney, 'Antecedents of Byzantine Iconoclasm.'

90 See Nersessian, 'Image Worship in Armenia'; and Alexander, 'An Ascetic Sect of Iconoclasts in Seventh Century Armenia.'

91 Mansi, 12:1031E, 13:157D–E, 172C–E, 181B, 196D–E, and elsewhere.

In addition, not only 'heretics' of Jewish, Muslim, monophysite, or docetic inclination opposed icons. In the sixth century the bishops of Asia Minor declared that they themselves 'had no delight in the icons.'[92] The bishops of Asia Minor were also instrumental in the eighth-century controversy.[93]

One of the most celebrated cases of early opposition to icons is that of Epiphanius. Epiphanius (d 403), Bishop of Salamis in Cyprus, is presented as an early banner-holder against the icons. Four writings in fragments, the 'Letter to Theodosius,' the 'Treatise against "Idol-makers",' the 'Testament,' and the 'Letter to John of Aelia,' were ascribed to him and used by iconoclasts as an example of early patristic rejection of the icons.[94] Epiphanius, a staunch traditionalist, was more concerned to combat heresies than to refine theological positions.[95] In one instance he is reported to have turn down icons, most likely because he was infuriated by the semi-Arians who were using icons to demonstrate that the Son, even though similar (*hômoios*) to the Father, is a creature and, therefore, depictable.[96] Beyond the dispute over the authenticity

92 Baynes, 'The Icons before Iconoclasm,' p 228.
93 See Ostrogorsky, 'Les Débuts de la querelle des images,' I, 235-255.
94 The reconstruction of these framents has been credited to Holl, 'Die Schriften des Epiphanius gegen die Bilderverehrung.' A more extensive version of these fragments with reference to their sources and codices has been reprinted by Hennephof, *Textus byzantinos*, pp 44-51. The authorship of these fragments is still under debate. Holl, Baynes ('The Icons before Iconoclasm' pp 227, n 2), and Kitzinger ('The Cult of Images before Iconoclasm,' p 93, n 28) consider them authentic. Ostrogorsky, *Studien zur Geschichte des byzantinischen Bilderstreites*, pp 68ff, has disputed their authenticity. Barnard, *The Graeco-Roman and Oriental Background*, p 89, finds Ostrogorsky's argument 'circular' and 'unconvincing' but he himself remains undecided. Even for Kitzinger, who has doubts about Epiphanius' opposition to icons, 'the problem of the disputed writings of Epiphanius is too intricate and too technical to be dealt with by a non-specialist.' For more on Epiphanius see below, 292D-296E. It is interesting that the iconoclastic Council of 754 made use of no other iconoclastic writings of Epiphanius, except for one short admonition attributed to him that survived only through oral tradition. The council, however, admonished those who want to find out to search for other possible works of Epiphanius (Mansi, 13:292D-E).
95 His written work is primarily heresiological: *Panarion*, PG 41:173-42:885; *Anchoratus*, PG 43:17-236.
96 See below, 292D, n 1. Images were also used by the Gnostics, who have been cited as one of the sources of influence on early Christian art. See Finney, 'Gnosticism and the Origins of Early Christian Art.'

and meaning of Epiphanius' iconoclastic writings and actions,[97] this whole episode confirms clearly the early use of icons by the Church.[98]

Prior to iconoclasm the defence of icons was, however, stronger than the opposition to them, although it was not expressed in a refined theological, Christological language, and was employed mainly for apologetic purposes against the Jews. Among those defenders of icons were Hypatius of Ephesus in the sixth century,[99] Leontius of Neapolis of Cyprus (d ca 650),[100] Hieronymus, a presbyter of Jerusalem, and others. In 691/2 the Council of Trullo in Constantinople with its eighty-second Canon fostered the practice of representing Christ; it promulgated that Christ, depicted symbolically in some icons as the Lamb of God and pointed to by John the Baptist, may now be painted with human features so that, in this way, 'we may perceive the height of the humility of God-the-Word and be led to the memory of his conduct in flesh, as well as of his redemptive passion and death.'[101]

By the middle of the eighth century the controversy had developed into a political as well as a theological-doctrinal dispute. It involved the imperial authority itself[102] in the person of the Emperors Leo III the Isaurian and his son, Constantine V the Copronyme, and the hierarchy of the Church in the person of such authorities as Germanus and Tarasius, Patriarchs of Constantinople. Constantine's monophysite

---

97 The Council of 787, although it questioned the authenticity of the iconoclastic writings of Epiphanius and absolved him of any such act, did ascribe to him a plea to the bishops of various districts urging them to remove the icons from their churches (Mansi, 13:293D–E). Barnard's statement that 'Epiphanius' protest against images is not part of a developed theological polemic. It was simply a protest against idolatry, an invasion of paganism into the Church' represents a reasonable, although partial, assessment of Epiphanius' 'iconoclastic' attitude: *The Graeco-Roman and Oriental Background*, p 91.

98 See André Grabar, *Christian Iconography*, and also his *Early Christian Art*; Kitzinger, *Byzantine Art in the Making*. Popular Christian piety has it (possibly in order to support the iconophile side) that the earliest icons were made by some of the Apostles. Icon-making is attributed to Luke, John, and Bartholomew: Nersessian, 'Image Worship in Armenia,' pp 73–74.

99 Baynes, 'The Icons before Iconoclasm,' pp 226–228 and n 3 for bibliography.

100 Ibid, pp 230–238. See also Nersessian, 'Une Apologie des Images,' for another defender of the icons, John Mayragometri. For an earlier defence of the icons, see Huskinson, *Concordia apostolorum*.

101 Mansi, 2:980B.

102 According to Theosterictus' observation, 'The other heresies had their origin from bishops and lower clergy, but this one from the rulers themselves': quoted by Gero, 'Notes on Byzantine Iconoclasm,' p 42.

sympathies found expression in the rejection of icons using theological arguments, in which he was well versed.[103] However, the iconophile position found a most articulate and ardent defender in John of Damascus, a monk and presbyter in the celebrated monastery of St Sabbas in Palestine, already outside the immediate reach of the imperial hand.[104]

As a theological-Christological issue the matter of the icons was taken up by two major councils, one condemning them (Constantinople, 754) and the other upholding them (Nicea, 787). East and West recognized the Council of Nicea as orthodox, and acclaimed it as the Seventh Ecumenical Council of the Christian Church. The controversy also involved large groups of people, from different social classes, professions, and vocations, who were identified by their opposition to or defence of the icons.[105] The military, in general, were iconoclasts,[106] while the members of the monastic community were the most fervent defenders of icons. The degree of polarization is manifested by the length and bitterness of the controversy and by the extent of physical and material destruction caused by the conflict. The military, which included those at the imperial court, had authority, power, and the means of destruction. The monks had conviction, determination, and the means of survival. The outcome of the controversy proved the latter more determined than the former.

LEO III

There is no consensus as to when iconoclasm officially began.[107] Iconoclasm must be seen more as a comprehensive and complex phenomenon than as an isolated incident in Byzantine history.[108] There is sufficient agreement, however, that the first Byzantine Emperor to take an official position against the icons was Leo III the Isaurian, the Emperor

---

103 Ostrogorsky, *Studien zur Geschichte des byzantinischen Bilderstreites*, p 25f.

104 John of Damascus, *Against those who defame the holy icons*, PG 94:1231–1420; in Kotter, vol III.

105 See, for example, Barnard, 'The Emperor Cult.'

106 Kaegi has shown, however, that the role of the armies was not consistently supportive of iconoclasm: 'The Byzantine Armies and Iconoclasm.'

107 For Ostrogorsky the era of the iconoclastic crisis begins in 711: *History of the Byzantine State*, pp 130–186.

108 For the philosophical-theological complexity of iconoclasm see Florovsky, 'The Iconoclastic Controversy.' For other aspects and considerations, and the relevant bibliography, see Haldon, 'Some Remarks on the Background to the Iconoclastic Controversy.'

who came from Germanicia in North Syria.[109] Theophanes, in the ninth
year of Leo's reign (i.e. 726), reports:

In this year the impious King Leo began speaking about abolishing the holy
and venerable icons. When Gregory, the Pope of Rome, heard of this, he withheld
the taxes of Italy and Rome and wrote to Leo a letter of doctrinal nature, that
the King ought not to talk on matters of faith and innovate on the doctrines
of the Church, which the Holy Fathers have taught.[110]

For some scholars the phrase 'Leo began speaking about abolishing
the holy and venerable icons' means that in 726 Leo issued an official
decree ordering the destruction of the icons, which he reinforced with
yet another decree, issued in 730.[111] They argue that Leo issued two
iconoclastic orders. For others the same phrase suggests that in 726
Leo began speaking openly against the icons but that he did not issue
any decree on the matter.[112] Patriarch Nicephorus of Constantinople
(806–815), a major defender of icons during the second phase of the
iconoclasm, seems to support the latter position when he writes that
in 726 Leo 'attempted to teach the people his own doctrine.'[113]

More important than the determination of the exact date of the official
beginning of the iconoclasm, and the dates of the number of iconoclastic decrees issued,[114] is the question of the content of such a decree

109 Theophanes calls Leo 'Syrian': de Boor, I, 412, line 3. An earlier reference of Theophanes
to Germanicopolis in Isauria (I, 391, line 5) as the birthplace of Leo is now considered
to be a later addition. The question of Leo's real identity has been raised by Head,
who has argued that Leo the Isaurian was in fact Emperor Leontius (695–698): 'Who
Was the Real Leo the Isaurian?' On Leo and the iconoclasm see Gero, *Byzantine
Iconoclasm during the Reign of Leo III*. On the question of the significance of the place of
origin of iconoclasm see Hélène Ahrweiler, 'The Geography of the Iconoclast World.'
110 De Boor, I, 404.
111 For example, Vasiliev, *History of the Byzantine Empire*, I, 258; Hefele, *History of the Councils of
the Church*, V, 272–273; Diehl, 'Leo III,' p 9; Anastos, 'Iconoclasm and Imperial Rule,'
p 68, n 2. See also Anastos, 'Leo III's Edict against the Images in the Year 726–27.'
112 For example, Ostrogorsky, 'Les Débuts de la querelle des images,' pp 235–255; as well as
several Byzantinists, like Brehier, Haller, Alexander, Andreev, and others.
113 *Opuscula Historica*, ed C. de Boor (Leipzig, 1880; repr New York: Amo Press, 1975), p 57.
Still the most important monograph on Nicephorus is Alexander, *The Patriarch
Nicephorus of Constantinople*.
114 For an attempted reconciliation of Theophanes' text and the thesis that iconoclasm
began officially in 726 with an imperial decree, see Gero, *Byzantine Iconoclasm during
the Reign of Leo III*, p 106. Barnard summarizes the evidence thus far with the
statement that 'the question whether there was one or two edicts against images
must be regarded as still open': *The Graeco-Roman and Oriental Background*, p 13, n 4.

and, thus, Leo's own iconoclastic views. Here again we are faced with a lack of concrete evidence, for no texts for such decrees are known.[115] One can discern Leo's iconoclastic ideas, and especially his iconoclastic policies, only indirectly, and then through the polemic iconophile literature.[116]

The earliest source of information, perhaps, about the Emperor's views on the icons are two letters of Pope Gregory II (715-731) to Leo 'On the venerable and holy icons.'[117] These letters are in response to what appear to have been annual briefs of the Emperor to the Pope on Church matters.[118] It seems that in his communications the Emperor used the opportunity to reaffirm his own orthodox faith and his determination to preserve the tradition of the Fathers.[119] A careful reading of the first letter in particular discloses a rather descriptive outline of the main points of Leo's thought and in some instances (if the text of these letters is accurate) possibly Leo's own wording.[120] Certainly these meagre

115 See Vasiliev, *History of the Byzantine Empire*, I, 258, for additional literature on the matter.

116 For a list of sources on the period of iconoclasm, and particularly of the iconophile literature, see the works of Martin, *A History of the Iconoclastic Controversy*; and Alexander, *The Patriarch Nicephorus*.

117 The text appears in Mansi, 12:959D-971B and 975D-979D, and there is a critical edition by Gouillard, 'Aux origines de l'Iconoclasme.' The references given here are to Gouillard's edition, with references to Mansi in parentheses. For a translation of Gregory's letters see Hefele, *A History of the Councils of the Church*, V, 289-295, 295-298. On Gregory II see Duschesne, *Le Liber pontificalis*, I, 396-414.

118 The authenticity of these letters, which have been used extensively by historians in the past, has lately been seriously questioned by Gouillard, 'Aux origines de l'Iconoclasme'; see esp. pp 259-260 for the bibliography on this debate. Anastos takes Gregory's letters, with possible alterations, as basically authentic: 'Iconoclasm and Imperial Rule,' p 71. Anastos seems to suggest that both letters of Gregory were written in 730. However, the preface of Gregory's first letter to Leo with its unequivocal condemnation of Leo's views makes it difficult for one to imagine that Gregory delayed making such a reply until 730. This is even more improbable if one maintains as Anastos does, that in 726 Leo issued an official edict against the icons! According to Diehl, what reached Gregory was an edict which the Pope denounced in his first letter: 'Leo III,' p 9. However, Gregory explicitly calls all the communications 'letters' (*Grâmmata*). Also Leo's statements, which can be reconstructed from Gregory's letters, are too direct and too personal to be part of an otherwise general and impersonal imperial edict. See Gouillard, 'Aux origines de l'Iconoclasme,' pp 287 (Mansi, 12:965C-D), 295 (Mansi, 12:971A), 295 (Mansi, 12:971B).

119 Gouillard, 'Aux origines de l'Iconoclasme,' pp 277-279.

120 Hefele, *A History of the Councils of the Church* , V, 295, states characteristically that with these extractions 'our desire to be acquainted with the tenor of the first edict, at least in outline, is satisfied.'

fragments do not reconstruct Leo's own text in its entirety. They reveal, however, the Emperor's own preoccupations with icons and his motivations for turning against them. If Gregory's letters are authentic and their wording accurate, there is little reason to doubt the accuracy of Leo's statements. It is not uncommon for an apologist to quote his opponent accurately for the sake of refuting him. One may also assume that the statements which are introduced with the words 'you wrote' may be actual quotations from Leo's letter; while those which follow the words 'you say' are probably Leo's thinking, as it is phrased by Gregory. This distinction, however, does not find support in all instances, and it is only hypothetical. Here are, therefore, Leo's views on the icons (italicized), extracted from the text of Gregory's response to him (printed in Roman):

BY GREGORY, POPE OF ROME TO EMPEROR LEO THE ISAURIAN, FIRST LETTER, ON THE HOLY ICONS:

For ten years you have been, by the grace of God, walking the right   279
path and you have made no mention of the holy icons. Now, however,   (959D)
you say that
they are in the place of idols
and that
those who venerate them are idolaters ...

You also wrote that   279
one should not venerate things made with hands, as well as any kind of likeness (959E)
neither in the sky nor on earth, as God said ...[121]
as well as,
let me know, who has taught us to venerate and bow down to things made with
hands, while God legislates not to do so? ...

You also say that   287
we [you] bow down to stones, walls and boards ...   (965A)

as you say   287
as if they were gods ...   (965B)

It is not as you say, O King, that   287
we [you] call the martyrs gods ...   (965C)

121 See Exod. 20:4-5.

You wrote that   287

After eight hundred years Hezekiah, the King of the Jews, drove the bronze serpent (965D)
out of the temple,[122] *so have I. After eight hundred years, I have driven the*
idols out of the churches ...

... however, as you boast, after eight hundred years you have driven   289
out of the churches the grace and the blessing of the martyrs and, as (965E)
you yourself confessed at the beginning,
intentionally, and not out of any need,
and later on
you signed so with your own hand ...

You wrote that   295
there should be an Ecumenical Council ...   (970A)

You also threaten us and say   295
I will send [army?] in Rome and shall have the icon of St Peter demolished. (971A)
Not only that, but I will have also Gregory the bishop of the city brought here
in bonds, as Constantine did to Martinus ...[123]

... as you say   295
If you (I) become serious and inflict upon us (you) threats ...   (971B)

BY THE SAME GREGORY, POPE OF ROME TO EMPEROR LEO –
SECOND LETTER

... you have not changed your way of thinking ... but rather you have   299
persisted in your stubborness and your inner passions, and you wrote (975D)
that
I am King and priest as well ...

You also wrote that   305
Why was nothing said (defined) on the icons in the Six Councils?   (279D)

No theological argument is to be found in Leo's position on icons. The
most that one can discern is, in the words of Gero, 'a simple reiteration
of the second commandment, with none of the later more sophisticated

---

122 See 2 Kings 18:4.
123 Constans II (641–668). Leo attempted to carry through his threat against Gregory's
     successor, Gregory III (731–741). In 732 he sent an expedition to force the Pope to
     comply with the imperial iconoclastic orders, after the Pope identified and
     disciplined those of his clergy who were against icons. The expedition failed, as the
     Byzantine fleet was destroyed during a storm on the Adriatic.

Christological and philosophical arguments.'[124] Leo was a military man rather than a thinker, a single-minded ruler and a pragmatist rather than an enlightened and articulate spokesman.[125]

The advice Leo sought from the ecclesiastics was only that which supported his views. Among the main supporters, or instigators, of Leo's iconoclastic ideas were Constantine, the Bishop of Nacoleia, and a certain Beser, convert from Christianity to Islam.[126] Germanus, the Patriarch of Constantinople (715–730) and the proper official adviser to the Emperor on matters of the Church, but an ardent supporter of icons, was subsequently removed and replaced by the iconoclast Patriarch Anastasius (730–753).[127] In 732/3 Leo removed from the ecclesiastical jurisdiction of the West the areas of southern Italy and eastern Illyricon (except Thrace), territories which were under the political administration of the East. He also removed Isauria from the jurisdiction of the Patriarch of Antioch, then under the Arabs. Thus he made the jurisdictional borders of the Church coincide with the borders of the State. The Church was now defined in terms of the *imperium*. From 'catholic' in the theological sense, meaning whole, encompassing, and all-inclusive, the Church becomes 'catholic' in the political sense, that

124 Gero, 'Notes on Byzantine Iconoclasm,' p 27. See especially his *Leo III*, pp 103–112.

125 Mango suggests that Leo attacked the icons because he was convinced that God was using the Arab Muslims against the Byzantine Empire, as a way of punishing the Christians for venerating the icons: 'Historical Introduction,' p 3.

126 Theophanes, ed de Boor, I, 402, 405. Thus, according to Theophanes, the Muslim iconoclastic decree of Yazid II against the Christian icons was instigated by a Jew (de Boor, I, 401, 402), while the Christian iconoclastic decree of Leo III was instigated by a Muslim! Vasiliev, 'The Iconoclastic Edict,' p 28, nn 12, 31, identifies Beser with 'Tessaracontapehys' [the Forty-yard-long-one] whom John the presbyter, the representative of the Eastern Patriarchates, in his report to the Council of Nicea (787), described as the Jew who influenced Yazid. However, the description by John the presbyter (Mansi, 13:197A–200B) does not seem to justify this identification.

127 There is a short account of a meeting in Constantinople, probably a *silentio* (a state council meeting of State and Church officials), at which were present Leo himself, Patriarch Germanus, Constantine of Nacoleia, and Beser. The suggestion that Germanus died a violent death, being hanged in the monastery of Chora along with Archdeacon Anthimus (Mansi, 12:269C), has generally been refuted by modern historians: see Vasiliev, *History of the Byzantine Empire*, I, 258; Diehl, 'Leo III,' p 11; Hefele, *A History of the Councils of the Church*, V, 277. They prefer the account of Theophanes that Germanus, after resigning from the throne in 730, retired to his family home where he lived peacefully (de Boor, I, 409). John of Damascus states that Germanus was beaten and exiled: *Against those who defame the holy icons*, II, 12 (PG 94:1297; Kotter, III, 103), but he does not refer to his death. The version of a violent death probably comes from martyrological sources.

is 'universal.' As a result perhaps, of this misunderstanding of the adjective 'catholic,' we see from the beginning of the eighth century, and especially in the context of the iconoclastic controversies, a more frequent use of the adjective 'Orthodox,' in the sense of 'upright,' 'unique,' 'balanced,' 'truthful'; an epithet with the same theological connotations as the original 'catholic.'[128] From then on 'Orthodox' became the official appellation of the Eastern Church. The theology of the icon, and its reaffirmation, was another manifestation of the 'catholicity,' that is of the wholeness of truth, that the Church embodies. That is why the victory of the Church over the issue of the icons was hailed in 843 as a triumph of 'Orthodoxy' for the entire Christian Church.

CONSTANTINE V

Unlike Leo, his son and successor, Emperor Constantine V (741–775), was a man of strong personal convictions on matters of faith. As Stefanidis has observed, while in Leo's times the veneration of the icons was combatted as idolatry, during Constantine's reign it was fought as heresy![129] Some exaggerated, utterly pietistic, and ignorant behaviour towards icons that was the result of Leo's iconoclasm must have aggravated the situation.

For Constantine the justification of icons stands or falls on the justification of the icon of Christ. If the icon of Christ has no theological justification, no other icon can be justified either. Thus the matter of the icons becomes an extension of the Christological controversies of the fourth and fifth centuries.[130] Constantine's own pointed and provocative theological Inquiries (Peûseis) provided the backbone for the theology adopted by the iconoclastic Council of 754.[131] As a matter of fact, if one compares Constantine's Inquiries and the text of the Horos of this council, there is no doubt, that at times, the council reports

---

128 See also below, 208B, n 12.
129 Stefanidis, Ekklesiastike Historia, p 258. On Constantine V and the Council of 754 see the excellent follow-up study of Gero, Byzantine Iconoclasm during the Reign of Constantine V; and also Ostrogorsky, Studien zur Geschichte des byzantinischen Bilderstreites, pp 7–45.
130 See Schanborn, L'Icône du Christ.
131 Only fragments of these Inquiries have survived and been transmitted to us through the Refutations (PG 100:205–533) of Patriarch Nicephorus (806–815). They have been collected by Ostrogorsky, Studien zur Geschichte des byzantinischen Bilderstreites, pp 8–11, and Hennephof, Textus byzantinos, pp 552–557. There is doubt as to whether the third Inquiry (which Hennephof has included with some reservation) is by Constantine or by a ninth-century iconoclast theologian. For a summary of Constantine's Inquiries see Gero, 'Notes on Byzantine Iconoclasm,' pp 28–32.

verbatim Constantine's own statements. In the first Inquiry Constantine wants to refute the claim that an icon depicting Christ is actually an icon of Christ, because Christ is of two natures brought together in one unconfused union.[132] Thus, in painting an icon of Christ, the painter either divides or confuses the two natures, since, according to Constantine, 'every icon ... is of the same substance with the subject depicted on it.'[133] Obviously Constantine identifies the icon of Christ with Christ himself. This line of thinking betrays a monophysite disposition which, however, Constantine avoids confirming by using the Chalcedonian thesis of the 'unconfused union of the two natures of Christ.'[134] Thus, according to Constantine, 'Either the divine quality is also depicted in that icon (i.e. in the icon of Christ) ... or you perceive Christ as being only a mere man ... For the icon is an icon of a person, and the divine one is indescribable.'[135] Constantine consistently prefers to use the word *prôsopon* (person), with Nestorian implications, rather than hypostasis: 'That which is given characteristics is one person, and he who describes that person obviously describes also the divine nature which is uncircumscribable.'[136]

The Nestorian leanings of Constantine's theology become more evident in his second Inquiry, where he maintains that the Church knows no other icon of Christ but the Eucharist which, according to Constantine, is Christ's own body 'by participation and convention.'[137] While in his first Inquiry Constantine seems to lean towards monophysitism, in the second one he leans towards Nestorianism.[138] Thus,

132 Hennephof, *Textus byzantinos*, p 52, fragment 141.
133 Ibid, fragment 142.
134 Ibid, fragments 162, 141.
135 Ibid, fragment 159.
136 Ibid, fragment 146. In the words of Mango, 'the Orthodox were clearly on more solid ground when they argued that an image was a symbol (*typos*) which, by reason of resemblance, reproduces the "person" (*prôsopon*), but not the substance (*ousia* or *hypostasis*) of the model': *The Art of the Byzantine Empire*, p 150.
137 Hennephof, *Textus byzantinos*, p 54, fragment 165. For a most thorough study of this point see Gero, 'The Eucharistic Doctrine of the Byzantine Iconoclasts and Its Sources,' in which the author concludes (p 21) that 'the iconoclastic doctrine of the eucharist was not necessarily *neoterismôs*, (innovation), or a wilful misapplication of the language of the liturgy. Rather, the iconoclasts, Constantine as well as the Council of 754, in propounding the doctrine of the eucharist as the true icon of Christ, depended upon certain, somewhat obscure, yet genuine, components of exegetical patristic tradition.'
138 For the affinity between Constantine's eucharistic theology and Nestorian theology see Gero 'Notes on Byzantine Iconoclasm,' pp 29–32.

the dilemma which Constantine wanted the iconophiles to face – that by depicting Christ on an icon they are professing either monophysitism or Nestorianism[139] – became his own: later iconophiles branded Constantine as an ardent Nestorian.[140]

THE COUNCIL OF 754

The iconoclastic views of Emperor Constantine V, with some modifications, found official sanction in a council convened by him in the year 754, in the palace of Hiereia, across from Constantinople, on the Asiatic side of the Bosphorus.[141] The council was presided over by Theodosius of Ephesus and Sissinius, or Pastillas, of Perga. Anastasius, Patriarch of Constantinople, who was subservient to the Emperor,[142] had died earlier that year. In spite of the large number of participating bishops (338), none of the 'Catholic thrones,' that is the patriarchal seats of Rome, Alexandria, Antioch, and Jerusalem, was represented. The works of this council lasted from 10 February to 8 August 754. The council concluded its works at St Mary's Church in Blacherna, a northern suburb of Constantinople.[143]

The records of the Council of 754, like the iconoclastic writings in general, have not survived. A few of them have been passed on in fragmentary form in the writings of the iconophiles, who quoted them for the purpose of refuting them. The ninth Canon of the Seventh Ecumenical Council (787) forbids the hiding of iconoclastic books and directs anyone possessing such writings to deliver them 'to the Bishop of Constantinople, in order that they may be placed together with other heretical books.'[144] Subsequently such books were destroyed. Testimonies heard during the same council confirmed that books by iconophiles, during the years in which the iconoclasts prevailed, suffered

---

139 See below, 260A–B.
140 See Theophanes, ed de Boor, I, 415, 435.
141 For the theology of the iconoclastic Council of 754 see Anastos, 'The Argument for Iconoclasm.'
142 Theophanes reports that, when for a moment Artavasdus took the upper hand in his revolt against Constantine, Anastasius supported the iconophiles in condemning Constantine and proclaiming Artavasdus as an orthodox Emperor; de Boor, I, 415.
143 Theophanes, ed de Boor, I 428.
144 Mansi, 13:430B. It seems that the suggestion for the destruction of the iconoclastic writings was proposed first by Peter the protopresbyter, the representative of the bishop of Rome, during the fifth session of the Council: Mansi, 13:200D–E.

the same fate.[145] In the edition of Mansi the iconoclastic Council of 754 is treated in less than twenty lines, or in less than a third of one column of one page! In this very brief account the council is called *âtheos* (godless), and its participants *mataiôphrones* (men of vain thinking), who 'called the venerable icons of Christ and those of all the saints "idols," rejected the prayers of intercession, and committed the relics, honoured by God, to fire.'[146]

The best source of information about the iconoclastic Council of 754 are the Acts of the Seventh Ecumenical Council of 787. From these Acts we learn that in the iconoclastic Council of 754 writings were presented as testimonies against the icons. Such writings included Nilus' *Letter to Olympiodorus, the sub-prefect* (but only those extracts which appeared to be against the icons),[147] and Anastasius of Theopolis' *Letter to a certain scholastic*. The iconoclastic council, however, paid no attention to the distinction made by Anastasius between 'worship' and 'veneration'[148] of an icon. Principal figures in the iconoclastic council were, according to Basil, Bishop of Ancara,[149] Theodosius of Ephesus, Sissinius of Perga, the so-called Pastillas, Basil of Pisidia, and Constantine of Nacoleia,[150] who became Patriarch of Constantinople under the name Constantine II (754–766).

After its deliberations the iconoclastic council promulgated on 27 August 754 its *Horos* or Definition, which was largely based on the theses of Emperor Constantine.[151] Vasiliev[152] seems uncertain whether the iconoclastic Definition has been faithfully reproduced by the Seventh Ecumenical Council 'in its complete original form,' although he maintains that it was preserved 'in parts and in a somewhat modified form.' There are no signs, however, of any abbreviation or distortion in the reading

---

145 Mansi, 13:184E–185A.
146 Mansi, 12:577A.
147 Mansi, 13:36A–D and 37B.
148 Mansi, 13:56C.
149 Basil was himself an iconoclast who, during the Seventh Ecumenical Council, asked to be accepted again into the Church, confessed the faith of the previous six Ecumenical Councils, and anathematized the iconoclastic Council of 754. Two more bishops, Theodore of Myra and Theodosius of Ammorium, submitted similar confessions and declarations and were admitted to the council. The text of one of these confessions of faith, that of Theodosius, is given in full in the Acts of this council: Mansi, 12:1014–1015.
150 Mansi, 12:1010D.
151 See above, pp 30–31.
152 Vasiliev, *History of the Byzantine Empire*, I, 251, 260.

of the Definition as it appears in the Acts of the Seventh Ecumenical Council. The format of the Definition is identical to that of other councils, even that of 787. The sequence of discussion follows a logical and uninterrupted order: an introduction to the purpose for which the council was convened; biblical and patristic testimonies and references to the practices of the Church which are against icons; decrees against the making and use of icons; review and confirmation of the faith of the previous ecumenical councils; renunciation of those who do not ascribe to the doctrines of this council; an expression of consensus from the participants; and the declaration of the council as Ecumenical. There is no reason to believe that the Council of 787 read a distorted text of the *Horos* of the Council of 754 at its sixth session.

The iconoclastic Council of 754 found no support from the other patriarchates. In 760 a local council, which was convened in Jerusalem and presided over by Patriarch Theodore I (735–770), condemned the iconoclasts.[153] In 767 Patriarch Theodore and the other Patriarchs of the East sent an encyclical letter to the Pope of Rome, Paul I (757–767), expressing their condemnation of the iconoclasts. This letter was read during a council convened in the Lateran in the year 769 by Pope Stephen IV (768–771). In 781 another local council, in Antioch, condemned the iconoclasts and particularly their argument that the icon of Christ divides Christ into two persons.[154] There is no record of this Council of Antioch except for a few fragments preserved by Theodore the Studite, which Mansi has included in his *Collectio*.[155]

Iconoclasm during Constantine's time did not remain merely a theological and dialectic controversy. Perhaps even more than in the times of Leo, the iconophiles were confronted with physical violence. The iconoclastic decree of the Council of 754 not only branded the veneration of the icons as a heresy, but made it an illegal practice as well. State employees were either dismissed or punished for inconophile sentiments and actions. The primary target of the iconoclasts were the monks, who were forced to abandon their monasteries, which subsequently were turned into social institutions.[156] The persecution against the iconophiles was intensified particularly after 766. Theophanes, an

153 Mansi, 12:679–680.
154 'In the same way as he is one from two opposite ones, and he is called together into one person, so is his icon one, which is of the same one Christ': Mansi, 12:899B.
155 Mansi, 12:899B–902A.
156 A number of monks fled to Rome. Consequently Pope Paul I ordered that some Greek be introduced in the services so that the refugees would be able to follow the prayers: Hefele, *A History of the Councils of the Church*, v, 317, n 2.

ardent iconophile himself and perhaps not an entirely objective historian of this period, depicts the actions of the iconoclasts during Constantine's reign in dark colours.[157]

BETWEEN TWO COUNCILS (754-787)

Constantine was succeeded by Leo IV (775-780), who was called 'the Khazar' because his mother, Irene, was the daughter of Khagan from Khazar. At the beginning of his reign he was sympathetic towards the iconophiles, but later he also turned against them. Many of his officials were punished for their iconophile views. It seems that Leo IV wanted to appear lenient towards iconophiles who did not hold a public position while officially he maintained an iconoclastic state policy.

With the death of Leo IV at the age of thirty the balance swung to the iconophile side. Leo's wife, Irene the Athenian, the controversial and ambitious mother of Constantine VI (780-798), made her iconophile sentiments immediately known. Acting as Empress in the place of her underaged son-Emperor, she neutralized all opposition to her son's rights to the throne. The effort of state officials to annul a previous agreement between themselves and Leo IV to respect the right of his son Constantine to reign after his own death was actually aimed at preventing Irene, who was known for her iconophile feelings, from influencing or changing the iconoclastic policies of her husband and his predecessors. It was, however, with the resignation of Patriarch Paul IV of Constantinople (780-784) that the veneration of icons became a matter of public discussion. Paul had been a pious Patriarch. Although at his ordination he had signed an agreement that he would neither condone nor venerate icons, he was distressed by the fact that the Church of Constantinople had been condemned by and isolated from the other patriarchates because of its iconoclastic position and he wanted reconciliation with them. According to Theophanes,[158] Patriarch Paul, in resigning from the throne, withdrew to the monastery of Floros to repent for his alliance with the iconoclasts. Before his death he pleaded for the convention of an ecumenical council that would uphold the teaching of the Church on icons, an act which would lead to the re-establishment of communion with the other Churches.

After Patriarch Paul's death Tarasius, a layman holding an official

157 See de Boor, I, 436-446. See also below, 329A-D.
158 De Boor, I, 457-458.

position and known, perhaps, for his iconophile views, yielded to the pressures of the Empress Irene and of the people, and was ordained Patriarch of Constantinople (784–806). Two years later, in August 786, a council was convened by Irene in the Church of the Holy Apostles in Constantinople. This council was violently interrupted by the iconoclasts, an indication of the extent of their power and influence, even at a time when an iconophile Empress and an iconophile Patriarch were in power.[159] This council was adjourned early and the representatives returned home to the delight of the iconoclasts, who were jubilant at their victory.[160]

THE COUNCIL OF NICEA (787)

It was during the next year, from 23 September to 13 October 787, that the council was convened again, this time away from Constantinople, in Nicea, the place of the first Ecumenical Council (325). Although the deliberations took place in Nicea, the council concluded its works, with its eighth session, in Constantinople. According to Photius, Patriarch of Constantinople (867, 868, 877–886), there were 367 bishops and representatives present at this council.[161] The Empress herself invited Rome to send representatives. To the eastern patriarchates both she and the Patriarch sent letters of invitation. Theophanes seems to explain the reason, indirectly: 'because the peace with the Arabs had not yet been dissolved.'[162] A letter to the heads of the Christian communities from the Byzantine Empress alone would have made the Arab authorities suspicious that a political alliance against them was meditated, and thus they would have prevented the Patriarchs from travelling to

159 Mansi, 12:990–991. The Seventh Ecumenical Council accepted bishops who had participated in the iconoclastic Council of 754, but gave grim consideration to those who persisted in their iconoclastic acts, and especially those who interrupted the convention of the Council in 786, even after they had repented. Considerable discussion took place during the first session of the council over the cases of Hypatius of Nicea, Leo of Rhodes, Gregory of Pisinus, Leo of Iconium, George of Pisidia, Nicholas of Hierapolis and Leo of Carpathos: Mansi, 12:1015–1050E. Two courses of action were suggested: to defrock them, or to accept them into the council; the latter, a moderate view by Patriarch Tarasius, prevailed.

160 Theophanes, ed de Boor, I, 461–462.

161 De Synodis, quoted by Mansi, 13:491D. Attending the council was a large number of heads of monasteries (archimandrites) – Nicodemos Hagioretes specifies 136: Pedâlion, 314.

162 De Boor, I, 461:1.

Constantinople. The signature of the Patriarch as well was an assurance that the content of the letter related to Church matters. However, even that scheme did not appease the Syrian monks who, not wanting to jeopardize the convention of a council in any way, or the participation of representatives from the eastern patriarchates, prevented the messengers from delivering the letters to the Patriarchs themselves, fearing that the Arab rulers would still not allow them to travel to Byzantium. Instead, they sent two monks-presbyters, John and Thomas, to represent the Patriarchs of Antioch and Alexandria, as well as the Patriarch of Jerusalem who at the time was in exile. John and Thomas signed the Definition of the iconophile Council of Nicea, 'attending for the three apostolic thrones of Alexandria, Antioch, and Jerusalem.'[163] Because these representatives were not sent by the Patriarchs of the East themselves, their presence at the council was therefore, strictly speaking, not in order. They represented correctly, however, the theology and the catholic sentiment of the eastern patriarchates, which were in favour of the theology of the icons and had taken a position against the iconoclasts. During the third session of the council the letters of Tarasius on the icons to the Patriarchs of the East, and their responses, were read as testimonies of the common faith of the eastern sees.[164] The representatives of the Pope of Rome (Hadrian I, 772–795) were also not in perfect canonical order, as they were sent to Constantinople for a different purpose, not for participation at an ecumenical council. For this reason, on their return they were disciplined for trespassing their assignment. However, during its second session the council heard two letters of Hadrian, Bishop of Rome; one to Constantine and Irene, 'which were sent in a conciliar manner' (or, 'as if to a Council'[165]) and another to Patriarch Tarasius stating the common faith of the Church of Rome on icons. Thus there was representation in the council of the faith of Rome expressed in the most official manner. According to Anastasius the Librarian, the translator of the Acts of the council into Latin for Pope John VIII (872–882),[166] the letters of Hadrian also contained the Pope's censure of Tarasius for the manner in which he became Patriarch, hastily, from the ranks of the laity; and for his calling himself 'Ecumenical' and 'Patriarch' against the provisions of the canons, a claim

163 Mansi, 13:380D.
164 Mansi, 12:1119E–1135B.
165 See Mansi, 12:1055A–1071B, 1054E.
166 Mansi, 12:981.

which reflects the later Roman attitude towards Constantinople, and the beginning of the clash between East and West over the matter of authority and primacy. These portions, according to this Anastasius, were eliminated from the text read at the council. And yet the second letter of the same Pope to Tarasius himself,[167] which expresses the dissatisfaction of the Pope over the manner in which Tarasius ascended the throne of Constantinople and makes the acceptance of Tarasius' ordination contingent upon his reinstating the veneration of icons in the Church of Constantinople, was read at the council in full! The Pope had been reassured about the orthodox of Tarasius' faith, and this prevented him from breaking relations with Tarasius.[168] Tarasius defended himself and explained his views on the episcopate in two letters to the Pope, reprinted at the end of the Acts of the council.[169]

Among those present at the Council of 787 were seventeen bishops who had participated in the iconoclastic Council of 754. They had now anathematized the iconoclastic council and rejected its teachings. The Fathers of the Seventh Ecumenical Council were actually pleased by the fact that 'there were some men left from the ill-gathered Council, refuting and destroying what they had wickedly done, and condemning their own shamefulness.'[170] A dominant figure among these was Gregory, Bishop of Neocaesarea, 'a principal of the past impious Council.'[171] Gregory was accepted at the council during its third session, after he had read a *libellus* of repentance and anathematized the iconoclasts and the iconoclastic council in which he had taken part.[172] It is interesting that it is he whom the council asked to read the Definition of the iconoclastic Council of 754! In doing so the Seventh Ecumenical Council underlined the authenticity of the iconoclastic Definition of 754, and expressed its intention to reverse it.

The Council of 787 convened in eight sessions. During the first session[173] the council heard the address of Patriarch Tarasius calling the participants to define the *isôrropon*, that is, the balanced or 'orthodox'[174] position of the faith. This address was followed by the address

---

167 Mansi, 12:1078c–1083d.
168 Mansi, 12:1078e–1079a.
169 Mansi, 13:458c–466b.
170 Mansi, 12:1118c.
171 Mansi, 12:1118b.
172 Mansi, 12:1114a.
173 Mansi, 12:991e–1051a.
174 Mansi, 12:1002b; see also above, n 128.

of the Emperors, the confessions of faith, and the declaration of repentance by some former iconoclast bishops. During the second session[175] the case of Gregory of Neocaesarea was discussed and the letters of the Pope of Rome to the council, as well as to Tarasius himself, were read.[176] During the third session[177] former iconoclast bishops, after reading their statements of renunciation, were admitted to the council. The council also heard the letters of Tarasius to the Patriarchs of the East, their responses, as well as the *synodikôn* (the report of their council of 760) with an accompanying letter by Patriarch Theodore of Jerusalem. These documents were confirmed personally by the participants as authentic.[178] With this session the formal reconciliation of the Church of Constantinople with all the patriarchal sees was achieved.

During the fourth session[179] the council heard, at the suggestion of Patriarch Tarasius, appropriate readings from the Bible and the patristic literature pertinent to icons. These readings constitute an interesting, although incomplete, list of source material on the tradition and the theology of the icons.[180] This session concluded with a series of condemnations (*anathêmata*) of those who were against icons, and a confession of the Orthodox faith, sealed with the signatures of the participants. During the fifth session[181] more writings in support of the icons were read.[182] Some participants had brought with them books of their own and demanded that excerpts supporting the tradition of icons be read in the council, but the presiding Patriarch Tarasius ruled that the council had heard enough evidence in support of icons. The council was also shown pages or remnants of iconophile books that survived destruction by the iconoclasts.[183] Subsequently John the presbyter, representing the eastern patriarchs, was called to read from a *Note* (*pittâkion*) 'how the destruction of the icons began.'[184] John attributed the beginning of iconoclasm to a certain Jew who convinced Caliph Yazid to issue a decree against icons,[185] and to Constantine, the

175 Mansi, 12:1051A–1111E.
176 See above, nn 165 and 167.
177 Mansi, 12:1114A–1154E.
178 Mansi, 12:1145C–1154B.
179 Mansi, 13:1A–156E.
180 See appendix, sections I and II, nos. 1–36.
181 Mansi, 13:157A–201E.
182 See appendix, section II, nos. 37–51.
183 See above, pp 32–33.
184 Mansi, 13:197A–200B
185 See above, p 19 and n 126.

iconoclast Bishop of Nacoleia, principal adviser to Emperor Leo III. The bishop of Messena also testified that the destruction of icons was begun by the Muslims and that he was a child in Syria when the Arabs were destroying icons.[186] Towards the end of this session the papal representatives asked that an icon be brought in to be kissed by all the participants, obviously as a demonstration of the faith of the council. The motion was accepted and acted upon in the next session. This session concluded with statements of condemnation of heretical teachings and with a declaration of the Orthodox faith.

The sole item of business during the sixth session[187] was the reading of the *Horos* or Definition of the iconoclastic Council of 754 and a Refutation of this Definition, point by point.[188] (It is these two texts in their entirety which we offer here in translation.)

During the seventh session[189] the council promulgated its own *Horos*. (This is the third text we offer here in translation.) During this session the council also anathematized the Council of 754, its participants, and those who accepted their teaching. In the manner of the iconoclastic Council of 754, it singled out and anathematized three major iconoclasts, Theodosius, Sissinius (or Pastillas), and Basil.[190] The council also anathematized by name the three iconoclast Patriarchs, Anastasius (730-753), Constantine II (754-766), and Nicetas I (766-780), 'who,' in the words of the council, 'successively presided over the throne of Constantinople as a new Arius, Nestorius and Dioscorus.'[191] The council also condemned Antonius and John 'as Manes, Apollinaris, and

---

186 Mansi, 13:200B.

187 Mansi, 13:204A-364E.

188 The author of this Refutation is unknown. A possible author is Deacon Epiphanius from Catanae, Sicily, a representative of Bishop Thomas of Sardinia, and the reader of the text in the Council. The Christological affirmations of Patriarch Germanus and of John of Damascus form the basis of the theological statements of this text, although, according to Meyendorff, 'Nicea II did not elaborate on the technical points of Christology raised by the iconoclastic Council of Hieria. The task of refuting this Council and of developing the rather general Christological affirmations of Germanus and John of Damascus belongs to the two major theological figures of the second iconoclastic period ... Theodore the Studite and Patriarch Nicephorus': *Byzantine Theology*, p 46.

189 Mansi, 13:364E-413A.

190 The phrase, 'The Trinity has abolished the teaching of these three,' is reminiscent of a similar phrase, 'The Trinity has abolished these three,' of the Council of 754, referring to Patriarch Germanus, Patriarch George of Constantia of Cyprus, and John of Damascus. See below, 356C-D.

191 Mansi, 13:400A.

Eutyches,' Theodore of Syracuse, John of Nicomedeia, and Constantine of Nacoleia. This session concluded with the formal submission of the Definition to the Emperors, Constantine and Irene, and to the priests of the Church.[192]

For its eighth and final session the council moved to Constantinople where it convened at the palace of Magnavra. During this session the *Horos* of the Council was signed by Constantine and Irene. The *Horos* and a portion of the fourth session of the council were then read in the presence of the people and of the army!

The council also promulgated twenty-two 'ecclesiastical canons' dealing with the office of bishop (bishops should not be elected by the rulers but by bishops alone, according to the Council of Nicea), local councils, the consecration of churches, the matter of accepting Jews into the Church after a proper conversion, the injunction against hiding away the books of the iconoclasts,[193] as well as matters pertinent to the office of the presbyter, to monasteries, and to laymen. With these canons the council was seeking to rectify situations caused by the iconoclasts during the period when they were in power. These canons, therefore, are interesting sources of information about ecclesiastical life during the iconoclastic era. This last session concluded with a speech by Epiphanius, the deacon, from Catanae in Sicily.[194]

The council was accepted and treated as Ecumenical, although Rome and the patriarchal sees of Jerusalem, Antioch, and Alexandria, because of the peculiarities in their representation, were reluctant to proclaim it officially as the 'Seventh Ecumemical Council.'[195] It was Photius of Constantinople who, in an encyclical letter of 866, and in front of a general council in Constantinople in 867, urged that the Council of 787 be officially proclaimed as Ecumenical.[196] The proclamation, however, took place later, during a general council of 383 representatives from

192 Mansi, 13:400c–413a.
193 See also above, p 32 and n 144.
194 Mansi, 13:442a–458b. The prominence given to this deacon by the council makes him the probable author of the text of the Refutation. See also above, n 188.
195 See the testimony of Photius of Constantinople in the fifth session of the Council of 879: Mansi, 17:493c.
196 Patriarch Photius was an ardent defender of the faith and the ecclesiastical rights of the Church of Constantinople. In his account of the councils he praises this council (Mansi, 13:491c–496a), and in a letter to Boris of Bulgaria he glorifies the role of the Church of Constantinople in the iconoclastic controversy (PG 102:649–656). See also Dvornik, 'The Patriarch Photius and Iconoclasm.'

all the patriarchal sees of East and West, in Constantinople (879/80).[197] Thus, the declaration of the Second Council of Nicea as the 'Seventh Ecumenical Council' took place about a hundred years after it was convened, after the consciousness of the entire Church – the main criterion of infallibility and authority – had testified through its experience to the orthodoxy of its Definition.[198]

In 813, twenty-five years after the Seventh Ecumenical Council, iconoclasm was revived. The iconoclastic emperors had proven to be good administrators, the iconophiles bad politicians. This is another phase of iconoclasm, with its own interests and intricacies, historical, cultural, and theological, but it is beyond the scope of this introduction. Let us note only that, during this phase and during the reign of Leo V the Armenian (813–820),[199] a second iconoclastic council was convened in Constantinople (in 815) which condemned the Council of 787 and restored the iconoclastic Council of 754.[200]

During the second phase of iconoclasm the main figures on the side of the iconophiles and the defenders of icons were Theodore, the abbot of the monastery of Studion (d 826), and Patriarch Nicephorus of Constantinople (806–815).[201] Emperor Leo V was assassinated. His successor, Michael II (820–829), who was instrumental in Leo's assassination, became Emperor with the help of the iconophiles, although he himself was an opportunist rather than an iconophile. Iconoclasm did not subside with his ascension to the throne. He sought to reconcile the two parties by seeking to abolish all the councils (754, 787, and 815) which dealt with icons.

---

197 This is a very significant council which was convened to restore unity between Rome and Constantinople, breached for a time by the conflict between Pope Nicholas I (858–867) and Patriarch Photius (867–868, 877–886). The council has been called the Council of Union and has been considered by many Orthodox to be Ecumenical, although it was not declared so officially. See Karmiris, *Ta dogmatikâ kai symbolikâ mnemeîa*, I, 262.

198 Some opposition to and condemnation of the Council of 787 by local councils in the West (Frankfurt in 794, and Paris in 823) must be attributed mainly to the growing mutual alienation and misunderstanding between East and West, and the weakening of a common theological thinking and language. See Vasiliev, 'The Iconoclastic Edict,' p 36. See also Munitz, 'Synoptic Greek Accounts of the Seventh Council.'

199 Notice the place of origin of this Emperor in reference to the previous iconoclast Emperors Leo III and Constantine V! See above, pp 24–32.

200 See Alexander, 'The Iconoclastic Council of St. Sophia (815) and Its Definition (*Horos*).' See also Anastos, 'The Ethical Theory of Images.'

201 On Nicephorus see Alexander, *The Patriarch Nicephorus*.

During the reign of Michael's successor, Emperor Theophilus (829–842), iconoclasm intensified, although it never reached the height of the first iconoclastic period. Theodora, the wife of Theophilus, was an iconophile. After the death of her husband, when she was regent for her underaged son, Michael (reigned 842–867), she influenced those developments which favoured the iconophile side. The iconoclast Patriarch John VII Grammaticos (836–842) was defrocked and replaced by the iconophile Methodius I (842–846). Less than a year after the death of Theodora's husband the iconophiles succeeded in calling a council (843). The main act of this council was to confirm the teaching and the canons of the Council of 787. On 11 March 843, the first Sunday of Lent, a solemn ceremony took place in the cathedral of St Sophia to mark officially the victory of the Church over the iconoclasts and 'the triumph of Orthodoxy.'[202] The event is observed even today in the Orthodox Church, on the first Sunday of Lent, which has been designated 'the Sunday of Orthodoxy.' It is a day of asserting the common faith of the Church. As the *synodikôn* of Orthodoxy,[203] that

202 Vasiliev, 'Sur l'année du rétablissement de l'Orthodoxie.' For the texts of the Council of 843 and the ceremonial confirmation of the triumph of Orthodoxy see Gouillard, 'Le Synodikon de l'Orthodoxie.' The two phases of iconoclasm provide the student with many events, personalities, and circumstances for comparison and contrast. However, the striking similarity in their circumstances and the decisive role played by the two Empresses, Irene and Theodora, in the restoration of the icons cannot pass unnoticed. In their capacity as regents to the throne both succeeded in neutralizing the power of the iconoclasts and regrouping the political and spiritual forces of the iconophiles. The iconoclasts were a minority but a capable and determined one. The majority iconophiles were weak and unprepared for a confrontation, although they were determined when the confrontation arrived. Both these Empresses, a little less than half a century apart from each other in time, succeeded in convening councils (787 and 843) in order to uphold the veneration of the icons and to define collectively the theology and praxis of the Church on this matter.

203 The Orthodox people prefer the term *synod* rather than *council*. Etymologically the word *synod* speaks of men 'walking together' rather than conferring together. Walking together implies an experiential participation, physical as well as mental and spiritual, and a committed commonality, a certain 'covenant.' 'Do two walk together, unless they know each other?' (Amos 3:3). The biblical scene of the resurrected Christ walking together with the frightened disciples towards Emmaus is the best and most characteristic image of the Church in Life, and the best way the Orthodox Church can express the notion of the Church in 'synod.' The fullness of communion of the disciples with Christ takes place when they recognize and confess Him as the same Christ, in the breaking of the break (Luke 24: 13–31). See the relevant papers in the special issue of *The Greek Orthodox Theological Review* on the forthcoming Pan-Orthodox Synod, 24 (Summer/Fall 1979), esp. pp 123–124, 215–216.

is the conciliar statement delineating the converging experience of the Church, puts it:

As the Prophets have known; as the Apostles have taught; as the Church has received; as the Teachers have defined; as the universe has consented; as the grace has shone; as the truth has manifested; as falsehood has been lashed out; as the wisdom has explicated; as Christ has praised, this way we also think of, this way we speak of, this way we confess Christ our true God and His holy saints: to honour them by means of words, of writings, of gestures, of sacrifices, of churches, of icons. And as far as Christ is concerned, to bow down to Him and revere Him as Lord; and as for the others, to honour them as true servants of His, and pay to them a relative veneration, for having, all of us, a common Lord.

THE TEXTS

Sixth Session

In the name of the Lord and Sovereign Jesus Christ, our true 204A God, during the reign of our most pious and Christ-loving sovereigns Constantine and his God-fearing mother Irene,[1] in the eighth year of their consulship, two days before the October *nonae*[2] of the eleventh indiction.[3]

After the holy and Ecumenical Council, which was convened by divine grace and according to a pious decree of these sov- 204B ereigns confirmed by God, had assembled in the splendid cathedral of the Niceans of the province of Bithynia (with Peter, the most reverend protopresbyter of the most holy Church of the holy Apostle Peter in Rome, and Peter, the most reverend presbyter, monk, and abbot of the holy monastery of Sabbas

---

1 These are Emperor Constantine VI (780–798) and his iconophile mother, Irene the Athenian, the wife of the iconoclast Emperor Leo IV the Khazar, or the Armenian (775–780).

2 *Nonae* is the Latin term for the fifth day of every month of the year, except March, July, and October; or for the *ninth* day (where the word *nonae* comes from) before *Ides* – *Ides* being the fifteenth day of March, May, July, and October. Two days, therefore, preceding the ninth day before the October *Ides* points to the fourth day of October. The works of the Seventh Ecumenical Council lasted from 24 September to 13 October 787. Thus the sixth session of the council began on 4 October 787.

3 An *indiction* is a cycle of fifteen years. It was Theophanes the Chronographer who first devised a system to synchronize the traditional chronology (which numbered from the year of the 'creation of the world') with a number of indictions, which system he used in his *Chronographia*, compiled 810–814. For more on Theophanes' system, as well as its shortcomings, see Ostrogorsky, *History of the Byzantine State*, pp 79ff. On calendars and calculations see the work of Grumel, *La Chronologie*; on indiction, pp 193–103.

in Rome, both occupying the apostolic seat of the most devout and holy archbishop Hadrian of the senior Rome; Tarasius, the most devout and most holy archbishop of the celebrated Constantinople, the new Rome; John and Thomas, the most pious 204C presbyters, monks, and representatives of the apostolic thrones of the eastern administration); and after everyone took his place before the most sacred pulpit of the great church named after Sophia,[4] in the presence and audience also of the most honourable and esteemed of those in authority, that is Petronas, famous among the consuls, patricius and count of the royal office guarded by God; and after the entire council was seated in the order established during the first session, in the presence also of their 204D graces the archimandrites and abbots and of the entire congregation of the monks; and after the sacred and immaculate gospels of God had been placed in front of the assembly; Leo, the celebrated secretary, said: 'The holy and blessed council is well aware of the fact that during the previous session we went through various statements made by those heretics, driven by evil, who have raised charges against the holy and immaculate Church of the Christians for having reinstated the holy icons. Today, however, we have in our hands the written blasphemy of these accusers of the Christians,[5] that is the absurd, refutable, and self-condemned Definition of the pseudo-gathering, which accords in every respect with the blasphemy of the heretics hated by God. We also have for this [Definition] an elaborate and most 204E effective Refutation which the holy Spirit has made available to us. For this [Definition] must be triumphantly defeated by refutations of wisdom, and shredded by a vigorous scrutiny. And this is what we are now submitting to the present gathering.'

The holy council said: 'Let this be read.'

---

4 The church of 'the divine Wisdom': the cathedral of the bishop of Constantinople.
5 What we translate here as 'accusers of the Christians' is the name *Christianocatēgoroi*. The name was employed by the Orthodox to refer to the iconoclasts.

Refutation of the Fabricated and Falsely Called 'Definition'   205A
of the Mob Assembly of the Accusers of the Christians

FIRST VOLUME

The misanthrope devil has always delighted in separating man,
who is in the image of God, from God and, through many devious   205B
deceptions, in leading him into error. In nothing is he more
diligent than in overpowering piety and upsetting the peace of
the Church. This, therefore, is what he has demonstrated to us
in our days, too, through a gang of conspirators who assembled,
introduced this statement, and praised themselves as 'the Seventh
Council.' By using the simple hatred of idols they snatched away
the simplest ones. Moreover, having forged anew the ancient
and corrupted word, I mean 'idolatry' – on account of which
those who have worshipped the devil and his wicked powers
and *the creature rather than the Creator*[1] by means of statues of the   205C
demons have been condemned, and rightly so, to be called
'idolaters' – they have attempted to smear with this those who
constitute the *royal priesthood and the holy nation;*[2] [they have
attempted], that is, to apply the name against those who *have
put on Christ,*[3] and who have rid themselves of idols and been
freed from their error. Would that the teachings propagated by
them had vanished like abortive creatures, as pollutants within
the Church. However, because they were nourished by the
frivolous repetition of some men – even though they did not
reach maturity – it is necessary for us to destroy them with the   205D
sword of the Spirit. But let Christ, our true God, be the Leader;
He who *enlightens every man coming into the world;*[4] the only Intellect
of those who think in piety and of that which is thought [in
piety]; the Reason of those who speak and of what is spoken;

---

1 Rom. 1:25. Biblical quotations in the texts of the Seventh Ecumenical Council of 787 are
   printed in italic type; since the text of the iconoclastic Council of Nicea of 754 is
   printed in italics in this translation, the biblical quotations in it are printed in Roman
   type.
2 Cf 1 Peter 2:9.
3 Gal. 3:25.
4 John 1:9.

Who is everything to everyone, and Who is and becomes; He Who gives a tongue of discipline so that one knows when he should utter a word. For *the manifestation of thy words will enlighten and instruct the simple,*[5] so that falsehood may be expelled and the truth may reach everyone, shining afar and joyful. It is the truth that the zealots of piety, having embraced it and remembering the divine Apostle who said, *Woe to me if I do not spread the good news,*[6] have an obligation to advocate and defend, as well as to refute what is false and stone it with the sling of the 205E Spirit. Having reviewed, therefore, what has been chattered about on the basis of the Scriptures and of the Fathers, diligently and with consideration, we shall be able, with the spear of the spirit, after the example of Phinehas,[7] and with one stroke of refutation, to pierce readily all those who are entangled with one another in this impiety, as well as to demonstrate to everyone, in clear exposition, that their tongues have spoken lies when they raised them against the knowledge of the only-begotten Son of God and against his Church, and when they spoke iniquities against the stature of his incarnation. After that, having broken their 208A bonds with *the sword of the Spirit, which is the word of God,*[8] and having dissolved their ignorance, we may make manifest to everyone the pretensions of their cunning. For even the Lord has ridiculed and mocked them, as He will also address them in his wrath, saying to them: *Go away from me; I do not know you.*[9] It is of them that He spoke through Jeremiah the prophet, too, saying: *They prophesied lies in my name; for I sent them not, and I commanded them not: for they have spoken false visions, and divinations, and auguries and devices of their own heart.*[10] For this reason *they* 208B *shall be cast out in the streets of Jerusalem,*[11] that is, cast out of the catholic Church,[12] and they will be trampled by all those who

---

5 Ps. 118(119):130. The number in parentheses indicates the numbering of the Psalms in the Hebrew version. The first number is that of the Septuagint version used by the Council.

6 1 Cor. 9:12 (RSV: 'if I do not preach the gospel').

7 Cf Num. 25:7f.

8 Eph. 6:17

9 Cf Matt. 7:23.

10 Cf Jer. 14:14.

11 Jer. 14:16.

12 In the early Christian literature the adjective 'catholic' was used to indicate clearly the whole, unique, and truthful character of the Church. Cf, e.g., Ignatius, *Epistle to the*

confess the Lord in piety. For *a man's own lips are a strong snare to him, and he is caught with the words of his own mouth*,[13] and a response to his words will be the refutation of his impiety; for *I will reprove thee*, it says, *and set thine offences before thee*.[14]

Smyrnaeans, VII; and Cyril of Jerusalem, *Catechetical Lectures*, No. 18, PG 33:1044–1045. As Christianity became the official religion of the Roman Empire and the borders of the Church coincided administratively with the borders of the Empire, the adjective 'catholic' lost gradually its qualitative meaning and it came to predicate only the visible dimensions of the *Civitas Dei* on earth. It is with this meaning that the adjective 'catholic' has been preserved and understood in the West ever since. Cf also below, 253A, n 18. The Fathers of the East, however, sensitive to this shortcoming and eager to disassociate the all-embracing Christian ethos from the claims of the state – which at times, as in the case of the icons, were different from the tradition and the practice of the Church – insisted upon another term, 'orthodox,' which explained and, in a figurative way, amplified the catholic quality of the Church. For a discussion of the meaning and implications of the catholicity of the Church see the papers presented at the Second International Conference of Orthodox Theology, 'The Catholicity of the Church,' published in *St. Vladimir's Theological Quarterly* 17 (1973) nos. 1–2.

Unlike the indiscriminate use and popular understanding of the adjective 'orthodox' as 'traditional,' 'conservative,' and the like, the word fundamentally points to the state of thinking, living, and behaviour resulting from that process which delicately balances the whole spiritual experience of human existence. *Orthos* means 'upright' rather than 'right.' Rightness is the outcome of 'uprightness.' Uprightness is the single state of being, after all 'inclinations' have been checked and balanced. *Doxa* is also a much more comprehensive and inclusive word than its common translation as 'faith.' *Doxa* means 'something which seems good.' Cf the use of the verb *doko* in Acts 15:22, 25, 28, 34, from which the word *dogma* derives, not as a rigid rationalistic teaching, but as the articulation of that which seems good to man *and* to the holy Spirit as well. 'Orthodox,' therefore, is to be contrasted with anything that 'inclines this way or the other' (cf below, 206B–C), 'to either the right or the left' (245A); that is, to anything particular, eccentric, solely individualistic, temporal; to anything that lacks the breadth of space and time, the depth of the human and the supernatural experience, the all-inclusiveness and comprehensiveness of life. It is in this sense that we encounter the word in the present text. Numerous epithets and expressions are used in the texts as contrasts for the adjective 'orthodox,' such as 'crooked,' 'allegorical,' 'fantastic,' 'unreal,' 'a base mind,' 'a mere sound,' 'a rotten voice,' 'corruption of one's thinking,' 'deceptive madness,' etc. Contrasts such as 'deception' vs 'reasonable thinking,' 'impious belief' vs 'right confession,' 'trenches, ravines, and cliffs' vs 'the well-paved and royal way' aim at further accentuating the qualities of balance and uprightness of orthodoxy. Other expressions such as 'those who think properly' (340B) or 'those who are straight in their heart' (356B–C) are common, and are used synonymously with the adjective 'orthodox.'

13 Prov. 6:2. The Bagster edition of the Septuagint reads 'with the *lips* of his own mouth' (*cheilesin* instead of *remasin*, used in this text).

14 Ps. 49(50):21.

This is sufficient so far. However, in order that we may not prolong this speech with longer introductory remarks, as we take up the road which is in front of us, we should make our refutation on the basis of this very writing. There is no other way to prove that their vain talking is dull and full of reproach but by exposing it. After that we shall juxtapose to them the superior wisdom. 208C As for ourselves, we gain nothing but the certainty that we, who have come to a reverence of God, introduce no innovation, but rather remain obedient to the teachings of the Apostles and Fathers and to the traditions of the Church. Thus we ask those who come across this treatise to read it diligently and not just in passing, in order that they may, after understanding the exact difference, clearly and emphatically, pay the tribute of victory to the Church of God.

This is, therefore, the preface they used:

GREGORY HIS GRACE THE BISHOP OF NEOCAESAREA read: 208D
The DEFINITION of the holy, great, and Ecumenical Seventh Council.

JOHN THE GREAT DEACON OF THE CHURCH OF GOD read:
Having started from a lie, which they have undertaken to defend with all this empty talk of theirs, these accusers of the Christians have also ended up with a lie. For how is this [council] 'holy,' since it did not even take into account what is holy? It is, rather, 208E cursed, profane, and intrusive, because those who assembled in it *did not distinguish between the holy and the profane*[15] – to speak with the words of the prophet – having called the icon of the incarnate Word of God and our Lord Jesus Christ 'idol,' as the icon of Satan.

Again, how is this council 'great' and 'ecumenical,' since those presiding over the rest of the churches did neither accept nor consent to it but rather dismissed it with an anathema? It did not have the collaboration of the Pope of the Romans of that time and his priests, by means of either a representative of his or an encyclical letter, as is the rule in the councils. Nor did it have the consent of the Patriarchs of the East, that is of Alex- 209A andria, of Antioch, and of the Holy City, or of their priests and bishops. Indeed, their word is a misty smoke that brings darkness to the eyes of the foolish, not a *lamp which is placed on the*

15 Cf Ezek. 22:26.

stand in order to give light to those who are inside the house.[16] As a result their teaching spread locally, as if from an obscure corner of a town, and not from the top of the mountain of orthodoxy; nor has *their voice gone out into all the earth* in the apostolic manner, nor *their words to the ends of the earth*,[17] like those of the six holy Ecumenical Councils.　　　　　　　　　　　　　　　　　　209B

And, again, how is it the 'seventh,' since it did not concur with the previous six holy and Ecumenical Councils? For whichever is placed as seventh must follow those which have been placed before it in the numbering; what shares nothing with those with which it is numbered is not counted as one of them either. If one has put down six golden coins, one after the other, and then puts down a copper one, he should not call this the seventh, because of its different substance; gold is expensive and valuable, while copper is cheap and worthless. So is it with this [council]. Having nothing golden or valuable in its teaching, but being actually inferior to copper, a counterfeit, full of deadly poison, it is not worthy to be counted with the six most reverend councils which are sparkling with the golden utterances of the　209C Spirit.

However, with the arrogance of him who said, *I will set my throne above the clouds*,[18] this council echoes out the following:

GREGORY THE BISHOP read:
The holy and ecumenical council, which was convened by the grace of God and in accordance with a most pious decree of our God-respecting 209D *and orthodox kings Constantine and Leo*,[19] *being gathered in this God-guarded and royal city, in the sacred church of our holy immaculate Lady Theotokos and ever-virgin Mary, which is surnamed after Vlacherna,* DEFINED *the following:*

HIS GRACE JOHN THE DEACON read:
If their gathering had convened by the grace of God, it would

---

16 Cf Matt. 5:15.
17 Ps. 18(19):4.
18 Cf Is. 14:13. The Septuagint version has it as 'above the stars of heaven.'
19 Obviously this Constantine is Emperor Constantine V the Copronyme (741-775). Whether, however, this Leo is Emperor Leo III the Isaurian (717-741) or Emperor Leo IV (775-780) is not clear. The order of the names would point to the latter.

have been adorned with words spoken by the grace of God, as it would also have been brightened with the joy of truth. For grace is conjoined with truth, and both are married to, and   209ᴇ commensal with, each other. A witness to this is John, the chief magistrate of theology, who says *grace and truth came through Jesus Christ.*[20] However, having abandoned the truth in which the author of the Proverbs takes pride when he says *I will produce right sayings from my lips,*[21] and having embraced falsehood, they have obviously fallen from grace. Nor is their word *seasoned with the divine salt*[22] so that it may convey grace to those who listen to it.

As for their having gathered in the most venerable church of our Lady Theotokos, that is not something to admire. They are not going to look better because of that, just as the fact that the unlawful deliberation against Christ took place in the Temple   212ᴀ did not benefit Annas, Ca'iaphas, and their Jewish Council. It is rather because of this that they have proven to be worthy of even greater condemnation, having fabricated the accursed slogan directed against God in holy places. And since they put as a preface the patristic words of Dionysius, the revealer of God,[23] would that they had preserved his teachings, as well as those of all our holy Fathers, unbroken. But this is not so with them, as continuing through their entire exposition will show. Furthermore, like wolves in sheep's clothing, they begin with a theological introduction, unfitting though this may be to them, saying:

GREGORY BISHOP OF NEOCAESAREA read: 212ʙ
Godhead, the cause and accomplisher of all, Who out of his goodness brought all things from non-existence into being, commanded them to conduct themselves in a proper and orderly manner, so that, by adhering to the well-being which was granted to them by grace, they may preserve their sojourn unwavering and inclining towards neither side from the position of truth.[24]

20 John 1:17.
21 Prov. 8:7.
22 Cf Col. 4:6.
23 The adjective *Theophantor* accompanies, usually, the name of the enigmatic fifth-century author disguised under the name Dionysius the Areopagite, the convert of Paul (Acts 17:34).
24 Cf above, 208ʙ, n 12.

EPIPHANIUS THE DEACON AND CHAMBERLAIN read: 212C
The entire creation, inanimate or animate, having been created
by God and having received the hypostatic power to exist from
the state of non-existence, moving now and directed by his order,
knows how to preserve the commandment of the Creator.
However, they have dared to anathematize what has been handed
down by Christ to us, his holy Church, for the remembrance
of his redemptive dispensation, failing to understand that nothing
that exists in the Church has been done without Him.[25] Thus
they prove to be more insensitive than inanimate creation and 212D
more irrational than irrational beings. Not only that, but thinking
that their tongue is on the right path even when it is involved
in improper words and teachings, they falsely accuse the holy
Church of God of being adorned with idols. With confidence
in their own falsehood they say to her: 'We do not want to know
your ways, nor do we choose to follow faithfully the tradition
which existed from the beginning.' Nevertheless, they will hear
from Christ, her founder: *I never knew you.*[26]

They even claim that the devil has triumphed, saying the
following:

GREGORY THE BISHOP read: 212E
When, however, Lucifer – who because of his previous splendour had
his place near God – raised his own mind high against his Creator, darkness
resulted from his apostatic power. Having of his own choice fallen from
the most glorious, light-giving divine order – an order even beyond light
– proving himself to be the perpetrator, inventor, and teacher of every
wickedness, he became dark. Since he could not tolerate seeing man, created 213A
by God, being introduced instead of him [Lucifer] into the glory in which
he had been ranked, he poured out all his wickedness against man, and
with deception he alienated him from the glory and splendour of God
by suggesting that he could worship the creature rather than the Creator.[27]

---

25 According to the Orthodox understanding, tradition is not a set of human customs,
  characterized simply by a local, individual, or temporary dimension, but rather the
  continuous and comprehensive experience of the Church in terms of faith, worship,
  spirituality, expression, and action in Christ and with Christ. For a brief and
  interesting discussion on tradition, see Scouteris, 'Paradosis.'
26 Matt. 7:23.
27 Cf Rom. 1:15.

EPIPHANIUS THE DEACON AND CHAMBERLAIN read:
If what they say were against idolatry or against the worship
of creatures – something which is forbidden and despised by
the holy Apostles who were vested with power from heaven,   213B
and by the divine prophets who spoke before them under the
inspiration of the holy Spirit, and then by our divine Fathers
who followed them – all those who have been nourished within
the Church would have consented. It would also have been
appropriate for them to have committed this [teaching] to writing.
However, they have abandoned her [the Church], and they
defend what is a falsehood. Pretending also that the devil – its
father – has triumphed, they sharpen their tongues against the
immaculate Church. Like tavern-keepers they mix water with
the wine. They do not even hesitate to offer their neighbour
as drink a muddy refutation. Because of this they will hear God's
voice of judgment, proclaimed through David, the revealer of   213C
God, as if it were addressed to them: *Why do you declare my
ordinances, and take up my covenant in your mouth? Whereas you have
hated instruction, and have cast my words behind you, having cast your
lot with those who have falsified the doctrines of truth.*[28]

    Thence, making pretensions of truth, they say:

GREGORY THE BISHOP read:
*Therefore, God the Creator, not wishing to see the work of his own hand
headed towards complete perdition after the care that He had taken for
man's salvation through the Law and the prophets – and with man unable*   213D
*to return to the previous kinship – deemed it worthy to send to earth,
in the last and predetermined days, his own Son and Word. He, by the
good will of the Father and the collaboration of the Spirit – his equal
in power, and the principle of life – having dwelt in a virgin's womb
and taken up in his own existence, or hypostasis, flesh consubstantial
with that of ours from her holy and spotless flesh, and having condensed
it and formed it with an intelligent and cogitating soul, and having been
born of her in a way which is beyond reason and understanding by
any mind, and having borne the cross wittingly, having chosen death*   213E
*and risen from the dead on the third day, He accomplished his entire
dispensation of salvation.*

28 Cf Ps. 49(50):16–18.

EPIPHANIUS THE DEACON AND CHAMBERLAIN read:
The holy Scripture, in the [narrative of the] creation of the world, declares that God said: *Let us make man according to our icon and our likeness.*[29] Great, therefore, is the magniture of [man's] dignity since, although earth-born, he has been honoured with the icon of God. Because, however, as a result of the deception, man was expelled and did not preserve the dignity of his original creation, mankind slipped into idolatry. It is this man whom God, the Word of the Father, recalled from decadence by becoming Himself a perfect man, without changing his own nature. After he delivered man from the error of the idols, He regenerated him to become immortal, granting him an irrevocable gift. This is a more Godlike [gift] than the one before, as the regeneration is greater than the creation, and the gift eternal. 216A

It is the greatness of these very gifts that they [the iconoclasts] want to obscure when they say audaciously that, with the making of icons, another idolatry has crept in, or that through themselves, as they boast, a new redemption has been accomplished. Having rhapsodized their own opinion with a variety of speeches, they actually condemn the Church of God as being in error – even though they make their words smoother than oil by pronouncing a few scriptural statements. However, their words are fraudulent and their tongues a piercing missile. For they sound conciliatory even though there is enmity inside them. Thus they add: 216B

GREGORY THE BISHOP read:
He removed us from the corrupting teaching of the demons, that is, from error and the worship of idols, and He handed over to us an adoration which is in spirit and in truth.[30] 216C

EPIPHANIUS THE DEACON AND CHAMBERLAIN read:
Unwittingly, most excellent ones, you are drawn towards the truth. For the entire divine congregation of the Apostles and the holy multitude of our Fathers proclaim that the Son and Word of God the Father came to mankind in order to deliver

29 Gen. 1:26. In this most important passage, what the RSV has rended as 'image,' the Septuagint has translated as 'icon' – the same word which is the subject of this controversy. Cf also the relevant discussion in the introduction, n 61.
30 John 4:24.

us from the error of the idols. We even have announcements   216D
proclaimed before their time through the prophets, who cried
out: *Behold, it shall come to pass on that day, saith the Lord, that I
will utterly destroy the names of the idols from all the land, and there
shall be no longer any resemblance of them.*[31] Therefore, you also have
been forced to confess that Christ our God delivered us from
the error of the idols. But if He has delivered us, how is it that
those who believed in Him have become idolaters again? Away
with your frivolous nonsense! God, by becoming flesh, provides
us with salvation. Do we, then, become captives again? Are we
now once more mastered by him who oppressed us? Listen to
the holy Scripture that says: *His kingdom is a kingdom of all ages,
and His dominion endures in every generation and generation;*[32] and   216E
The Lord shall reign for ever, even thy God, O Zion, to all generations.[33]
In no way is God like the kings of earth, who at times win and
soon after are defeated. His victory endures forever. Nor, as it
is written, *is God deceived, like man, or, like a son of man, will he
be threatened.* The Apostle agrees with this, too. *The gifts*, he says,
and the call of God are irrevocable.[34]

However, they repeat the same things, thinking that they are
making themselves solemn. For they pursue this matter, fighting
actually against themselves:

GREGORY THE BISHOP read: 217A
Afterwards He ascended into heaven in that which He had assumed,[35]
*having left behind his holy disciples and Apostles as teachers of this
redemptive faith. They, having beautified our Church as his bride with
various brilliant doctrines of piety, raised her to be beautiful and splendid,
surrounded by and decorated with golden tassels. It is this beauty of hers
that our renowned Fathers and teachers, and the six holy and Ecumenical*   217B
Councils, have received and preserved undiminished.

---

31 Cf Zech. 13:2.
32 Cf Ps. 144(145):13.
33 Ps. 145(146):10.
34 Rom. 11:29.
35 The phrase 'that which He had assumed' is a translation of the word *proslemma*, which
   implies not only the form or the flesh but the entire human nature which God the
   Word assumed to Himself.

59 The Church and the dogma

EPIPHANIUS THE DEACON AND CHAMBERLAIN read:
Being ignorant and undisciplined in their thinking, these chat-
terers of the new empty talk do not even sense their own intrusive
arrogance. In their desire to conceal their opinion behind a
deceitful shadow, out of carelessness they render themselves
utterly ridiculous. Praising repeatedly and highly the tradition
of the Church, they agree – even unwittingly – that the holy   217C
six Ecumenical Councils have preserved this tradition undiminished. And while with words they pretend piety, with their minds
they fabricate evil. *They honour this [piety] with their lips, but with
their heart they are far from it.*[36] They do not even come close to
accepting the tradition admitted by so many saints throughout
history. They ought to feel ashamed before the multitude of
present-day Christians, and all those who have been Christians
since the gospel was first proclaimed, for rejecting and debasing
the recounting of the gospel through painting. For no more than
seventy years have passed since the time of the holy Sixth
Ecumenical Council, when they gathered to speak against the   217D
venerable icons. That it was not during those years that the
tradition of the reproduction of icons was handed down is clearly
evident to all. Rather, it was long before the Sixth Council; or,
to say the truth, it was since the time of the preaching of the
Apostles, as we learn from looking at the holy churches in every
place, as the holy Fathers have testified and as the historians,
whose writings have survived until today, relate.

Thus, in the year 5501, Christ our God came to men and lived   217E
with us for thirty-three years and a little less than five months.
After He accomplished the great and redemptive mystery of our
salvation, He made his way to heaven – He ascended, that is,
to the place from which He had descended – charging the Apostles
to teach everything that He had commanded them. From those
years till the time of Constantine the King – the first king of
the Christians, because before him it was the Greeks who were
in power[37] – there passed almost three hundred years. When
most Christians were fighting the good battle and leaving this   220A

36 Cf Is. 29:13.
37 Literally, who were the tyrants. The name 'Greeks' signifies the pagan emperors rather
than the nationality of the emperors. In most of the instances in this text, the
adjective 'Greek' is used to mean 'pagan.'

life as martyrs, after standing up against idols, the [surviving] Christians, moved with divine zeal in building churches, some of them in the name of Christ and others in honour of saints, painted in them scenes related to the incarnation of our God, as well as other stories related to the contests of the martyrs. Others, who wanted to preserve the memory of them forever, painted on boards the icon either of their desired martyr or even of Christ Himself. Icons were also reproduced by our holy Fathers and pious men on holy veils and utensils which they used to perform bloodless sacrifices.[38] All these are clearly preserved up to our own time and will remain forever.   220B

Subsequently the heresies sprouted up, full of gall and bitterness against the Church. The six Ecumenical Councils, which convened under God's inspiration at different times in order to destroy them, confirmed and supported everything – either written or unwritten – that had been handed down to the catholic Church from earliest times, including the presentation of venerable icons. As for the Sixth Ecumenical Council – this was during the reign of Constantine who, by his decree and the will of God, convened the council, and shortly afterwards departed from life,   220C and who was succeeded on the throne by his son, Justinian – after it promulgated its Definition against those who maintain that there is one will in Christ our God, the same [Fathers] who had assembled for that council gathered together again, under the inspiration of God, four or five years later, and promulgated about two hundred and two canons to rectify matters of the Church. Included in these canons is one – the eighty-second – regarding icons, in which they [the Fathers] promulgated the following:

In some venerable icons, and pointed to by the finger of the Forerunner, there is the drawing of a lamb, which has been received as the figure   220D of grace, making what is for us the true Lamb – Christ our God – glimmer

---

38 'Bloodless sacrifices' implies the celebrations of the Eucharist. The bloody sacrifices of the Old Testament at the Temple are replaced in the New Testament by the bloodless sacrifice of the Lamb of God. Cf the prayer of consecration in the divine liturgy of John Chrysostom: 'Again we offer Thee this *reasonable and bloodless worship,* and we ask and pray and supplicate ...' Cf also below, 249D, n 11. On the veils and the utensils used during the liturgy cf below, 329E, 332B.

through the Law. Although, therefore, we totally embrace the old forms and figures as symbols and foreshadowings which have been handed down to the Church, yet we prefer to honour Grace and Truth, because we have welcomed this as the fulfilment of the Law. We, therefore, decree that the human figure of Christ, the Lamb of our God, who has taken away the sin of the world, be painted with colours as perfectly as possible, in view of everyone, and from now on be reinstated in icons in the place of the former lamb. This way we may perceive the height of the humility of God the Word, and be led to the remembrance of his conduct in flesh, his suffering, his redemptive death, and the salvation which   220E
resulted from it for the world.[39]

We all, therefore, see and understand that the painting of icons is something that has been handed down to the Church before the holy councils, as well as after them, like the tradition of the gospel. Thus, as when we receive the sound of the reading with our ears, we transmit it to our mind, so by looking with our eyes at the painted icons, we are enlightened in our mind. Through two things following each other, that is, by reading and also by seeing the reproduction of the painting, we learn the same thing, that is, how to recall what has taken place. The operation   221A
of these two most basic senses is also found conjoined in the Song of Songs, where it says: *Show me thy face, and cause me to hear thy voice; for thy voice is sweet, and thy countenance is beautiful.*[40] In agreement we say with the words of the Psalms: *As we have heard, so have we also seen.*[41]

Be this as it may, it is now the proper time to say of those who have stammered against the venerable icons: *Every one has spoken vanity to his neighbour: their lips are deceitful, they have spoken with evil in their heart;*[42] from whom may we be guarded, by the grace of our Saviour Christ, the true God.

39 Mansi, 11:977E–980B.
40 Song 2:14.
41 Ps. 47(48):8.
42 Cf Ps. 11(12):12.

SECOND VOLUME

EPIPHANIUS THE DEACON AND CHAMBERLAIN read: 221B
Oblivious of the Lord's unmistaken promise regarding his Church,
that *the powers of death shall not prevail against her,*[1] with the head
uncovered and the mouth unguarded, and with opinions which
are most controversial, they fight against her.

Also, having stolen statements from the Fathers, which they 221C
put forth as their own, they say the following:

GREGORY THE BISHOP read:
*But, again, the aforesaid creator of evil, not wishing to see her [the Church]
being comely, did not refrain from using at different times different means
of wicked ingenuity in order to subdue the human race to his power;
thus, with the pretext of Christianity, he reintroduced idolatry unnoticeably
by convincing, with his subtleties, those who had their eyes turned to* 221D
*him not to relinquish the creation but rather to adore it, and pay respect
to it, and consider that which is made as God, calling it with the name
'Christ.'*[2]

EPIPHANIUS THE DEACON AND CHAMBERLAIN read:
Those who fight against the spiritual Jerusalem, that is the catholic
Church, conform in a way with those who fought the earthly
Jerusalem. They, too, are eager to make use of the words of the
Fathers, in the manner that Rab'shakeh at one time used the
language of Judah.[3] Thus, these heretics arm the teaching of the 221E
Fathers and the word of the Church against the Fathers, as well
as against the catholic Church. But *you will know them by their
fruits,*[4] says the Lord. For they resemble *whitewashed tombs, which
outwardly appear beautiful* to men, like these accusers of the
Christians, who take cover, supposedly, under the words of the
Fathers, *but within they are full of dead men's bones and all uncleanness*[5]
– I mean of dead and stinking teachings.

---

1 Matt. 16:18.
2 Cf Gregory of Nyssa, *Funeral Oration to his Own Brother, Basil the Great*, PG 46:796B. This is an
  encomium rather than a funeral oration. On this oration, as well as on Gregory of
  Nyssa, see Quasten, *Patrology*, III, 254–296, at 278–279.
3 Literally, the Hebrew dialect. Cf 2 Kings 18:26ff.
4 Matt. 7:16.
5 Matt. 23:27.

But we, having discovered their tomb, will reveal their entire uncleanliness, that according to their own desire they distort the teaching which the Fathers promulgated to the catholic   224A
Church. Although they use the same words, they deceptively alter their meaning. For what they [the Fathers] decreed against the Arians, these used instead to attack the painting of venerable icons. Thus Gregory, the memorable one, who presided over the church of the Nyssaeans,[6] in his *Funeral Oration to St Basil*, his own brother in flesh and spirit, made a statement against the Arians, which they took to be against the venerable icons. This can be detected from the very introduction of the passage, which reads as follows:

Certainly no one ignores the purpose of the emergence of our teacher   224B
at this time. When men's insanity with the idols had been extinguished by the preaching of Christ, and all the objects of the vain worship were already ruined and abolished, the preaching of piety was spread in almost the entire world, in such a way that he who prevailed over the human deception was expelled by the name of Christ, driven away from the world. However, the inventor of wickedness, being wise in what is evil, did not lack a wicked idea as of how to make mankind subject to himself   224C
again, by deception. Thus, with the pretext of Christianity he reintroduced idolatry unnoticeably by convincing with his subtleties those who had their eyes turned to him, not to relinquish the creation, but rather to adore it, and pay respect to it, and venerate[7] the creature as God, calling it with the name 'Son.' And as for the creation that was made from non-existence and was estranged from the divine essence into its own nature, [he convinced them] not to make any reference to this, but, instead, by putting the name 'Christ' to the creature, to venerate, worship, entrust his hope of salvation to it, and expect judgment from it. Thus the apostate, throwing himself wholly upon men, managed to pour out all his wickedness into a number of men – I mean Arius, Aetius, Eunomius, Eudoxius, and in addition to these   224D

---

6 Notice the expression used to indicate the title and the function of the bishop. Unlike the non-theological expression prevailing today (e.g., 'such and such, bishop of Salonica'), which makes the bishop an overseer (*epīscopos*) of a city (and, what is worse, sometimes of a non-existent city in the case of titular bishops), the usage of the early Church identified the bishop with the people and the clergy over whom he presided, and with whom he constituted the 'catholic' Church.

7 It should read 'to consider,' or 'to believe.'

many more – through whom he brought back idolatry, under the name of Christianity as we said, at a time when idolatry had already vanished. Thus the disease of men who worshipped the creature rather than the Creator prevailed, to the extent that the deception was strengthened even by the alliance of the ruling kings. All the high authorities were defending the disease. When only a little was needed for men to change to what was prevailing, then Basil the Great was raised by God-like Elijah during the time of Ahab.[8] After he laid hold of the priesthood, 224E which in some ways had tumbled, he made the word of faith rekindle like a lamp, through the grace residing in him.[9]

Let us notice, therefore, that the entire content of what the Father says refers to the Ariomaniacs.[10] Thus, he says that St Basil lived during the time of Arius, Eunomius, Eudoxius, Macedonius, and those around them, Anhomians and semi-Arians, who were saying that our God, the Son and Word of the Father, is a creature. Since, therefore, they worship the creature as God, they are rightly called idolaters by him and by the catholic Church. 225A For they say that he whom they worship came into being from non-existence, like all created creatures. As for the icons, Christians do not call them 'gods,' nor do they worship them as gods, nor do they entrust the hope of their salvation to them, nor do they expect judgment to come from them. They have kissed them and have ascribed to them a veneration of honour, only for the sake of recalling and of being reminded, and out of zeal for their prototypes. But in no way do they worship them, nor do they bestow a divine reverence upon them, or upon any of the creatures – away with such accusations. The Arians, however, 225B did so by including the Son and Word of God among the creatures. They maintained that they had the faith of their salvation in him, and that the coming judgment will be made by him. It is for this reason that the divine Father, criticizing them, said: 'to venerate this [the creature] worship, entrust in this the hope of salvation, and expect judgment from it.'[11]

---

8 Cf 1 Kings 17, 18, 19.
9 Gregory of Nyssa, *Funeral Oration*, PG 46:796A–D.
10 Greek *Ariomanitae*: the name refers to the followers (called 'maniacs') of Arius. It was used by Epiphanius, *Panarion*, 49(69), PG 42:201–336, and repeated by John of Damascus, *On the Heresies*, PG 94:720; Kotter, IV, 38. Cf also below, 253B.
11 Cf above, 224C.

Consequently, the promoters of this empty talk are proven forgers of the truth, tavern-keepers, according to the prophet, *who have mixed the wine with water.*[12] Not only that, but they have become also falsifiers of the words of the Fathers. For, while this same Father said, 'calling it with the name "Son",' they said falsely, 'with the name "Christ!",' instead of 'with the name "Son",' because they wanted to make the meaning apply to his iconographic re-presentation. It is clear that when he says, 'calling it with the name "Son",' he criticizes the Arians for blaspheming against the heavenly and divine birth of the Son. That is why he condemns the principals of this heresy, saying: 'I mean Arius, Eunomius, Eudoxius, and Aetius.' However, they, by saying 'Christ,' instead of 'Son,' attempt to ascribe the blasphemy to the impression of the venerable icons. Even in this respect, therefore, some of them have proven to be falsifiers and liars.

225C

Then, they continue on the same subject with things which are improper:

GREGORY THE BISHOP read:

225D

For this reason, therefore, Jesus, the author and agent of our salvation, as in the past he had sent forth his most wise disciples and Apostles with the power of the most holy Spirit in order to eliminate completely all such things, so also now He raised his devotees, our faithful kings – the ones comparable to the Apostles, who have become wise by the power of the same Spirit – in order to equip and teach us, as well as to abolish the demonic fortifications which resist the knowledge of God, and to refute diabolic cunning and error.

EPIPHANIUS THE DEACON AND CHAMBERLAIN read:

225E

Who has ever spoken an iniquity of this magnitude? What impiety could be worse than this? What a shameless and wicked blasphemy! What a hidden deception and a diverse machination! They speak as if they have been taught this way by the devil himself. For they had the audacity to call the sight and the countenance which leads us to the glory of God, 'through which we perceive the height of the humility of God the Word, and are led to the remembrance of his conduct in flesh, as well as

228A

---

12 Cf Is. 1:22.

of his suffering and of his redemptive death,'[13] 'demonic fortifications which resist the knowledge of God' and 'diabolic cunning
and error.' Indeed, *they have bent their bow maliciously to shoot in
secret at the blameless.*[14] For, since they confessed that the holy
disciples, vested with power from on high after the holy Spirit
came upon them, were sent out to abolish the idols, they should
not have said that eight hundred years later, after their tradition   228B
and teaching had prevailed, other men and holy Fathers rose
in order to confirm and stabilize this [tradition and teaching]
as a safe anchor. For once we have been totally saved from idols
by Christ, we do not need to be charged with idolatry unless
they dare to say that a change has occurred in the Church, and
that different laws and institutions have been handed down –
thus attributing to us irrational and totally negative excuses. For
this is what these excellent ones have spread as rumour saying,
in the same way as long ago Jesus, the author and agent of our
salvation, said.[15] Thence it follows for them to say: *What is becoming
obsolete and growing old is ready to vanish away,*[16] and that 'the teaching
of the Apostles has grown old; we have chosen, therefore, to
produce a new one. For Moses and Aaron were also priests. When,   228C
however, grace came in their place, the Apostle says that another
priest arose.'[17] When, therefore, they say, 'to equip and teach
us,' they must be thinking that they are offering now a certain
great grace, greater than that of the holy Apostles. However,
since the participants of that council were bishops, entrusted
with the perfection of the apostolic commandments, they ought
not to have taught otherwise, nor to have been taught by others.
Instead, they refused with contempt to be disciples of the teaching
and of the tradition of our holy Apostles and our illustrious
Fathers. They have proven, therefore, that they have nothing
in common with their quality as teachers, since they do not align
themselves with what they [the Apostles and Fathers] have
handed down. To them David the psalmist says: *The Lord shall*   228D
destroy all the deceitful lips, and the tongue that speaks great words.[18]

13 Cf above 220D–E.
14 Ps. 63(64):4.
15 Cf Matt. 9:17.
16 Heb. 8:13.
17 Cf Heb. 7:11ff.
18 Cf Ps. 11(12):3.

Truly, let the same David sing with us, and we with him: *The swords of the enemy have failed utterly: and thou hast destroyed cities.*[19]

When did the 'swords' and the 'cities' – that is, the fortifications – of the enemy vanish? Was it not when Christ became man? Of Him it was written: *He shall divide the spoils of the mighty.*[20] Was it not of their pseudo-gathering, of their gang, that it was written, *the swords of the enemy have failed utterly*? If *the swords of the enemy have failed utterly* and completely, and the 'cities' of impiety *have been destroyed*, why have they babbled that these cities have been rebuilt anew? Have they, perhaps, done so in order to attribute to themselves the abolition [of the 'cities'] and the redemption of mankind from those 'cities'? In so doing they belittle the great mystery of our salvation – the dispensation of Christ, the God of all, Who is, indeed, blessed throughout the ages, Amen. 228E

Then, using flatteries for the rulers, they say the following:

GREGORY THE BISHOP read: 229A
Moved by the divine zeal which was in them, and not tolerating the ravaging of the Church of the faithful by the deception of the demons,

EPIPHANIUS THE DEACON AND CHAMBERLAIN read:
By saying this they [prove that] they have neither learned of the promise which the catholic Church has received from Christ who established her, nor confessed that mankind was saved through redemption in Jesus Christ our Lord. For those whom Christ redeemed with his own blood they sell back to the devil. Those to whom He gave life with his own death they kill with the poison of their lips, and lead them down to the prison of Hades. Let them listen to the clear songs which are sung to the Church as by Christ Himself: *Thou art all fair, my companion, all fair and there is no spot in thee.*[21] They have just heard that she is *all fair* and a *companion of Christ*, free from any spot. It is to her, also, that He speaks through Isaiah: *I have painted thy walls on my hands, and thou art continually before me.*[22] How then is she 229B 229C

19 Ps. 9:6.
20 Is. 53:12.
21 Cf Song 4:7.
22 Is. 49:16.

who has received these promises ravaged by the adverse power of the demons? Also, who can take her as a spoil since Christ is her head, according to the divine Apostle?[23] He *has presented her to Himself without spot or wrinkle.*[24] How, then, is she again defiled? How reprehensible! For it is obvious that such a notion implies a denial of his dispensation. They have hastened to bring the Church to nought. For this reason the Lord will bring them to nought, and they will be scorned and anathematized by all those who have been born within her; for she has remained un-ravaged, unbroken, and unshaken.   229D

Yet, with mouths full of flatteries, they refer to their own actions with pride.

GREGORY THE BISHOP read:
they called together the entire sacerdotal congregation of the bishops who love God, in order that, after they gathered together into a council, and after they searched the Scriptures together about the deceptive work of likenesses with colours which lowers the human mind from the high worship proper to God down to the base and material worship of creatures, motivated by God this [council] may pronounce that which seemed good to it. They did so because they knew what is written in [the book of] the Prophets: For the priest's lips should keep knowledge, and they should seek the law at their mouth: for they are the messengers of the Lord Almighty.[25]   229E

EPIPHANIUS THE DEACON read:
Because they have been oblivious of the birth of God the Word   232A
from a virgin, and of his great and redemptive mystery which He granted to us when He came in flesh, delivering us from the error of the idols and from the insane worship of them, and because they have misappropriated this salvation in their desire to gain glory for themselves, they are publicized by the catholic Church ingloriously. Suitably, then, Christ our God addresses them through the prophet: *The priests have set at nought my law, and profaned my holy things: they have not distinguished between the*

23 Cf Eph. 4:15
24 Cf Eph. 5:27.
25 Cf Mal. 2:7.

holy and profane, nor have they distinguished between the unclean and the clean.[26] For they did not distinguish the icons of the demons 232B from the icons of the Lord and of his saints, which they called by the same name, 'idols.' They slandered with accusations the Church whom Christ our God *obtained with his own blood,*[27] for they idly called the narrative from the gospel[28] 'a deceptive work of colours,' which the faithful confess and call 'venerable' and 'holy,' as they look not at what is seen but at what is signified in it. For, when they hear the gospel with the ears, they exclaim 'glory to Thee, O Lord'; and when they see it with the eyes, they send forth exactly the same doxology, for we are reminded of his life among men. That which the narrative declares in writing 232C is the same as that which the icon does [in colours].

Let us now consider what they have chattered about without restraint, and with arrogance: 'which lowers the human mind from the high worship proper to God down to the base and material worship of creatures.'[29] What a derangement! With a tongue pointed like a knife and sharpened with falsehood, they think that the immaculate faith of us Christians has changed into one of icon-adoration. To this they add insult, calling it a 'base and material worship of creatures.' Not one Christian who has ever lived under the sky has worshipped an icon. This is a fable of the pagans, an invention of the demons, and its undertaking an act of Satan. This is something that has been 232D vanquished by the coming of Christ. Worship now is *in spirit and in truth.*[30] The Church possesses various things dedicated to God, which are placed there for the remembrance of God and of his saints: the making of icons is one of these.

However, they criticize themselves when they say: 'it may pronounce that which seemed good to it.' They have forsaken that which is in the Scripture from the mouth of the Lord: *He who speaks of his own authority seeks his own glory.*[31] They themselves, therefore, confess that they speak from their own authority and

26 Cf Ezek. 22:26. The Septuagint version reads: 'between the sacred and the profane.'
27 Cf Acts 20:28.
28 That is, the iconographic representations of New Testament scenes which one finds painted inside a church.
29 Cf above, 229E.
30 John 4:24.
31 John 7:18.

not from the Spirit. Can there be anyone who will listen to them, if what they say is not of the Spirit?

Then taking pride – not in the Lord but in their own tongues – they say this:

GREGORY THE BISHOP OF NEOCAESAREA read: 232E
Thus we, this holy council of ours, which has now convened and has reached the number of three hundred and thirty-eight [participants], following the institutions of the councils, gladly accept and proclaim the doctrines and the traditions which they confirmed and decreed so that we would keep them safe.

EPIPHANIUS THE DEACON read: 233A
They take pride in having many in their gathering, boasting of their number. However they only courted a mob which, with unguarded mouth, babbled against the Church things which are improper, telling great iniquities. They even surpassed the crowd of the Jews and became vulgar. However, the Lord did not esteem them. Why? Because, having forced themselves out of the Church into a waterless land, they wandered in a desert without the   233B
spiritual wine that *makes glad the heart of man.*[32]

And again, they say the same things on the same subjects, pretending that with their words they follow the traditions of the councils, while they deny them with their deeds. They also enumerate the Ecumenical Councils, saying:

GREGORY THE BISHOP read:
First to be mentioned is the holy and Ecumenical great Council of Nicea, in the reign of the great King Constantine, who is among the saints.   233C
This council unfrocked the most impious Arius from the dignity of the priesthood for saying that the uncreated Son of God, Who is of one substance with the Father and with the holy Spirit and Who shares in the same glory and honour, is a creature. It pronounced also the creed[33] of our redemptive faith, delivered by God.

32 Ps. 103(104):15.
33 The Greek word for 'creed' is *sȳmbolon* (symbol!) from a verb, *symbállein*, which means 'to contribute.' The symbol of faith, or the creed, contributes; it does not prescribe, nor does it exhaust, the faith of man about God, Who is beyond a definitive description. The creed contains statements of faith which define the 'boundaries' (*hōros*: landmark, definition) of faith.

Afterwards, similarly, there is the Council of the one hundred and fifty holy fathers, who convened in this royal city, in the reign of Theodosius the Great. This condemned Macedonius, the Pneumatomachian,[34] *for blaspheming against the most holy and uncreated Spirit, as well as for teaching irreverently that He is not of one substance with the Father* 233D *and the Son. It also strengthened and expanded the creed of our redemptive faith by affirming that the holy and omnipotent Spirit is God.*

EPIPHANIUS THE DEACON read:
Even Nestorius, the impious one, and his fellow-heretics accepted those two holy Ecumenical Councils. So, even though the council of this mob of theirs accepts these [councils], it has introduced another heresy, because of which those who adhere to it were called by the holy catholic Church of God 'accusers of the Chris-   233E tians.' They differ in no way from insane men who, when they see the sun over the earth, say to each other: 'The stars are hidden because of the brightness of the sun'; and 'it is daytime, not night.' That is, they draw conclusions after deliberating about obvious and manifest things with idle thinking.
   Then they add:

GREGORY THE BISHOP read:
After these there is the Council of the two hundred holy fathers, which 236A *convened originally in Ephesus in the reign of Theodosius the Younger. This condemned the Jewish-minded and man-worshipping Nestorius for maintaining that Christ, the Word of God, is one in particular, while the one born of woman is another Christ; thus placing God the Word, at one place, and on his own, and at another place the man. Thus he taught that there are two hypostases in the one Christ, denying the hypostatic union.*[35] *According to this [hypostatic union], the one [Christ] is not co-adorned with the other, as if the one were the other, but rather it is understood that there is one Jesus Christ, the only-begotten Son, honoured with one adoration, along with his own flesh.*

34 'Pneumatomáchian': 'he who fights against the Spirit' or 'the offender of the Spirit.' By this name were called the followers of Macedonius who denied the consubstantiality of the Spirit to God the Father.
35 That is, the union of the two hypostases, divine and human.

EPIPHANIUS THE DEACON read:

Even Eutyches and Dioscorus, the 'confusers,'[36] and their follow-   236B
ers accepted this [council]. Yet they remained heretics, because,
they introduced another heresy. Therefore these present ones
will be counted together with those others, because they brought
into the catholic Church a novelty of empty talk. As children
mimic to each other what their fathers expressly say and do,
they think that they pronounce as teachings what everybody
knows very well; they even commit it to writing. However, they   236C
have become ridiculous to all.

Again, with their own empty fable, they say:

GREGORY THE BISHOP read:

*Then there is the great and renowned Council in Chalcedon, which convened
in the reign of Marcian, the God-loving king. This anathematized Dioscorus
and the unfortunate Eutyches[37] for teaching that the one and the same
Christ and Lord, after the perfect union of God the Word with the flesh,
did not have two natures; rather, although the union was made of two*   236D
natures, it nevertheless resulted in a single one, mixed and confused.

*In addition to these there was the Council of the one hundred and
sixty-five fathers, which convened in Constantinople during the divine
assignment[38] of Justinian. This anathematized Origen (who is also called
Adamantius), Evagrius, and Didymus along with their pagan[39] writings;
Theodore of Mopsuestia and Theodore,[40] Nestorius' teacher; Severus, Peter,*

36 That is, those who confuse the two natures in Christ and mingle them into one. Cf below,
    236C–D.
37 The name Eutyches means 'the fortunate one.' With the expression 'the unfortunate
    Eutyches' the authors of the text are playing with the two words for reasons of irony!
38 That is, the period in office.
39 Literally, Greek.
40 He is better known as Diodorus [of Tarsus]. Diodorus is the latinized form of the name
    Theodore. Diodorus of Tarsus (d ca 394) and Theodore of Mopsuestia (d 428) are
    considered the originators of Nestorianism. Nestorius (d after 450) received his
    theological education in the School of Antioch, probably under Theodore of
    Mopsuestia himself. The Antiochian school was interested in showing in its theology
    that in Christ there are two *natures*, unconfused and unchangeable, the one subject to
    passion and the other beyond passion. The Alexandrian school, however, was
    interested in showing that Christ is one *person*. The Alexandrian theologians made a
    distinction between 'person' and 'nature'; the Antiochians did not. They were,
    therefore, speaking of two 'persons' in Christ, in the same way as they were speaking
    of 'two Sons.' Theodore was speaking of a perfect nature of God the Word and a
    perfect person, and also of a perfect human nature and a perfect person!

and Zooras, with their impious doctrines; [it anathematized] also the so-
called Iba's letter to Mares the Persian. It also reaffirmed the pious doctrines
of the holy and great Fourth Council.

EPIPHANIUS THE DEACON read: 236E

Even Sergius of Constantinople, Cyrus of Alexandria, Honorius
of Rome, and their associates, who are called Monothelites,
accepted these holy and Ecumenical Councils and those before
them. Yet they have been anathematized by the catholic Church
as heretics, because they gurgled emptiness into this Church.
So is it with them. Even though they have accepted these holy   237A
councils, yet they are expelled from the catholic Church because
of their heresy. Vain, therefore, and idle is their word and
unworthy of any response. For, while they acknowledge the holy
councils, they oppose them and are antagonistic to them. If they
did so out of ignorance, it is wholly silly and stupid. But if they
did so in full awareness, it is impious, something done out of
a completely absurd conscience. For they should either show
us one council contradicting another – unless it is one of those
which was alien to the catholic Church and has been anathematized, like that of theirs – or follow the holy and approved ones,
and accept what they have bequeathed to the Church. If they
accept the venerable icons, it means that they follow the catholic   237B
Church, because they [the icons] have been accepted by the holy
six Ecumenical Councils. But if they do not follow the catholic
Church, no one will listen to them, since they do not adhere
to her tradition, meet for God.

GREGORY THE BISHOP read:

Similarly, there is the Council of the one hundred and seventy holy fathers
which convened in this city guarded by God, during the time of Constantine,
the pious king. This council anathematized and denounced Theodore of   237C
Pharan, Cyrus of Alexandria, Honorius of Rome, Sergius, Paul, Pyrrus,
and Peter (who had presided over this city),[41] *as well as Macarius of*
Antioch and Stephen, his disciple, for saying that there is one will and
energy in the two natures of the one Christ, our God.

---

41 That is, the Patriarchs of Constantinople: Sergius I (610–638), Pyrrus (638–641, 654), Paul II
   (641–653), Peter (654–666).

EPIPHANIUS THE DEACON read:
There is no reason to refute these petty words, because they have been refuted earlier.

However, with a forged sophism, they bring again to the fore 237D
the holy councils, saying the following:

GREGORY THE BISHOP read:
These six holy and Ecumenical Councils, therefore, having made a pious and pleasing to God, exposition of the doctrines of the immaculate faith of us Christians - instructed by the gospels which are delivered by God - have handed down that in the one Christ, who is our Lord and God, there is one hypostasis in two natures, wills, and energies. They have also taught that both the miracles and the sufferings have been of the 237E
one and the same [Christ].

EPIPHANIUS THE DEACON read:
What arrogance and presumptuous thinking! They attempt to instruct the Church as if she were ignorant and had never known the divine doctrines; she who is testified to be full of all wisdom, as her priest, the divine Apostle, cries out with the loud voice 240A
of the Spirit, saying that *through the church the manifold wisdom of God may be made known to the principalities and powers.*[42] By bringing into consideration what is not under question, they have made not a right, but rather quite a perilous, judgment. For the catholic Church has received and confirmed these doctrines as a safe anchor, and she has no need to be taught about them. However, along with these doctrines our Fathers accepted the venerable icons, deemed them worthy of a certain respect and honour, and reproduced them as iconographies in the venerable churches they built. They also reproduced them in every appropriate place, and kissed them. These one, however, have dared to overstep the entire congregation [of the Fathers] and set their throne in 240B
opposition to them, with their neck arched proudly like the devil, the father of falsehood. They have also defiled and insulted things which are sacred, committing them to the fire. What an endeavour! What daring thoughtlessness! May their thinking recede, and the Lord spare his people from this corruptive wickedness of theirs. In addition, may everyone follow faithfully the catholic Church,

42 Cf Eph. 3:10.

accept every iconographic representation of the gospel, as well as the reproductions of the labours of the martyrs, and embrace them, as the holy catholic Church of God has from the beginning.

They, however, continue the same artifices, talking frivolously as follows:

GREGORY THE BISHOP read:
Having looked into these matters with great diligence and deliberation, 240C
under the inspiration of the all-holy Spirit, we have also found that the
unlawful art of the painters constitutes a blasphemy against this very
fundamental doctrine of our salvation, that is, against the dispensation
in Christ, and that it subverts these very holy and Ecumenical six councils,
convened by God,

EPIPHANIUS THE DEACON read: 240D
There is diligence and deliberation which is for evil – as Absalom attended to and deliberated with Ahithophel against his own father,[43] and as they did against the holy Fathers. Ahab also thought of accepting the prophecies of the pseudo-prophets as being of divine inspiration, but he, too, was deceived in his hopes. The author of Proverbs has also said this: *There is a way which seems to be right with men, but the ends of it reach to the depth of hell.*[44]

This is what has happened with them, too. Conquered by the passion of pleasing men, and speaking from their own belly,[45] 240E they think that their ways are right, while those who believe in them are led down to the traps of Hades. For how does the making of icons by the painters constitute, as they say, 'a blasphemy against this very fundamental doctrine of our salvation'? Or, again, how does the art of the painters violate the six holy Ecumenical Councils? Or how were the icons placed 241A inside the churches against their opinion since – unlike what they say – it was those very divine Fathers of ours who, for the purpose of teaching and in their desire to accentuate the mystery of our salvation, and using the art of the painters,

43 Cf 2 Kings 15, 16, 17.
44 Prov. 14:12.
45 This is the literal translation of what could be translated freely as 'talking off the top of their heads.' The expression is obviously used sarcastically to criticize the lack of critical and diligent thinking of the iconoclasts. Cf also below, 272F.

reproduced them inside the venerable churches? Which of the divine Fathers has declared that the art of the painters is incompatible with this very crucial doctrine of our salvation, that is, the dispensation of Christ? What one accepts, one cannot afford to condemn. Therefore, they know how to talk frivolously but not how to defend their talk. It seems that they thought that no one would notice them making a fraud out of the word of truth. Every vulgar art which deviates from the purpose of God's commandments must be renounced. However, those arts which do not do so but are useful in our life, if there is nothing improper 241B in them, were neither despised nor rejected by our holy Fathers. Thus, the art of painting, if used in order to depict obscenities, is despicable and harmful. Painting pornographic designs and scenes, the gyrations of dancing and scenes of horse-races, or anything similar presented through art, is a dishonourable endeavour. But if we want to paint the life-stories of virtuous men, the narratives of the contests of the martyrs and the explanation of their sufferings, as well as the mystery of the dispensation 241C of God almighty and our Saviour, and if in these cases we use the art of the painters, we find ourselves doing something which is wholly proper. Thus, the painter paints the cross and no one of right thinking rejects an iconographed cross, nor is this [cross] void of grace because it is presented through colours by a painter.

The same principle applies to books. If one describes in books shameful stories, these books are shameful and to be rejected, alien to what a Christian should hear. But if they contain words and narratives which are inspired by God and lead to piety, they are worthy of praise and acceptance, and worthy of the Church of God. It is necessary to think in the same say – as we have 241D already said – about the icon of our Lord Jesus Christ and those of his saints. When one makes guitars and flutes, his endeavour is shameful. But if he makes any of the holy utensils, this is acceptable. No one of right thinking condemns an art if one uses it to make something that is necessary for this life. One should think of the purpose as well as of the means through which art accomplishes its result. If the purpose is for piety, the result is acceptable; if it is for a certain shamefulness, it is despicable and to be rejected.

However, being fixed firmly in their accusations, they continue, saying:

GREGORY THE BISHOP read: 241E
while it reinstates Nestorius, who divided the one Son and Word of God,
Who for us became man, into a duality of sons.

EPIPHANIUS THE DEACON read:
Again, as we said before, they make pronouncements without 244A
providing proofs. For how does he who reproduces with colours
the icon of Christ reinstate Nestorius? Nestorius introduces two
sons, one being the Word of the Father, and a different one, the
one from the Virgin. True Christians, however, confess one and
the same Son as Christ and Lord, and when they produce an
icon with colours, in so far as *the Word became flesh* – that is a
perfect man – *and dwelt among us,*[46] they do something perfectly
proper. For God the Word circumscribed Himself when He came
to us in flesh.

No one, of course, has thought to reproduce with colours his
divinity, for *No one,* it says, *has ever seen God.*[47] He is uncircumscribable, invisible, and incomprehensible, although circumscrib- 244B
able according to his humanity. For we know Christ to be of
two natures, and in two natures, that is, a divine and a human
one, without division. The one, therefore, which is uncircumscribable and the one which can be circumscribed are seen in the
one Christ. The icon resembles the prototype, not with regard
to the essence, but only with regard to the name and to the
position of the members which can be characterized. Nor does
one who paints the icon of a man seek a soul in it – although
the difference between a human soul and the divine nature is
one beyond comparison. For the one is uncreated, creative, and
beyond time, while the other is created, bound to time, and created
by it [the divine nature]. No one of sound mind who sees an 244C
icon of a man thinks that, through the art of the painter, man
is separated from his soul. An icon lacks not only a soul but
also the very substance of the body, I mean flesh, muscles, nerves,
bones, and elements, that is, blood, phlegm, fluid, and gall, the
blending of which it is impossible for one to see in an icon. If
these were seen in the icon, we would call this a 'man,' and
not an 'icon of a man.'

46 John 1:14.
47 John 1:18.

Surely, then, this present hair-splitting goes along with the rest of their problems. What follows is also worthy of laughter.

GREGORY THE BISHOP read: 244D
Not only he, however, but also Arius and Dioscorus, and Eutyches and Severus, who, with regard to the two natures of the one Christ, teach that these were confused and mixed.

EPIPHANIUS THE DEACON read:
What thoughtless myths of old women, and what a hidden deception! They like to dwell again upon the same chatter. Either 244E they are ignorant of the diversity which exists among the heresiarchs whom they enumerate, or, wittingly, they choose to talk nonsense. For the heresies of Arius, Dioscorus, and Eutyches are markedly contrary to that of Nestorius, and in opposition to each other, although equivalent with regard to impiety. Thus, Arius, by teaching that the pre-eternal and uncreated Word of God the Father came into being from non-existence, adds to his impiety another heresy, saying that Christ does not have a cogi- 245A tating soul, but that the divinity is in place of the soul – to which [divinity] he ascribed also passion. Dioscorus and Eutyches, however, are opposite to Nestorius, who teaches that there are two natures and hypostases in Christ, and they confuse the natures, teaching idly that there is one nature. Having walked far from the royal way which does not incline either to the right or to the left,[48] they deviated from the teaching of the Apostles and of the Fathers. What is, then, the relationship and agreement of the holy catholic Church of God towards Arius, Dioscorus, and Eutyches in regard to descriptive iconographies? These are only empty and fading words, different from those which the 245B Apostle recommends when he says: *Let your speech always be gracious, seasoned with salt.*[49] Job also, the man of many contests, who detested such words, used to say: *Shall bread be eaten without salt? or again, is there taste in empty words?*[50]
One, therefore, must deal with their random accusations made in vain against the Church of God. At one place they say that,

48 Cf above, 208B, n 12.
49 Col. 4:6.
50 Job 6:6.

when the Church depicts with colours the incarnation of the Lord, she is carried away along with Nestorius, the impious one who divides the natures; and at another place that she is carried away along with Eutyches and Dioscorus, the accursed ones who confuse the natures. But as has been shown, it is clear that these oppose each other, although together they fight against the Church. If we accept what they say, that the Church follows 245C Nestorius, then they are proven liars, because they say that she is in agreement with Eutyches and Dioscorus. And the opposite: if we concede that she is in agreement with Eutyches and Dioscorus, they are also proven, in this regard, to be liars. For, as the previous discussion has shown, Nestorius and Eutyches differed from each other in impiety. Thus, this fallacy of theirs is irrational and useless.

THIRD VOLUME

EPIPHANIUS THE DEACON read:

Having ploughed on thorny ground, they make pronouncements 245D
which are alien to what the Apostles have seeded, while they
germinate weeds of heresy. For this reason God cries out to them
through the prophet: *Many shepherds have destroyed my vineyard:*
they have defiled my portion[1] by saying to it:

GREGORY THE BISHOP read:

We considered it, therefore, right to demonstrate in detail, through our
present Definition, the error of those who make and those who pay respect
[to the icons]. 245E

Thus, whereas all the God-bearing Fathers and the holy and Ecumenical
Councils have handed down the pure and immaculate faith and confession,
proven by God to be such, that one should not contrive any means of
dividing or confusing that which is beyond reason and cogitation, the
unspeakable and unknowable unique hypostastic union of the two natures
of a person who is signified as absolutely one,

EPIPHANIUS THE DEACON read: 248A

Indeed, what the conceited ones have shown in every detail is
their own error. For, while all our Fathers who gathered in the
six holy Ecumenical Councils accepted and instituted the venerable iconographic representations in the holy churches and
other appropriate places, they, on the contrary, have renounced
them publicly through certain intrusive, petty words, suggesting
that they are, and calling them instead, an 'error' and 'another 248B
idolatry' next to the demonic one. Where there are two things,
exclusive of each other, they made no distinction between the
one and the other.[2] They circulate in their mouth the same name
both for the things which are for the glory of Christ our God
and have a place in order to remind us of his conduct in the
flesh and also for those things which are for the glory and memory
of the demons and are made by the Greeks and the Jews who
worship them. Neither did they have any shame in committing

1 Jer. 12:20.
2 That is, the icon and the idol.

these things to writing, mixing what cannot be mixed and making sinful pretensions. They hum idle talk about division and confusion in the knowledge of God[3] by the catholic Church, and they babble that no one should contrive any means of dividing 248C the union between the hypostasis of God the Word with the flesh.

It appears that they have never read what the Fathers say. If they have, they have done so in passing and not diligently. Thus Gregory the Theologian refutes their totally empty recitation when he says, 'Whenever the natures are distinguished from one another in our thoughts, the names are also distinguished.'[4] All our holy Fathers who do not accept the confusion [of the natures] say that, in our thinking, the two natures are separate because they are different, not because they are divided. Therefore, they either fail to understand this – and along with this the precise 248D meaning of the doctrines – or they assume that in no way do our holy Fathers speak of a division in the union of the two natures of the dispensation of Christ. Thus while Nestorius, when he says that God the Word is one, and the one from the Virgin another, actually divides the natures into a man on his own and God on his own, the catholic Church, by confessing that the union took place without confusion, distinguishes the natures only in the thinking without dividing them, confessing that Emmanuel is one and the same, even after the union.

However, breathing insults from their nostrils, they pursue their attack:

GREGORY THE BISHOP read: 248E
what is this senseless contrition on the part of the painter of caricatures who, for the sake of cheap profiteering, has occupied himself in doing something that cannot be done, that is, with profane hands giving form to things that are believed with the heart and confessed with the mouth?

---

3 What we render here as 'knowledge of God' reads *theologikē epistēme* in the text. Today this wording is used for theology or, more accurately, for theological scholarship. Obviously the text is not referring here to the discipline or the academic study of theology, but rather to the way in which the Church 'knows' and experiences the Godhead. Cf also below, 300A, n 19.
4 Gregory of Nazianzus, *On the Son*, Oration 30, PG 36:113B. Cf also below, 257C, 341B.

EPIPHANIUS THE DEACON read:

It is madness to say and think this way. To accuse persons who
are not at fault is not characteristic of sensible men. What an awkward notion on their part to apply these fables to the consecrated   249A
things of the Church! If they have said that it is for profiteering
that the painter depicts our Lord in so far as He became a perfect
man, and his saints, it is also time for them to accuse those who
copy the holy gospels, and to call those who design the cross
with colours 'painters of caricatures,' and to say that they do this
for profiteering! What? Will the mason of a cross also be called
a 'builder of a caricature'? Will the stone-mason who carves out
and makes a holy altar be called a 'stone-mason of a caricature,'
or the goldsmith, the silversmith, and the weaver similarly? According to their madness, this is the implication regarding every
discipline and art given by God for his glory, and for the constitution
of our life. Since they reached an ultimate point of ignorance and
wickedness, let them hear the holy Scripture and our holy Fathers
praising the wisdom which was given to our nature by the munif-
icent God who created us. First, Job, speaking of God: *Who has
given to women skill in weaving?*[5] The holy Scripture also testifies
that God gave wisdom to Beseleel for every knowledge of work.
For this is what it says: 249C

*And the Lord spoke to Moses, saying, Behold I have called by name Beseleel
the son of Urias, the son of Or, of the tribe of Jude. And I have filled him
with a divine spirit of wisdom, and understanding, and knowledge, to invent
in every work, and to frame works, to labour in gold, and silver, and brass, and
blue and purple, and spun scarlet, and the spun flax,[6] and works in stone and
for artificer's work in wood, to work at all works. And I have appointed him
and Eliab the son of Achisamach of the tribe of Dan, and to every one understanding
in heart I have given understanding; and they shall make all things as many
as I have appointed thee.*[7]

In harmony with these Gregory, the renowned in theology, says   249D
also: 'A spirit of the Lord descended and guided them. A spirit

---

5 Job 38:36. The word 'skill' in the Septuagint version reads 'wisdom' (*sophīa*).
6 The words 'and the spun flax' are not found in Bagster's edition of the Septuagint
   version or in the English translation.
7 Exod. 31:1–6.

of understanding filled Beseleel the mason of the Tent.'[8] Having, therefore, disparaged and reprehended the disciplines which God gave to men, they are added to the heretics who are contemptuous of God, and they are called so, having, according to the words of the Scripture, *added a sin to a sin.*[9]

Thus the authentic, not illegitimate, sons of the adorned bride of Christ, the catholic Church, which is *without spot or wrinkle*,[10] offering the reasonable sacrifice[11] and worship to God alone, when through the sense of sight they see the venerable icon of Christ   249E or of the holy Theotokos who is properly and truly our Lady or the icons of the angels and of all the saints, are sanctified, and they set their mind to the remembrance of them. They also *believe in one God with their heart and so they are justified, and they confess with their lips and so are saved.*[12] So it is when they hear the gospel. They fill their sense of hearing with sanctification and grace, and thus *they understand with their heart*[13] the narrative of the Scriptures.

Then, puffing up in vain, what do they say?

GREGORY THE BISHOP read: 252A
For he has made an icon which he has called 'Christ.' But 'Christ' is a name [indicative] of God as well as man. Consequently, along with describing created flesh, he has either circumscribed the uncircumscribable character of the Godhead, according to what has seemed good to his own worthlessness, or he has confused that unconfused union, falling into the iniquity of confusion. Thus, in two ways, with the circumscription and the confusion, he has blasphemed the Godhead. The one who has venerated them [the icons] is also responsible for the same blasphemies. 252B
Both are equally to be condemned because they have fallen into error

---

8 Cf Gregory of Nazianzus, *Funeral Oration to Basil the Great, Bishop of Caesarea*, Oration 43, PG 36:553B. This passage reads as follows: 'That Beseleel, the mason of the Tent of God, made use of every material and every art to accomplish the work, as he implicated everything to create an abundance and harmony of a single beauty.' The author refers to Beseleel in order to relate him to Basil the Great typologically.
9 Cf Is. 30:1.
10 Eph. 5:27.
11 The liturgy of John Chrysostom. Cf also above, 220A, n 38.
12 Cf Rom. 10:10.
13 Cf Is. 6:10; Matt. 13:15.

along with Arius, Dioscorus, and Eutyches, and into the heresy of the Acephaloi.[14]

EPIPHANIUS THE DEACON read:
The making of icons is not an invention of the painters but an accepted institution and tradition of the catholic Church; and that which excels in antiquity is worthy of respect, according to the divine Basil.[15] Antiquity itself and the teaching of our Fathers, who bear within themselves the Spirit, testify that they   252C
[the Fathers] were gratified to see icons inside the venerable churches. They were the ones who, having built venerable churches, iconographed them and offered inside them prayers to God and bloodless sacrifices which are accepted by Him, the Master of all. The idea, therefore, and the tradition are theirs, not the painter's. Only the art is of the painter, whereas the disposition is certainly of the holy Fathers who erected [churches].

As to the name 'Christ,' this is indicative of divinity and of humanity as well, the two perfect natures of the Saviour. Christians have been taught to depict the icon of that nature of his according to which He has been seen, not of that according to which He is invisible; the latter is uncircumscribable. For we   252D
have heard from the gospel that *No one has ever seen God.*[16] Therefore, since Christ is depicted according to his human nature, it is obvious, as the truth has shown, that Christians confess that what the icon has in common with the archetype is only the name, not the essence.

However, these senseless men say that there is no distinction between an icon and the prototype, and, although these are of

---

14 *Acéphaloi* means 'those lacking a head,' that is, a bishop. This name was applied to the extreme Monophysites, who after the Council of Chalcedon (451) continued arguing in favour of 'one nature' in Christ, rejected the *Henoticōn* (a 'Volume of Union' drafted by the Emperor Zeno in 482 to bring the Orthodox and the Monophysites together), and finally broke away from their Patriarch of Alexandria, Peter III the Dumb (482–490), a moderate Monophysite who had signed the *Henoticōn* – thus remaining 'headless.' The same name was afterwards used for all the Monophysites who did not accept the *Henoticōn*, which among other provisions declared a moratorium on any further discussion of the wording of the state of the divine and the human natures after their union in Christ. Against the *Acéphaloi* John of Damascus wrote a treatise, *On the Composite Nature. Against the Acephaloi*, PG 95:112C–125B; Kotter, IV, 409–417.
15 Cf Basil of Caesarea, *On the Holy Spirit*, ch 29, PG, 32:204D–205A.
16 John 1:18.

a different essence, they deem them to be of the same. Who would not laugh at their ignorance or, rather, lament their impiety? Having deviated with a base mind, they say things that are improper, fabricating that the holy Church of God, on account   252E of the venerable icons, is the cause of the confusion [in the natures of Christ] and that she ascribes to the Godhead the quality of circumscription.

Then, adding lawlessness to lawlessness, they launch condemnations. However, that which they inflict will return upon their own heads. For if *he that curses the ancient Israel is cursed and he that blesses him, blessed,*[17] how much more cursed is he who curses the new Israel - the Church of God - that sees God in a spiritual sense? He is totally accursed. Who would not detest them for saying that she is led astray by Arius, Dioscorus, Eutyches, and the heresy of the *Acephaloi,* while they themselves have had those   253A as teachers and patrons of their own heresy? Thus, later on they bring forth as a witness Eusebius of Pamphilus, whom the entire catholic[18] Church knows as a supporter of the heresy of Arius, as is evidenced by all his writings and publications. He is so by saying that God the Word is second in adoration, subordinate to the Father, and second in dignity - in opposition to the doctrine of consubstantiality [*homoousios*] - and that the holy flesh of the Lord changed into the divine nature. Consequently, in adherence with his confusion [of the two natures], he does not accept the   253B icon either; nor does the entire accursed group of Ariomaniacs.[19] For they believe that our Lord became man without a rational soul and that in him divinity took the place of the soul. They believe so in order - as Gregory the Theologian testifies[20] - that they may attach suffering to the divinity. Therefore, they do not accept the icon either, because they are Theopaschites.[21]

---

17 Cf Num. 24:9.
18 That the adjective 'catholic' is not used in the Christian literature of the East in the sense of geographical or political universality becomes evident in cases such as this, where the two adjectives 'entire' and 'catholic' - the one referring to quantity and size, and the other to the wholeness and orthodoxy of the Church - occur together. Cf also above, 208B, n 12.
19 Cf above, 224E, n 10.
20 Gregory of Nazianzus, *Second Letter to Cledonius,* Epistle no. 102, PG 37:196C.
21 *Theopaschites* (from *Theōs,* God, and the verb *paschein,* to suffer): 'those who maintain that God is subject to suffering.' The name was given to the Scythian monks and their

Similarly, Severus the confuser [of the natures] did not accept
the icon of Christ our God in the Church, as many historians
relate. Therefore, it is a wonder that they say that the catholic
Church follows Arius, Dioscorus, Eutyches, and the heresy of
the *Acephaloi*, since she has accepted iconographic representations! 253C
They throw out with their unguarded tongue nothing else but
petty words which are spread through the air. Truly, let them
listen to this: [in Christ] the divine nature is beyond description,
as we have said: the human nature, however, has been circumscribed. No one of sound thinking, when he says that [Christ's]
human nature is describable, describes together with it the one
which is beyond description. Thus, the Lord, in so far as He
was a perfect man, when He was in Galilee, was not in Judea.
This is something to which He Himself gives testimony when
He says: *Let us go into Judea again.*[22] Also, talking to his disciples
about Lazarus, He said this: *And for your sake I am glad that I was
not there.*[23] In so far, however, as He is God, He is present at 253D
every place of His sovereignty, and He remains altogether
uncircumscribed.

Why, then, talking empty babbling words, do they stammer
with an undisciplined tongue, saying that the painter 'has circumscribed the uncircumscribable character of Godhead, according to what has seemed good to his own worthlessness'? If the 253E
divine nature was circumscribed together with the human nature
by his being laid down and wrapped in swaddling clothes inside
a manger, so is his uncircumscribable divinity in the depicted
icon of his human nature.[24] So is it on the cross. If the divine
nature was circumscribed with the human nature, so is his

---

followers, who under the influence of Monophysitism maintained that it was God
Who suffered on the cross. The Orthodox side maintained that suffering is applicable
to the human nature alone; the divine nature is beyond passion. However, the
Godhead did not remain unaffected. God suffered, not in his divine nature, but in the
person of the human nature with which the divinity was united in Christ (*metádosis
idiomáton*, i.e., 'communication of properties' of the two natures). The Monophysites,
by making no distinction between 'nature' and 'person' (*prósopon*), ascribed the
suffering to the divinity. The controversy is known as *Theopaschite* and it lasted from
519 to 533. Cf also below, 261B–C, 320A.

22 John 11:7.
23 John 11:15.
24 Cf n 21 above for the reference to the 'communication of properties.'

uncircumscribable divinity together with the depicted icon of
the human nature. If the former did not happen, neither did
the latter. Would that they had heard the statement of Dionysius,
who bears God in him, from his *Oration of the Hierarchy*,[25] who
says this:

There is no exact likeness between those things which are produced
by a cause and the things which are the causes. Yet the effect bears
the image which is contingent to the cause, although the cause super-
sedes and stands above the effect, to the degree of its own nature.

Therefore, it has been shown – even to those who can under   256A
stand very little – that the rhapsody of their words attempts
to introduce vain, empty talk aimed at combatting the Church,
not the painter.

And as they are shameless, they say, insolently:

GREGORY THE BISHOP read:
*Then, when they are criticized by those who think rightly about engaging
in painting the incomprehensible and uncircumscribable divine nature
of Christ, they always resort to another mischievous defence, that 'It is*   256B
*the icon of the flesh alone which we have seen and touched and were
in company with that we depict' – something impious and an invention
of the Nestorian misfortune.*

EPIPHANIUS THE DEACON read:
The falsifiers of truth, having turned to shameless polemics,
continue with the same contrivances. However, by expressing
thoughts of their own they fall into the snare of blasphemy. First,
with irrational words they accuse Christians of describing the   256C
incomprehensible and undescribable nature of Christ. Then, in
a rhetorical way, they impersonate them and declare falsely that
'it is the icon of the flesh alone, the one which we have seen
and touched and were in company with that we depict,' in order
that they may push the Church again into the slander of Nestorius. That is why they conclude that this is 'something impious
and an invention of the Nestorian misfortune.'

25 Dionysius the Areopagite, *On the Celestial Hierarchy*, PG 3:120–369. Cf also above, 212A,
   n 23.

Therefore, let them listen to the truth: Christians, knowing that Emmanuel is one Lord Christ, iconograph Him in so far as *the Logos became flesh.*[26] In doing so they dispel anything that in itself is complicated chatter, because they accept with a simple heart everything that has been handed down to the Church. 256D When they see the iconographies, they understand nothing except what is signified in them. Thus, when they see in an icon the Virgin giving birth and angels standing around with shepherds, they bring to mind that when God became man He was born[27] for our salvation, and they make a confession, saying: 'He Who is without flesh, became flesh. The Word assumed density. The uncreated One was made. The impalpable One was touched.' They also confess that He is one and the same, perfect in divinity, and perfect in humanity, truly God and truly man. As to the accursed heresy of Nestorius, it has already been said that the 256E painting of icons is not compatible with it – and sufficient has been said on this. Should there be a need, however, it will be said again.

Thinking, then, that there is something in them to understand, they say:

GREGORY THE BISHOP read:
It is necessary, even on this point, for one to consider that if, according to the orthodox Fathers, the flesh is flesh, and at one and the same time flesh of God the Word, never subject to any notion of partition, but rather assumed as a whole within the divine nature and deified as a whole, 257A how can it be split into two, or be given a hypostasis of its own, by

26 John 1:14.
27 Does the phrasing 'when God became man He was born' suggest two spheres of operation in the manifestation of the divine dispensation? Perhaps yes; the taking up of the human nature by God the Word, something which only God can do to Himself (cf the phrase 'He emptied himself' in Phil. 2:7); and, further, his birth of a woman (cf Gal. 4:4); for it is not possible for the Godhead to be converted and change into the nature of matter (cf Cyril's statement below, 320D). This distinction is essential in understanding the soteriological concept of *synergeia* (the co-operation of God with man in man's salvation), as well as the actual meaning of the name 'Theotōkos' given to Mary – a name, which, according to John of Damascus, *On the Orthodox Faith*, vol III, ch 12, PG 94:1029, 'constitutes the entire mystery of the [divine] dispensation.' Cf also the wording of the Nicene Creed: 'And in one Lord Jesus Christ ... who for us men and our salvation came down from heaven and was incarnated by the holy Spirit *and* the virgin Mary and became Man.' Cf also below, 320D, 336B, n 21, 377A.

those who try impiously to do so? So it is with his holy soul, too. For, when the divinity of the Son assumed the nature of the flesh in its own hypostasis, the soul played the role of the mediator between the divinity and the density of the flesh. In the same way as the flesh is at one and the same time the flesh of God the Word, so is the soul at one and the same time the soul of God the Word – both these together: that is, the soul is deified just as is the body. Divinity remains inseparable from them, even at that very separation of the soul from the body at the voluntary Passion. For, wherever the soul of Christ is, there is the divinity as well; 257B
and wherever the body of Christ is, there is the divinity too.

EPIPHANIUS THE DEACON read:
When those who deviate from the catholic Church are about to say something wicked, they begin with what everybody confesses. By being right on this, they hope not to be disbelieved on the rest. Thus, having stated a few things properly, they now mix gravel with the pearls. Having returned to their own vomit, they now say that those who accept the venerable iconographic 257C
representations 'split the one Christ into two and give each one a hypostasis of its own.' They also slander that [the flesh] is never subject to any notion of partition. Obviously they are unaware of what the Fathers say. For all of them speak expressly of a division of the two natures in thought, as we have said above,[28] although not in actuality, as Nestorius dared to say blasphemously.

Indeed, the fact that the Lord has been iconographed in so far as he became a perfect man is not a cause of separation and individualization, or of any kind of division, or again – the opposite – of confusion, as they have falsely said in many ways. For the 257D
icon is one thing and the prototype another. No one of sound mind looks in any way to the icon for the qualities of the prototype. In the icon the true discourse knows nothing else but how to communicate in name, not in essence, with the one who is in the icon, as we have said in many ways when we were challenged by their disputations.

Having nothing justifiable to say against the catholic Church, they repeat the same words about the same things, gibbering empty things and making those who listen to them talk idly

28 Cf above, 248C.

as well. For this reason everybody knows how ridiculous they are, saying one time 'division' and another 'confusion,' with a   257E
tongue ready only to utter sinful things.

Thence they say:

GREGORY THE BISHOP read:

If, therefore, at the Passion the divinity remained inseparable from them [the soul and body of Christ], how can these insane and completely unreasonable men divide the flesh, that had been interwoven with the divinity and deified, and try to draw an icon as if it were that of, supposedly, a mere man? For in this respect, too, they fall over another precipice   260A
of lawlessness, by separating the flesh from the divinity and presenting it as if it had a hypostasis of its own, and by attaching to the flesh a different person, which they claim to depict in an icon. By this they show that they add a fourth person to the Trinity; and even more, they describe that which was assumed[29] and deified as being without divinity.

From those, therefore, who think that they are drawing the icon of Christ, it must be gathered either that the divinity is circumscribable and confused with the flesh or that the body of Christ was without divinity and divided; and also that they ascribe to the flesh a person with a hypostasis of his own – thus, in this respect, identifying themselves with the Nestorian fight against God.

Those, therefore, who make, and those who desire, and those who pay   260B
respect to the icon of Christ, which falsely is made and called so by them, should feel ashamed and embarrassed, and should be reproached for falling into such an impiety and blasphemy. Let them be far from us – Nestorius' division and Arius', Dioscorus', Eutyche's, and Severus' confusion – two evils diametrically opposite to each other, but equal in impiety.

EPIPHANIUS THE DEACON read:

In no sense do the propagators of the offensive heresy against the Christians follow the only way, as it is the tradition of those who are orthodox with regard to divine doctrine – to follow, that is, the royal way, and not lean either to one side or the   260C
other.[30] On the contrary, by distorting the ways of the Lord, they, guided by their own mind, collect the most adverse ideas

29 In Greek *prōslemma*.
30 Cf also above, 208B, n 12.

on their own, thinking that they are wise in every respect. They are the ones for whom Isaiah, the outspoken one, says: *Woe to them that are wise in their own conceit, and knowing in their own sight.*[31] For they take as confessions what the orthodox Christians have never said. Drawing untenable syllogisms, they criticize the Church by using sophistry. The result of all this is simply insult and scorn, and, in addition to these, impiety. For that which Diodorus and Theodore of Mopsuestia, Nestorius, Eutyches,   260D Dioscorus, and Severus maintained, raging against the truth, they ascribe to the catholic Church. Mixing evil with evil, they accuse her, with the most idiotic and foolish words, of being entangled with those most impious heresiarchs. Like pedlars they mix water with the wine, the word of distortion with that of truth, and produce a mixture of bitter gall. For we have just described the way in which the heresy of Dioscorus is opposite to that of Nestorius. It is not likely that opposing heresies will have the same opinion and confession, just as it is impossible to have white and black, warm and cold, in one thing at the same time.   260E Warmth is never found in the snow, nor cold in the fire.

However, we shall make even clearer the ineptitude of their foolishness. They who are quick to make accusations say that 'icon' and 'prototype' are the same thing. For this reason they label those who depict through designs the narrative of the gospel with the names of 'confusion' and of 'division' of the natures of Christ. Thus the deviation from the truth by the Eutychians, those, that is, who believe that there is one nature in the hypostatic union of Christ and who as a consequence promulgate confusion,   261A consists in nothing else but in defining 'hypostasis' and 'nature' as the same thing – things which we, reared in the catholic Church, know to be different one from the other. We call hypostasis a substance with properties of its own, beyond subsistence; while we call nature something self-existing, which is in need of nothing else in order to be constituted, beyond birth. In the same way also they say that the icon of Christ and Christ Himself do not differ from each other in essence. If they had known the difference, they would not have spoken of these novelties with exaggerations. For it is quite clear to everyone that 'icon' is one thing and 'prototype' another; the one is inanimate, the other animate.

31 Is. 5:21.

Having departed from reason, and chattering that in the icon   261B
the divine nature is described, *they gave themselves up to a base
mind.*[32] Thus, when Peter and Paul are depicted, one can see
them. Their souls, however, are not present in the icons. Even
if the body of Peter were present, one could not see his soul.
Since one cannot see it [the soul], who then of those who adhere
to the truth can say – unless in thought only – that the body
of Peter is separated from his soul? How, even more, [could one
say this] with regard to the uncircumscribable nature of God
the Word, which is described by the flesh which was assumed
by Him? Thus, when He became tired from his walk and asked
for water from the Samaritan woman, or when He was stoned   261C
by the Jews, it was not the divine nature that was tired and
attacked with stones – far from this blasphemy.[33]

Such are the complicated contortions which, in their desire
to spit upon iconographic representations, the celebrated vanity
of the accusers of the Christians introduced sideways with
uncontrolled tongues. In such a manner, introducing other things
indirectly and collecting iniquity upon iniquity, they chattered
that a fourth person has been added to the holy Trinity. However,
we, who as legitimate children have been born within the catholic
Church – accepting everything pertinent to the dispensation of
our Lord Jesus Christ, and despising Arius, Nestorius, Apollinaris,   261D
and their disciples Eutyches and Dioscorus – do accept the
venerable icons. We acknowledge these to be nothing more than
icons, in so far as they bear the name only, not the essence, of
the prototype.

However, moving suspiciously like a cancer, they adopt
another line of blasphemy, saying:

GREGORY THE BISHOP read:
Let those who enact, desire, and respect the true icon of Christ with a   261E
*most honest heart, and who offer themselves to salvation, both soul and
body, rejoice, exalt, and become outspoken. It is the Celebrant Himself
and God Who, when He assumed from us our entire composition, handed
this [icon] down to his initiates, at the time of his voluntary Passion,
in place of [Himself] and as a most vivid remembrance [of Him]. For,*

32 Cf Rom. 1:28.
33 Cf above, 253B, n 21.

when He was about to offer Himself voluntarily to his ever memorable
and life-giving death, taking the bread He blessed it and, after He gave
thanks, He broke it, and passing it on, He said: Take, eat, for the
remission of sins; this is my body.[34] *Similarly, passing on the cup,*   264A
He said: This is my blood; do this in remembrance of me.[35] *He*
did so, because there was no other kind or form under the sun selected
by Him which could depict his incarnation. Here is, therefore, the icon
of his body, the giver of life, which is enacted honestly and with honour.
For what else did the all-wise God want to achieve through this? Nothing
else, but to show, to make abundantly evident to us, the accomplished
mystery of the dispensation in Him. That is, in the same way as that
which He assumed from us is a mere matter of human substance, perfect
in every respect, which, however, is not characterized as a person with
a hypostasis of its own – in this way no addition of a person may occur
in the Godhead – so did He command that the icon also be matter as   264B
such; that is, He commanded that the substance of bread be offered which
does not yield the shape of a man's form, so that idolatry may not be
introduced indirectly. Therefore, as the natural body of Christ is holy,
as it has been deified, so, obviously, is the one which is in its place
[by convention]; that is, his icon is also holy as one which becomes deified
by grace, through an act of consecration. For this is what the Lord Christ
specified, as we have said; so that, in the same way that He deified the
flesh which He assumed by the union of it with the sanctity of his own
nature, so did He the bread of the Eucharist. He consented that this become
a holy body – as a true icon of the natural flesh – consecrated by the
descent of the holy Spirit and through the mediation of the priest who   264C
makes the offer[36] *in order that the bread be transferred from the state*
of being common to that of being holy.[37] *Thus, the physical and cogitating*

34 Cf Matt. 26:26–28.
35 Cf Luke 22:17–19.
36 The word used here is *anafora*, which is the term for the elevation (*ana*) and offering
    (*ferein*) of the gifts of the Eucharist by the priest, before the prayer of consecration –
    their transfer 'from the state of being common to that of being holy.'
37 The Orthodox understanding and appreciation of the eucharistic elements as the deified
    body of Christ is only the consequence of its Christological teaching of the hypostatic
    union of the divine nature of God the Word with the human nature and the
    deification of human nature which resulted from this union. In the Eucharist, which
    is the re-enactment of the divine dispensation, this union and transformation are
    represented through the 'elevation' and 'offering' of the material elements and their
    sanctification through the invocation of the holy Spirit. Cf also the discussion that
    follows, 264D–268A.

*flesh of the Lord was anointed with divinity through the holy Spirit.
Similarly also the icon of his flesh, handed down by God, the divine
bread along with the cup of his life-giving blood from his side, was filled
with the holy Spirit. This is, therefore, the icon that has been proven
to be the true icon of the incarnate dispensation of Christ our God, as
it has been stated before; and it is this one which the true Creator of
the life of the world has handed down to us with his own words.*

EPIPHANIUS THE DEACON read: 264D
It seems that once a discourse has deviated from the truth it
is carried along to many and dangerous improprieties by the
course of error. This is what has happened to these instigators
of novelty. After they deviated from the truth on the issue of
making icons, they were led to another apoplectic madness. This
happened because they delivered these ambiguous and sinister
teachings as oracles coming from a Delphic tripod. Thus the words
of the Proverbs are for them: *A man's own lips become a strong
snare to him, and he is caught with the words of his own mouth,*[38] 264E
for they put forth wood, hay, and stubble, which end up on
fire.

None of the holy Apostles – the trumpets of the Spirit – or
of our every-memorable Fathers called our bloodless sacrifice,[39]
which is celebrated in memory of the suffering of our God and
of his entire dispensation, 'an icon of His body.' They did not
receive such a thing from the Lord either to say or to confess.
Let them rather hear Him saying with the words of the gospel:
*Unless you eat the flesh of the Son of man and drink of His blood,
you shall not enter the kingdom of heaven;*[40] and *He who eats my flesh* 265A
and drinks my blood abides in me, and I in him;[41] *and He took bread,
and blessed, and broke it, and gave it to the disciples and said, 'Take
eat; this is my body.' And he took the cup, and when he had given thanks
he gave it to them, saying, 'Drink of it, all of you; for this is my blood
of the covenant, which is poured out for many and for the forgiveness
of sins.'*[42] He did not say "Take; eat the icon of my body."[43] Paul

---

38 Cf Prov. 6:2; cf also above, 208B, n 13.
39 Cf also above, 220A, n 38, and 249D, n 11.
40 Cf John 6:53.
41 John 6:56.
42 Matt. 26:26–28 (cf also Luke 22:17–19).
43 In the Orthodox Church, although the celebration of the Eucharist is confirmed as an act
   of 'remembrance,' it is understood and lived as an actual re-enactment of the entire

also, the holy Apostle who has drawn from the divine words
of the Lord, said: *I received from the Lord what I also delivered to*   265B
you, that the Lord Jesus on the night when he was betrayed took bread,
and when he had given thanks, he broke it, and said, 'This is my body
which is broken for you. Do this in remembrance of me.' In the same
way also the cup, after supper, saying, 'This cup is the new covenant
in my blood. Do this as often as you drink it, in remembrance of me.'
For as often as you eat this bread and drink the cup, you proclaim the
Lord's death until he comes.[44]

Thus, it has been clearly demonstrated that nowhere did either
the Lord, or the Apostles, or the Fathers call the bloodless sacrifice,
offered through the priest, 'an icon,' but rather 'this very body'
and 'this very blood.' Some of the holy Fathers out of piety
thought that it was proper for the elements of the sacrifice, prior   265C
to the completion of the consecration, to be called 'antitypes.'[45]
Among them was Eustathius, the steadfast[46] champion of the
orthodox faith and destroyer of the Arian misfortune, as well
as Basil, the abolisher of the same superstition, who rightly taught
those under the sun the level basis of the doctrines. Both of
them spoke through one and the same Spirit. The former,
interpreting the saying in the Proverbs of Solomon, *Eat of my*

cycle of the divine dispensation, that is of the incarnation, ministry, transfiguration,
crucifixion, and resurrection of Christ. And while events of the human life – which is
subject to time and change – can be re-enacted only in a figurative way, the re-
enactment of the 'story' of the dispensation in Christ is believed to be an actual one,
as the Church which celebrates it, and which is the mystical and living body of
Christ, involves along with the human the divine element as well, which is beyond
the limitation and the predication of time, space, and density. And although visible
means and common elements are used at the Eucharist, these are actually
transformed into mystical and holy realities which are shared by man here and now;
thence the present tense and the antinomical language which characterize the
Orthodox worship. This last point is particularly illustrated by the confession which
the priest recites immediately after the consecration of the gifts and while he cuts
and divides the Lamb, i.e., the consecrated piece from the bread of the Eucharist: 'The
Lamb of God is portioned and dismembered – He Who although portioned, He is
never divided, and although distributed, He is never consumed, but Who sanctifies
those who partake.' Thence the objection here to the understanding of the Eucharist
as an 'image' or 'icon' of the body of Christ.

44 1 Cor. 11:23–26.
45 That is, something which is in the place of (anti-) and corresponds to something else.
46 The name Eustathius means 'the well-based one' or the 'steadfast one.' The authors of
this text, for reasons of emphasis, complement the name with the consonant
adjective *eustathēs*. Cf also above, 236C, n 37.

bread, and drink wine which I have mingled for you,[47] says this: 'By "wine" and "bread" he proclaims the antitypes of the physical members of Christ.'[48] The latter, who has drawn from the same   265D
fountain, in the prayer of the holy offering, as all the initiates of the priesthood know, say this: 'taking courage, we approach the holy altar; and placing before Thee the antitypes of the holy body and blood of your Christ, we entreat Thee and supplicate.'[49] What follows makes even clearer the meaning of the Father, because the elements before the sanctification are called 'anti-types,' but after the sanctification they are called the 'proper body and blood of Christ,' as they are, and are believed to be.

These noble ones, however, in their desire to abolish the sight of the venerable icons, have introduced indirectly another icon – which is not an icon but body and blood. Possessed by wicked-   265E
ness and deception, and deceiving themselves with forged sophistry, they have said that the connection with the divine takes place by convention. Just as to state this clearly constitutes a madness, so to call the body and the blood of the Lord 'an icon' constitutes instability, which, in addition to being naïve, is also impious.

Afterwards, leaving aside falsehood, they touch for a moment upon the truth, saying that the bread does become the divine body. But, if the bread is an icon of the body, it is impossible for it to be the divine body itself. This turning from one side to the other makes their chattering utterly unreliable. What has   268A
happened to them is what happens to an eye, which, when disturbed, cannot see properly. Having disturbed and confused their own mind with wicked thinking, they imagine – like madmen – one thing instead of another. At one time they call our holy sacrifice an icon and at another a body by convention. This has happened to them, as we have just said, because they want to see the iconographic representations abolished from the Church, rejoicing, furthermore, at distorting the traditions of the Church.

47 Prov. 9:5.
48 Eustathius of Antioch, *In Proverbs* IX:5, PG 18:684–685. On Eustathius (d ca 337) see Quasten, *Patrology*, III, 302–306.
49 Basil of Caesarea's Divine Liturgy, in Panagiotes N. Trempelas, *Hai treis leitourgiae*, p 183.

FOURTH VOLUME

EPIPHANIUS THE DEACON read: 268B
Insisting again on the same slander, they sharpen their tongues
and move them to insult the holy Church of God; and they say:

GREGORY THE BISHOP read:
On the contrary, the ill name of the falsely called 'icon' neither has its 268C
existence in the tradition of Christ, or the Apostles, or the Fathers, nor
is there any prayer of consecration for it to transpose it from the state
of being common to the state of being sacred. Instead, it remains common
and worthless, as the painter made it.

EPIPHANIUS THE DEACON read:
With a magniloquent tongue they proliferate evil by further
additions, with no fear of God. Having attempted empty things
with unrestrained audacity, they have declared that icons, which
bear the name of Christ, have a false and ill name. If they had 268D
dared to say this about the icon of a king, they would have
received the death sentence. And this will indeed happen to them,
as they will receive such a sentence when the reward for words
and deeds takes place.

Among the many things which have been handed down to
us in an unwritten form, that of the painting of icons in the
Church has spread everywhere, since the time of the preaching
of the Apostles. The account of the woman in haemorrhage –
a story which is testified to by different accounts – states that
the woman built a statue of the Lord and, touching the edge
of it, as the gospel has narrated,[1] was healed; also, that between
her and the icon of the Lord a plant with the power to avert 268E
every disease had grown at the feet of the statue.[2]

---

1 Cf Matt. 9:20–22; Mark 5:25–34.
2 The tradition of this information belongs to Eusebius, *Ecclesiastical History*, ed E. Schwartz
(Leipzig, 1903), VII, 18. According to Eusebius, in Caesarea of Philippi, or Paneas
according to the Phoenicians, there is a house shown to be that of the biblical woman
in haemorrhage (Matt. 9:20–22). In front of this house there is a statue made of copper
showing a woman kneeling and extending her arms in supplication towards another
figure, which according to the popular belief depicts Christ himself. This figure is also
presented with hands stretched out towards the woman. By the feet of the statue of
Christ grows (again according to Eusebius) 'a strange kind of weed of qualities

Most of our holy Fathers also have conveyed to Christians, even in writing, instructions to entertain icons: Basil the Great – whose teaching is heard to the ends of the world – mentions icons in various discourses; Gregory, his brother in flesh and spirit, the one presiding over the Nyssaeans, in his oration to Abraham; also Gregory, the one surnamed after theology, in his poems, among which there is a discourse entitled *On Virtue*; John,   269A the one with a mouth more precious than gold, in his funeral oration to Meletius, bishop of Antioch, as well as in his discourse entitled *That the Law-giver of both, the Old and the New Testament, is one*; Cyril, the demolisher of Nestorius, in his first letter to Acacius, bishop of Skythopolis; as well as Anastasius of Theopolis, Sophronius, and Maximus. But, why do we have to mention all of them by name? All our holy Fathers accepted the painting of icons.

Thus, they are lying when they say that there is not such a tradition from the Fathers. Naturally there is not. If they did not hand down to us [exhortations] to read the gospel, neither did they to depict icons. If they had done the former, they would have done the latter, too. The representation of scenes in colours   269B follows the narrative of the gospel; and the narrative of the gospel follows the narrative of the paintings. Both are good and honourable. Things which are indicative of each other undoubtedly speak for each other. If we say 'the sun is over the earth,' it is certainly daytime. And if we say 'it is daytime,' the sun is certainly over the earth. So it is in this case. When we see on an icon the angel bringing the good news to the Virgin, we must certainly bring to mind that *the angel Gabriel was sent from God to the virgin. And*   269C *he came to her and said: 'Hail, O favoured one, the Lord is with you Blessed are you among women.'*[3] Thus from the gospel we have heard of the mystery communicated to the Virgin through the angel, and this way we are reminded of it. Now when we see the same thing on an icon we perceive the event with greater emphasis.

---

healing many kinds of diseases.' This same account, drawn obviously from Eusebius, is given by Antipater of Bostra in his *Oration on the woman in haemorrhage*, a small portion of which was read during the fourth session of the Seventh Ecumenical Council (Mansi, 13:13E). The same tradition is also known to Pope Gregory II, *Letter to Germanus of Constantinople* (Mansi, 13:93D), and to Germanus, *Letter to Thomas of Claudiopolis* (Mansi, 13:125D-E).

3 Cf Luke 1:26-28.

However, they have deviated to another way of ignorance, saying:

GREGORY THE BISHOP read:[4]
... nor is there any prayer of consecration for it to transpose it from the state of being common to the state of being sacred. Instead, it remains 269D
common and worthless, as the painter made it.

EPIPHANIUS THE DEACON read:
Let them listen to the truth of the matter: many of the sacred things which we have at our disposal do not need a prayer of sanctification, since their name itself says that they are all-sacred and full of grace. Consequently, we honour and embrace them as venerable things. Thus, even without a prayer of sanctification, we revere the form of the life-giving cross. The very form of it is sufficient for us to receive sanctification. By the veneration 269E
which we offer to it, by the making of its sign on our forehead, and also by the making of its sign on the air with the finger, like a seal, we express the hope that it dispels demons. In the same way, when we signify an icon with a name, we transfer the honour to the prototype; and by embracing it and offering to it the veneration of honour, we share in the sanctification. Also we kiss and embrace the different holy utensils which we have, and we express the hope of receiving a blessing from them. Therefore, either they [the iconoclasts] must say idly that the cross and the holy utensils are common and worthless – since 272A
it is a carpenter, or a painter, or a weaver who has made them, and because there is no prayer of consecration for them – or they will have to accept also the venerable icons as sacred, holy, and worthy of honour.
However, in their desire to sow more seeds of weeds, they – as from a spirit of divination – say even further:

GREGORY THE BISHOP read:
And should any of those who have been caught in this error admit that, 272B
although what we have said against the so-called icon of Christ has been said rightly and with piety, because the two natures are undivided and unconfused and brought together into one hypostasis, yet they wonder

4 Repetition of the above, 268C.

on what basis we forbid the making of the icons of the all-pure, all-glorified One, Who is indeed Theotokos, or of the prophets, apostles, and martyrs, who are mere men – not of two natures, divine and human, in one hypostasis, as in the case of Christ, Who is One –

EPIPHANIUS THE DEACON read:

No one who has been nourished within the catholic Church would   272c
ever think or say that these have made a right and pious judgment
on this novelty. All bishops and priests of the East and of the
West, of the North and of the South, have committed those who
maintained this opinion to anathema. They have led astray only
a small portion of these communities here, and they have cut
them off from the wholesome body of the Church, either because
they did not know, or because they disregarded, the voice of
the Lord, which says: *Whoever causes one of these little ones to stumble,
it would be better for him to have a great millstone fastened round his
neck and be thrown into the sea.*[5]

Since, by raging against his icon they did not show any shame   272d
for Him, they have no regard for his saints either. They have
moved their tongues even against them, saying this:

GREGORY THE BISHOP read:

*... yet they wonder on what basis [we forbid the making of the icons]
of the all-pure, all-glorified One, Who is indeed Theotokos, or of the prophets,
apostles, and martyrs, who are mere men – not of two natures, divine
and human*[6] *– we must say to them, too, that since the former*[7] *has
been abolished, there is no need for the latter either.*

EPIPHANIUS THE DEACON read:

To begin with, they have produced no refutation on the basis   272e
of the gospel, or of the Apostles, or of the Scriptures, or of the
Fathers, or on the basis of proofs, or even, simply speaking, on
the basis of piety; rather, speaking from their own belly,[8] they
set themselves against the catholic Church of God. Nor do they
have any word of truth or of piety to pose against the present

5 Cf Matt. 18:6.
6 Repetition of the above, 272B.
7 That is, the icon of Christ.
8 Cf above, 240E, n 45.

icons of our immaculate Lady Theotokos, or of the saints, as 273A
we have proved with the words which God has provided us.
For, as we have just said, drawing upon the holy Fathers, the
honour of the icon is conveyed to the prototype. When one looks
at the icon of a king, he sees the king in it. Thus, he who bows
to the icon bows to the king in it, for it is his form and his
characteristics that are on the icon. And as he who reviles the
icon of a king is justifiably subject to punishment for having
actually dishonoured the king – even though the icon is nothing
but wood and paints mixed and blended together with wax –
so does he who dishonours the figure of any of these [saints]
transfer the insult to him whose figure is [on the icon]. Even
the very nature of things teaches that when an icon is dishon- 273B
oured, it is certainly the prototype that is dishonoured. Everybody knows that, as everybody also knows that they have
revolted against the Fathers, they oppose the tradition of the
catholic Church, and they do not subscribe to what is natural.[9]

With a tongue again full of falsehood they think that they
strike the truth, saying:

GREGORY THE BISHOP read:
Nevertheless, we shall say what must be said in refutation of them, too: 273C
Because the catholic Church of us Christians stands in the middle
between Judaism and paganism,[10] she shares the usual ritual of neither.
Instead, she walks the new path of piety and of worship handed down
by God, without acknowledging the bloody sacrifices and holocausts of
Judaism; despising also the sacrifices as much as the entire practice of
making and worshipping idols – of which abominable art paganism is
the leader and inventor. For, having no faith in the resurrection, it [pagan-
ism] invented a plaything worthy of itself in order to present, by means
of mockery, something that does not exist. 273D

If, therefore, there is nothing foreign in her, this also – an invention
of men who have demons in them – must be diverted from the Church
of Christ.

EPIPHANIUS THE DEACON read:
Shocking and altogether ridiculous is their writing, of immeas-
urable vulgarity and rife with futilities. While earlier they brought

---

9 Literally, they do not follow the nature of things.
10 Literally, Hellenism.

themselves down to cliffs and ravines, now, by declaring that
the Church of the Christians stands in the middle between
Hellenism and Judaism, they have led themselves down into the   273E
trap of Hades. Then, returning to themselves, they say that the
Church shares the usual ritual of neither. Therefore, either they
were lying in the first instance, or they do not speak the truth
now. In fact, they are lying to themselves, because falsehood
stands not only against truth but also against itself, as David
the divine psalmist said. *Injustice*, he says, *has lied within herself.*[11]

Thus Basil, the one presiding over the Caesareans, whose *voice
is gone out into all the earth,*[12] in the very foreword of his discourse
against Sabellius, says this: 'Judaism combats Hellenism, but both   276A
combat Christianity.'[13] These, however, thinking that they are
wiser than the Fathers, decree that the faith of the Christians
stands in the middle between the two extremes, that is, Judaism
which introduced an absence[14] of divinity, and Hellenism which
introduced polytheism. Gregory, surnamed the Theologian, in
renouncing both of them, says the following:

When I say 'God' I mean Father, Son, and holy Spirit. That is, that
the Godhead does neither overflow beyond these so that we may not
introduce a crowd of gods, nor is defined within their framework so
that we may not be condemned for impoverishing the Godhead. This
way we think neither like the Jews, on account of monarchianism, nor
like the pagans, on account of proliferation. For evil is the same in both
of them, even though it is found in two things which are opposite.[15]

What is included in the Old Testament, of which the Israelites   276B
were part, has been God's tradition, while the practices of the
Greeks were those of demons. Thus, at this point also they have
reckoned among the commandments given by God demonic ones,
which they mixed together; in the same way as they have declared
the icon of the Lord to be an idol equivalent to images of the
demons. Therefore, they shall have to accuse Abel, Noah, and

---

11 Ps. 26(27):12.
12 Ps. 18(19):4.
13 Basil of Caesarea, *Against the Sabellians*, PG, 31:600B.
14 *penia*: literally, poverty, or lack.
15 Gregory of Nazianzus, *On Theophany, that is the Nativity of the Saviour*, Oration 38, PG
36:320B.

Abraham, on account of having brought forward sacrifices of animals; as well as Moses, Samuel, David, and the rest of the Patriarchs, because they, too, offered sacrifices to God which were alien and pagan – in spite of the fact that the Scripture testifies, as to their sacrifice, that *the Lord smelled a smell of sweetness.*[16] Would 276C they had known the truth, that what is dedicated to God is acceptable to Him, because it is written that *they sacrificed to God, the Lord.*[17] However, what is dedicated to demons is abominable and detested, for *they sacrificed to the devils and not to God,*[18] says the Scripture. What is evil, therefore, as well as its opposite, comes from us and through us, not from the matter that is used. For *what is an idol,* asks the Apostle, or *what is the food offered to idols, but that which the Gentiles sacrifice to demons and not to God?*[19]

However, being in great error and fabricating insults and falsities, they think and add the following:

GREGORY THE BISHOP read: 276D
Let, therefore, every mouth that speaks iniquities and blasphemies against our opinion and our vote, which have been approved by God, be silent. For the saints who have pleased God and been honoured by Him with the dignity of sainthood live with God forever, even though they have departed from here. Thus, he who thinks to reinstate them on the poles,[20] *by means of a dead and accursed art which has never been alive but rather has been invented in vanity by the adversary pagans, proves himself blasphemous.*

16 Cf Gen. 8:21.
17 2 Chron. 7:4.
18 Deut. 32:17.
19 1 Cor. 10:19–20. The rendering of this passage in the RSV is inaccurate and confusing.
20 What we translate here as 'to reinstate on the poles' is the verb *anasteloūn*. The icons were originally fixed on the poles of a low screen which divided the nave from the altar. The space in between the icons was taken by screens or curtains (*vēla*), which at different instances – especially during the consecration of the eucharistic elements – were drawn closed. From this pattern the modern-day *iconostāsion* has developed, which is a more rigid divider between these two parts of a church. The icons now occupy the spaces between the poles which were earlier closed by the *vēla*. There is a signigicant concern today regarding the validity of this development of the icon-stand, particularly in relation to the liturgical life of the Orthodox Church and its renewal. Arguments in favour of abolishing the *iconostāsion* and returning to the early Christian architectural designs are matched by an able defence of its integral liturgical role and its theological meaning. Cf Labrecque-Pervouchine, *L'Iconostase.* Cf also below, 340D, n 33.

EPIPHANIUS THE DEACON read:

On the basis of what they have just said, they prove themselves to be foreign and alien to the peace of God, which our Lord bestowed upon those who believed in Him genuinely and sincerely, saying: *My peace I give you; my peace I leave with you.*[21]

How can there be peace if the catholic Church, strengthened and assured by her traditions, revolts against their opinion and vote? Those who are motivated by a divine zeal always agree with the Fathers and with the Church institutions which have been handed down, and they avoid as enemies those who oppose them. It is those, therefore, who cut themselves off from the wholesome body of the Church, that the true worshippers – those, that is, who worship God *in spirit and in truth,*[22] and who have iconographic representations only as a means of explanation and remembrance and who embrace and kiss them – dressed with the breastplate of truth against their opinion and vote which is unacceptable to God, cease not stinging with the probe of the Spirit.

Those holy men of all times who pleased God, whose biographies have remained in writing for our benefit and for the purpose of our salvation, have also left to the catholic Church their deeds explained in paintings, so that our mind may remember them, and so that we may be lifted up to the level of their conduct. Thus St Basil, in his *Encomium to the Holy Forty Martyrs*, says this:

Let us, therefore, by being reminded of them, bring them here to the middle and make the benefit which derives from them common to those present, showing to everyone, like a painting, the excellence of these men. Many times writers and painters mark out feats of arms, some by embellishing them with speech and others by painting them on panels; and it has happened that both have aroused the bravery of many men. For that which speech presents through hearing by giving an account, painting does show, although silently, by the art of representation.[23]

276E

277A

277B

277C

---

21 Cf John 14:27.
22 Cf John 4:24.
23 Basil of Caesarea, *To the Holy Forty Martyrs*, Homily 19, PG 31:508C–509A.

However having mixed their praises with cunning, they say the following:

GREGORY THE BISHOP read:
How do they also dare to depicit through the vulgar art of the pagans the all-praised mother of God, upon whom the fullness of the Godhead cast his shadow[24] *and through whom the inaccessible light did shine* 277D *on us – she who is higher than the heavens and holier than the Cherubim? Or, again, those who will reign with Christ and sit along with Him to judge the world, and who will be as glorious as He*[25] *– of whom, as the Word says, the world was not worthy?*[26] *Are they not ashamed to depict them through a pagan art? For it is not lawful for Christians, who have their hope in the resurrection, to use the customs of nations that worship demons, and to treat so spitefully, by means of worthless and dead matter, the saints who will be resplendent with such glory. We certainly do not accept from the alien ones ways of demonstrating our faith. Thus Jesus rebuked the demons, even when they were confessing* 277E *Him as God, because He deemed it unworthy to be witnessed to by demons.*[27]

EPIPHANIUS THE DEACON read:
They start with an encomium in their desire to seduce towards their own vain thinking those who are of the simplest mind. Those, however, who have the craftiness – although not the cunning – of the serpent[28] and the purity of the dove know how to honour the most immaculate and irreproachable one, she who 280A is truly and properly Theotokos, and the saints, with words and praises, as well as how to recollect their virtues through books which tell their stories. On the other hand, however, [they also know how] to express their feats and braveries through iconographic paintings, as well as how to exalt them with the highest of honours. They also know that, according to the divine Apostle, *they set themselves free* [from the body] *and they are with Christ,*[29] and they intercede on our behalf; as they also know how to

24 Cf Luke 1:35.
25 Cf Phil. 3:21.
26 Heb. 11:38.
27 CF Mark 1:24.
28 Cf Gen. 3:2.
29 Cf Phil. 1:23. The RSV rendering of the verb *analÿsai* as 'to depart' is inexpressive of the meaning of the Apostle, both etymologically and contextually.

offer the sincere and pure faith and worship to God alone – and not to any of the creatures whatsoever that are under the sky – *in spirit and in truth*.

Also, why is it, that, taking matter as evil, they want to reproach   280B
the truth? They ought rather to have disregarded what is utterly evil and have chosen what is utterly good, and to have reminded themselves of those holy sacrifices which are praised by the Scripture. The same [sacrifices] which were offered to God at one time were offered to demons at another – in which case they were totally defiled, even though the same matter was used. Looking only at what is underneath, they accuse the Church of using symbols which are after pagan[30] models. The usefulness of matter should not be overlooked, just because it happens that matter is used in many utterly objectionable ways, thus becoming reproachable, or shown to be evil. If matter was to be thought of and taken this way, it follows – according to them – that every-   280C
thing that is dedicated to God is so [reproachable and evil], as well; we mean holy covers and utensils.

Thus the followers of paganism made idols from gold and silver and used to offer libations of wine, just as those of the Jews, who relaxed [their faith], became idolaters, and offered flour to the celestial host. What is left, therefore, is for them to charge that, because the pagans[31] praise their deities and demons through books containing their stories, the catholic Church should not praise the God of all and his saints through books, as the pagans do, because this way we accept outside suggestions. What per-   280D
version and madness! As men with senses, we make use of the means of perception to identify things, as well as to remember everything holy and pious that has been handed down to us.

Afterwards, as counterfeiters of the truth who distort the ways and the meanings of the Lord, they say:

GREGORY THE BISHOP read:
*In addition, therefore, to this diligent and carefully thought out teaching of ours, we shall provide also the testimonies which are from the Scripture inspired by God and from our eminent Fathers, which are in accord with   280E
us and confirm this pious purpose of ours; testimonies which he who*

30 Literally, Greek.
31 Literally, Greeks.

knows cannot contradict, but he who does not should learn and keep,
as being from God.

First of all [the testimonies] from the very word of the Lord, which
says: God is spirit, and those who worship him must worship
him in spirit and truth;[32] *and again,* No one has ever seen God;[33]
and His voice you have never heard, his form you have never
seen;[34] *which also blesses* those who have not seen Him and yet
have believed.[35]

EPIPHANIUS THE DEACON read: 281A
No one should be surprised at men who, when they attempt
to distort true doctrines according to what they think, make use
of words from the Scriptures. All the heresiarchs collect excuses
for their error from the Scripture inspired by God, forfeiting what
has been rightly said through the holy Spirit with their own   281B
vile thinking. This is what Peter, the supreme trumpet among
the Apostles, proclaimed, forewarning: ... *which the ignorant and*
unstable twist according to their own desires.[36] It is characteristic of
those who indulge in heresy to twist the knowledge of divine
and true doctrines according to their own desires. Thus, while
the holy Fathers in general understood the phrase *The Lord made*
me the beginning of his ways for his works[37] to refer to the dispensation of Christ in the flesh, Arius, Eunomius, and their followers
took it to refer to a divine birth above, and, as a consequence
of this, they were diverted from knowledge. Apollinaris also
misunderstood the word of the gospel, *No one has ascended into*
heaven but he who descended from heaven, the Son of man,[38] and he   281C
deviated to absurdity, saying that God the Word descended with
the flesh which He had when He was in heaven, a flesh which
was pre-eternal and joined essentially with Him. He was also
deceiving himself with his own thinking, proposing the phrase
of the Apostle which says: *the second man, the Lord, is from heaven.*[39]

32 John 4:24.
33 John 1:18.
34 John 5:37.
35 Cf John 20:29.
36 Cf 2 Peter 3:16.
37 Prov. 8:22.
38 John 3:13.
39 Cf 1 Cor. 15:47.

It is not surprising, therefore, that the heretics of this empty foolishness pronounce statements which are taken from the holy Scripture. For they adopted the excuse of their own teachers. They reversed the statements that referred to the invisible and incomprehensible divinity, as if they were the incarnate dispensation of our Lord Jesus Christ, one of the holy Trinity. For who among those of right thinking does not know that the phrase 281D *No one has ever seen God* was written in reference to the divine nature? Also [who does not know] that to understand the phrase *you have neither heard His voice, nor have you seen His form,*[40] as if it were referring to humanity, is like subverting the entire gospel? Where, then, shall we place the sayings, *The Lord said to his disciples,* and *The Lord said to the Jews who came to him,*[41] and *The Lord said: Woe to you, Scribes and Pharisees?*[42] Or, again, how shall we understand the phrase *And he opened his mouth and taught them?*[43] Obviously, these sayings refer to humanity, while the former, *You have neither heard His voice, nor have you seen His form,* refers to the divine essence. For, as we said earlier, in as much 281E as God the Word became a perfect man, we heard his voice and we saw his form, even after the resurrection – for He was touched, and it was while the disciples were looking at Him that He was telling them about the Kingdom.[44]

Afterwards they equated also divine worship and adoration, which Christians preserve in themselves with a true and sincere faith, to the relative veneration of honour.[45] These are the two matters which they have distorted, for which they are called, and truly are, 'accusers of the Christians.' For they say that Chris- 284A

---

40 Cf John 3:13.
41 Cf Matt. 24:2; John 8:31. These phrases are not direct quotations from the New Testament but rather standardized liturgical sentences which are used to introduce the appropriate Bible readings during the Orthodox service.
42 Cf Matt. 23:13.
43 Matt. 5:2.
44 Cf Acts 1:3.
45 There is a crucial and essential distinction made here by the defenders of the icons between the 'divine adoration and worship' (*theia latreia*), which is due to God alone, and the 'relative veneration of honour' (*timetike proskynesis*), which is proper to everything sacred and dedicated to God. Because the iconoclasts made no such distinction, they considered and called their opponents 'iconolaters' (worshippers of icons), which is the exact opposite of what the defenders of the icons maintained. Cf also below, 309C-E.

tians offer the adoration and worship which is due to God to the venerable icons, and that they describe the incomprehensible nature. What derangement and stupidity, and everything else that results from these two! There is no place for their word. It is, instead, full of insult and slander. Christians have not attributed the adoration *which is in spirit and truth* to the icons or the divine form of the cross, nor have they ever made an icon of the invisible and incomprehensible nature. Rather, in as much as *the Word became flesh and dwelt among us*,[46] they have represented and iconographed what is pertinent to his dispensation as a human. Also, because they know that *God is spirit* 284B *and those who worship him must worship in spirit and in truth*,[47] they have offered, according to their faith, the adoration and the worship to Him alone, Who is God of all and Who is praised in the Trinity. We kiss and offer the veneration of honour to the divine form of the cross and to the venerable icons, because we are moved by a desire and affection to reach the prototypes.

Therefore, their shallow words are proven by the truth to be vain, totally empty, and entirely rotten, as is the rest of what they say, which they understood with a mind alien to piety:

GREGORY THE BISHOP read: 284C
In the Old [Testament] also, where He says to Moses: Thou shalt not make to thyself an idol,[48] nor likeness of any thing, whatever things are in the heaven above, and whatever are in the earth beneath; *for* in the mountain you heard the sound of words coming from the midst of fire, but you saw no likeness, except the voice.[49]

EPIPHANIUS THE DEACON read:
It is from this that they grab the excuse of impiety to frighten 284D Christians – as if there were children – with their sophistry: 'If you are recalling Christ or his saints through the means of iconographic representations, you are slipping into idolatry.' Added to every imaginable injustice in what they have already

---

46 John 1:14.
47 John 4:24.
48 Deut. 5:8. The text of the Septuagint uses the word 'idol' (*eidolon*), which the Bagster translation has rendered as 'image.' Cf also above, 213E, n 29.
49 Cf Deut. 4:12.

said – the noble ones! – they now resort to the edict! *Thou shalt make no likeness.* They exercise themselves in impiety, *supressing the truth by their own wickedness,*[50] *seeking to establish their own righteousness.*[51] They also alienate themselves from the truth by taking pride in the nonentity of falsehood. For, by reversing the   284E commandments which were given in olden times to the Israelites, who worshipped the calf and who had experienced the Egyptian abominations, and by applying these [commandments] to the divine community of Christians, they speak of marvels to themselves, acting like actors, and *they are caught by the lips of their own mouth.*[52] They ought to have realized that it was because God was about to lead the Israelites into the promised land – where lived nations which worshipped idols and venerated demons, the sun, the moon, the stars, and other creatures, even birds, quadrupeds, and reptiles, and not the living and true God – that He gave them the law: *Thou shalt not make to thyself an*   285A *idol, nor likeness of anything, whatever things are in the heaven above and whatever are in the earth beneath* – diverting them from idolatry, as is clear: *Thou shalt not bow down to them, nor shalt thou worship them.*[53] However, when his faithful servant Moses was making the Tabernacle of the Testimony under the commandment of God, he, in order to show that everything is to the service of God, made perceptible Cherubim in the form of men – antitypes of the spiritual ones. These Cherubim were to overshadow the seat of expiation,[54] a seat which was an antecedent type of Christ; for, as the divine Apostle says, *He is the expiation for our sins.*[55] Therefore, he introduced them to the knowledge of God through two actions: by saying *Thou shalt bow down to God and Him only*   285B *shalt thou worship,*[56] and by having made Cherubim of molten gold which were overshadowing the seat of expiation, that is, bowing to Him. He led them up *to bow down to God the Lord and Him only to worship* by both sight and hearing!

50 Rom. 1:18.
51 Rom. 10:3.
52 Prov. 6:2.
53 Deut. 5:8–9. The Bagster edition has erroneously rendered the word *ei̅dolon* (idol) as 'image,' and the verb *proskȳneseis* (you shall worship) as 'you shall serve.' Cf also above, 284C, n 48.
54 Cf Exod. 25:17–21.
55 1 John 2:2.
56 Cf Deut. 6:13.

However, because their thinking is full of distortion, they bring forth the following statement of the Apostle:

GREGORY THE BISHOP read:
And, they exchanged the glory of God, who is incorruptible, with the likeness of an image of man who is corruptible ... and they paid respect to and worshipped the creature rather than the Creator;[57] *and again,* Even though we once knew Christ according to the flesh, yet we no longer know him this way,[58] for we walk by faith, not by sight;[59] *and from the same Apostle who said:* So faith comes from what is heard, and what is heard comes by the word of God.[60]

285C

EPIPHANIUS THE DEACON read:
One must expressly say that they are the ones who, like the gentiles, exchanged the glory of God and worshipped the creature rather than the Creator, because they have exchanged and dis- torted what the Apostle meant, according to their own desires. For it is quite clear to everyone that, when the Apostle says *they exchanged the glory of God who is incorruptible with the likeness of an image of a man who is corruptible,* he is, obviously, ridiculing the pagans; for he continues: *or of birds, quadrupeds, or reptiles.*[61] Even though they cut off a whole phrase deceitfully in order to lure the simpler ones [to believe] that the Apostle addresses himself to the issue of the iconographic representations of the Church, what follows makes the clarification manifest. For he also makes reference to birds, quadrupeds, and reptiles, as well as to the fact that *they worshipped the creature rather than the Creator.*[62] Thus, those who are most experienced in historical books know that in olden times the Egyptians used to honour bulls and other mammals, various kinds of birds, insects, wasps, and even less worthy creatures.

285D

285E

57 Rom. 1:23, 25. The English translation of the RSV is too distorted and interpretive at this point to be produced verbatim.
58 2 Cor. 5:16. The RSV rendering of the passage is incorrect. The use of the verb 'we regard' for the definite *ginōskomen,* as well as of the expression 'from a human point of view' for the existential category *katā sārka,* allows a docetic reading of the passage.
59 2 Cor. 5:7.
60 Cf Rom. 10:17.
61 Cf Rom. 1:23.
62 Rom. 1:25.

The Persians also worshipped the sun and fire, while the Greeks, in addition to these, worshipped the entire creation. So did even some of the Jews, as the book of Kings and the narratives of the Prophets describe.

Let them, therefore, say how and when the nations *became futile and their senseless mind was darkened*,[63] before or after they believed in Christ? Certainly before; this is quite clear. For, if they say that 'the nations worshipped the creation and the idols after they believed in Christ,' that is, after the dispensation of Christ our God, it means that according to them the foretelling of the prophets about the Church – *Jerusalem shall be holy, and strangers shall not pass through her anymore*,[64] and, *my mercy I will not utterly remove from him ... neither will I by any means profane my covenant; and I will not make void the things that proceed out of my mouth*[65] – is false. But if the nations, because they worshipped the devil, exiled themselves from the knowledge of God and *gave themselves up to a base mind*[66] before the coming of Christ, the accusation which they make now against the Christians is futile. Isaiah will speak outspokenly against them, crying: *Woe to them that write wickedness; for when they write they do write wickedness.*[67]

They take, therefore, the words of the Apostle and of the Scripture wickedly and maliciously, and they hasten to subvert the great mystery of salvation – that of the dispensation of Christ our God, through which we were freed from the error of the idols – and to ascribe the glory to themselves. However, none of the Christians takes heed of them. For all of us confess that Christ, our true God, by his advent in flesh, separated us from the error of idols and from every pagan[68] religion. If they do not confess that this has happened, they do not bear his name either [i.e., 'Christians']. It is to them that the Apostle says: *What have you that you did not receive?*[69] However, if they did receive it, they ought to confess this redemption and accept icons, which have become a comeliness in the churches for our sight and

288A

288B

288C

---

63 Cf Rom. 1:21.
64 Joel 3:17.
65 Ps. 88(89):33–34.
66 Cf Rom. 1:28.
67 Is. 10:1.
68 Literally, Greek.
69 1 Cor. 4:7.

have undertaken to bring to our mind the gospel narrative, for the purpose – as we have said many times – of reminding us of the gospel and explaining its story.

However, since they propose other sayings of the Apostle, such as *Even though we once knew Christ according to the flesh, yet* 288D *we no longer know him this way,* for *we walk by faith, not by sight,* let us bring into our midst the eloquent teachers who have interpreted these sayings. Thus John, gifted with teaching more valuable than gold or a precious stone, interprets this same passage of the Apostle – *From now on, therefore, we know no one according to the flesh, and even though we once knew Christ according to the flesh, yet we no longer know him this way*[70] – by saying the following:

We know no one of the faithful according to the flesh. What? Even if they are in flesh? That life, the carnal one, has perished and we are born in spirit from heaven, and we know another way of life, another behaviour, another life and situation which exists in heaven.

And again by the same [Father]:

He shows Christ to be the Leader; that is why he went on: *Even though* 288E *we once knew Christ according to the flesh, yet we no longer know him this way.* What is this, then? Tell me. Did He put away the flesh and is He without a body now? Far from it. He has flesh even now. For *this Jesus who was taken up from us into heaven will come in the same way.*[71] 'In the same way.' Which way? In flesh, along with the body. How, then, does he say *Even though we once knew Christ according to the flesh, yet we no longer know him this way?* He says so, because even though we knew Christ as being subject to suffering, we no longer know him this way. Thus for us the expression 'according to the flesh' means the state of sin; and the expression 'not according to the flesh' means the state without sin. With regard to Christ, however, the expression 'according 289A to the flesh' means the state of the passions of [human] nature, that is of thirst, hunger, fatigue, sleep; for *He committed no sin, nor was any craft found in his mouth.*[72] That is why He said: *Which of you convicts me*

70 2 Cor. 5:16.
71 Acts 1:11.
72 Is. 53:9. The Bagster edition has rendered this passage as follows: 'He practised no iniquity, nor craft with his mouth.'

of sin?[73] And again: *The ruler of this world is coming; but he has no power over me.*[74] On the other hand, the expression 'being not according to the flesh' means that from then on He is free of these passions; not that He is without it. For He is coming to judge the world in an incorruptible flesh which is not subject to suffering. This is the state towards which we, also, are heading – *our body becoming like the body of his glory.*[75]

Also Cyril of Alexandria, the arch-defender of our pure faith, in   289B
clarifying for us the same saying, interprets it this way:

Because the only-begotten Word of God became man and a second root appeared of the race, which is not the same as the first one from Adam, but one which is and is to be understood as incomparably superior even among the best ones, our elements have changed towards life. For we are not under death, but under the Word who gives life to everything. No one is 'in flesh,' that is, under the limitation of the flesh, which is corruption. Paul does not say that Christ did not have flesh. For although he says *we have known no one according to the flesh,*[76] he   289C
does not mean that. Otherwise, how did He die? Death is a limitation of the flesh. What he says, therefore, is this: The Word became flesh and He died for everyone; this way we have known Him according to the flesh. Nevertheless, we no longer know Him this way, for He is not in flesh now. He was risen after three days and He ascended into heaven. Yet He is understood to be beyond the flesh, for He no longer is subject either to death or to any other limitation of the flesh but, as God, He is beyond all these.[77]

See, therefore, you who are opponents; you not only distort the words of the Apostle, but you oppose also all the saints. For they, on the basis of the words of the Apostle, show that Christ after the resurrection was free of suffering. They also urge   289D
us that, since *we have become like the body of his glory,* we should not walk 'according to the flesh,' that is, we should not follow

73 John 8:46.
74 John 14:30.
75 Cf. Phil. 3:21. John Chrysostom, *Homily in II Corinthians*, Homily, 11, PG 61:475.
76 Cf 2 Cor. 5:16.
77 Cyril of Alexandria, unidentified reference.

carnal desires. However, having thought otherwise than the Fathers, and not bearing to follow in their footsteps, you introduce a new faith. Also, walking on a pathless road and guiding yourselves and those who follow you to cliffs and ravines, you lead them down to the trap of Hades. However, no one believes in you, for you are not following the teaching of our holy Fathers.

As for [the phrase] *we walk by faith, not by sight*, the same John in interpreting this says:

So that you may not say: 'What is this? Since you say that *while we are at home in the body we are away from the Lord*?[78] Why do you say this? Are we separated, therefore, from Him while we are here?' So that no one would say this, he [the Apostle] explained this further, saying: *for we walk by faith, not by sight*. We know Him while we are here, but not clearly. This is what he says in another place: *Now we see in a mirror dimly, but then face to face.*[79]   289E

This is what both divine Fathers have said. The Apostle himself in other statements of his makes the meaning clear to us, saying: *Who hopes for what he sees? But if we hope for what we do not see, we wait for it with patience.*[80] It is obvious, therefore, that *we walk   292A by faith, not by sight*, for we do not see God here, but we believe in Him. By faith also we proclaim that his creatures were made by Him, as the same Apostle proclaims with the loud voice of the Spirit, saying: *By faith we understand that the world was created by the Word of God, so that what is seen was made out of things which do not appear.*[81] Also, when we consider the orderly movement of the universe, we come to an understanding of God, Who created everything with wisdom. This is what the phrase *we walk by faith, not by sight* means; not what those who out of ignorance twist the meaning of the Apostle, taking the saying to refer to the   292B making of venerable icons.

Thus, having heard the teaching of the Fathers, let us follow it, and let us detest this present novelty, saying: *I have hated the assembly of wicked doers; and I will not sit with ungodly men.*[82]

78 2 Cor. 5:6.
79 1 Cor. 13:12. John Chrysostom, *Homily in II Corinthians*, Homily 10, PG 61:469.
80 Rom. 8:24.
81 Heb. 11:3.
82 Ps. 25(26):5.

FIFTH VOLUME

EPIPHANIUS THE DEACON read:

Because their feet run towards wickedness, they have been en-   292C
tangled in their own snares. It has already been shown that none
of those who have been nourished within the Church has
exchanged the glory of God for the making of icons, or for any
other creature whatsoever. Let us, therefore, proceed now with
the refutation of the rest, having with us as an ally the truth
which is never defeated. For, in their effort to make evil abundant
with additional arguments, they have also brought into their
midst the holy Fathers, maintaining insultingly that they speak
against the reproduction of venerable icons, adding the following:

GREGORY THE BISHOP read: 292D

Analogous also is what our God-revealing Fathers, the disciples and
successors of the Apostles, teach outright. Thus, Epiphanius of Cyprus,
renowned among those who hold the banner,[1] says:

1 On Epiphanius see Quasten, *Patrology*, III, 384–396, and in the introduction. Epiphanius
(315–403), bishop of Constantia – the ancient city of Salamis near the present-day
Famagusta – is one of the most significant and prolific church writers of his times,
and, reportedly, the first opponent of the icons; this is, at least, what has been widely
accepted. This thesis is based upon the celebrated incident according to which
Epiphanius, upon seeing an icon of Christ (or of a saint? – he was not sure even
himself) embroidered on the door-curtain of a church, violently tore it down. The
incident is, reportedly, confessed by Epiphanius himself in a letter to John, bishop of
Jerusalem, which, however, exists only in a Latin translation (PG 43:379–392) made by
Jerome. This version was criticized very early as a falsification of the original,
although Jerome defended the reliability of the sense rather than the wording of the
letter (letter 57 in Jerome's collection). The debate over the authenticity of this
incident and its source of information has produced a considerable amount of
literature. What has also been debated is the authenticity and the value of three other
treatises against the icons, which are a reconstruction of fragments attributed to
Epiphanius' pen. The minutes of the present councils (Constantinople in 754, and
Nicea in 787) constitute one of the main sources for this material, which the reader
will now have the opportunity to analyse and evaluate for himself. At the time of
Epiphanius icons were used especially by groups which adhered to and were
interested in exemplifying and promoting the teachings of Arius and Nestorius,
which Epiphanius mercilessly combatted as heresies. One wonders, therefore,
whether Epiphanius combatted the icons as such (especially with their theological
content of the eighth century) or rather, through them, those who had particular
motives in making and using them.
Here, for example, is what he writes about the semi-Arians of Acacius of Caesarea –

Take heed to yourselves, and keep the traditions, which you have received. Do not incline either to right or left.

To which he adds:

And remember this, dear children. Do not bring icons into the churches, or into the cemeteries[2] of the saints. Instead, always remember God in your hearts. Neither into a public place. For the Christian must not be lifted up through the eyes or through the reverie of the mind. 292E

He wrote other discourses as well, to refute the making of icons, which those who search diligently will be able to find.

EPIPHANIUS THE DEACON read:
Those who are diligent in examining matters of the Church know that those of contrary opinion, *who seek to establish their own righteousness*[3] and to oppose that of God, are fortified behind forged

those, that is, who rejected the consubstantiality (*homooūsios*) in favour of the similarity (*homoioūsios*) of the Son to the Father. He reports that in their council in Seleucia they amended the Nicene Creed accordingly: 'We believe in one God, the Father Almighty' and so on. 'And in the Son of God,' plainly, without any emphasis. Afterwards, and in order to demonstrate their action, they said that 'We reject the *homooūsion* as being alien to the divine Scripture, while we anathematize the *anhōmoion* [i.e., the teaching that the Son is not similar to the Father] of the Son to the Father. But this was a lure by deceitful hunters. For, when they came to themselves, they said and taught that, while the Son of God is a creature, He is similar to the Father, in the sense which was current among the people. For the moulders also produce statues and make icons of likeness, either with gold, or silver, or other matter, or with colours on wood. But these are resemblances, having, however, nothing equivalent to that which is depicted. This was, therefore, their deception too: to confess on the one hand that He [the Son] is similar to the Father, and on the other hand that He shares nothing whatsoever in the divinity of the Father.' *Panarion*, PG 42:448B-C
For a summary in English of Epiphanius' major work against the heresies see Sahas, *Epiphanius' Panarion.* Cf also below, 293C–296E.
2 The word 'cemetery' is a transliteration of the Greek word *koimetērion*, which in classical Greek means 'sleeping-room' but which became the Christian term for a graveyard. Under the influence of the Christian understanding of death in light of the resurrection, the graveyard became 'the place of those who have fallen asleep,' and the dead 'those who have fallen asleep' (*kekoimemēnoi*). Cf Matt. 27:52; 1 Cor. 15:6; 1 Thes. 4:13, 15.
3 Cf Rom. 10:3.

and intrusive writings. It is these men whom the authentic sons 293A
of the catholic Church do not accept as brothers, since they are
illegitimate, but rather dismiss with the words: *You offspring of
Canaan and not of Judah*,[4] being aware of what the Evangelist has
said: *They went out from us, but they were not of us; for if they had
been of us, they would have continued with us;*[5] and also what the
divine Apostle says: *That after my departure fierce wolves will come
in among you, not sparing the flock, … to draw away the disciples after
them;*[6] and also, *See to it that no one makes a prey of you by philosophy
and empty deceit.*[7] The same Apostle [sic] also says: *Do not believe* 293B
every spirit.[8]

Every Christian, therefore, when he happens to hear of spurious
books, must spit upon them and not accept them in any way.
Thus, there is a forged 'Letter to the Laodiceans' which is
attributed to the divine Apostle, found in some books containing
writings of the Apostle,[9] which our Fathers renounced as not
his. The Manichaeans also introduced, indirectly, the 'Gospel
according to Thomas,' which the catholic Church, out of piety,
despises as foreign. Such is also the statement, which although
said to be of our holy Father Epiphanius, is not. This divinely
speaking Father wrote a treatise composed of eighty chapters,
in which he combatted triumphantly all the heresies – Hellenistic, 293C
Jewish,as well as all the others which have been contrary to
Christianity – without omitting any of them.[10] If he had considered
the making of icons to be in opposition to Christ, he would have
included this among the heresies. Moreover, if the Church had
accepted these writings against the venerable icons, there would
have been no venerable icons painted to serve both as decorations
of the holy churches and as reminders for us. The writings
themselves, which the instigators of this vain talk offer as

---

4 Susanna (Daniel 13):56.
5 1 John 2:19.
6 Acts 20:29, 30.
7 Col. 2:8.
8 1 John 4:1.
9 The New Testament Canon of the Paulicians (a heresy of the seventh century which
   combined the heresy of the followers of Marcion in the second century and the
   heresy of the Massalians in the fourth century) contained the four gospels and fifteen
   epistles by Paul, one of which was addressed to the Laodiceans.
10 This is the *Panarion*, PG, vols 41, 42. Cf also above, 292D, n 1.

testimonies, provide the refutation: St Epiphanius was active during the years of Theodosius and Arcadius.[11] From that time to this heresy there is a period of almost four hundred years, 293D during which none of the Christians has accepted these writings against icons, except the false advocates of this vain talk. If so many years have not allowed these writings into the Church, they will not be accepted now either, because they were never acceptable. As to the writing which some of them bring forth, and which falsely bears the title 'Epistle of Saint Epiphanius, who presides over the Cypriots, to King Theodosius,' we have taken it in our hands and read it, not in passing but carefully, and we found at the end of the letter an emphatic note containing this: 'Having many times suggested to my cocelebrants[12] that the icons should be removed, I was not welcomed by them; they 293E did not even want to listen to me for a moment.' Let us consider, therefore, who were the ever-memorable teachers and unshaken supports of the Church at the time of our Father Epiphanius, who has been mentioned here: Basil, the Great in works and words; Gregory, who is surnamed after theology; Gregory, presiding over the city of the Nyssaeans and who is called by everybody 'the Father of the Fathers'; as well as John, from whose tongue flows a speech of sweet honey and who, for this reason, has been given the name 'Golden Mouth';[13] and in addition to 296A these Ambrose, Amphilochius, and Cyril of Jerusalem. Therefore, if the author himself who wrote these treatises against the venerable icons says that he was not welcomed by the holy Fathers who were living at that time, how can we, who have reached the end of the ages and who are deficient in words and knowledge – because we are not even worthy to be called disciples of them – accept what has been forged against the Church, which those holy Fathers themselves did not accept? Let this accursed and daring treatise be dismissed. Those who have striven thus against the Church have separated themselves from reason. 296B However, let those of us who love Christ keep the saying of the Apostle, *Let us hold to the traditions which we have received*,[14]

---

11 Emperor Theodosius I the Great (379–395); Arcadius (395–408).
12 The expression implies the bishops presiding over other churches.
13 *Chrysōstomos* (Chrysostom).
14 Cf 2 Thes. 2:15.

declining from profane vain talk, and let us know that these writings are false and fabricated. The books of our holy Father Epiphanius, the so-called *Anchoratus*[15] and the rest of them, have become well known all over the world and have spread to almost every church. As to the petty words – the two or three books – with which these ones buzz against the venerable icons, they are not found anywhere in the world, unless they were written recently. If the catholic Church had known them, they would have been as widely circulated as St Epiphanius' so-called *Anchoratus*, which is spread among all the churches. Being foreign, however, different and forged, they have never been accepted by the catholic Church; they have never even appeared; nor can they be accepted now. In this way the peace of God and ancient tradition may prevail in all the churches. Let not the slanderers resort to their tongues either, accusing those of right faith that those who accept the ancient practice of the catholic Church go contrary to St Epiphanius – not at all. For we reject the writing, while we acknowledge the holy Father as teacher of the catholic Church. Similarly, the holy Fathers who gathered in Chalcedon for the holy Fourth Ecumenical Council – so did the Fathers of the holy Fifth Council – anathematized the so-called 'Letter of Iba, bishop of Edessa, to Mares the Persian,' as being in agreement with Nestorius; not Iba himself. For it was not proven to be true that the letter was Iba's. Consequently, in the anathemas, they did not anathematize Iba himself, but the so-called 'Iba's Letter'; for although it was called so, it was not. Neither are these false writings against the venerable icons. For although some say that they are of St Epiphanius, yet, as has been shown, they are not, nor do they exist anywhere. As a matter of fact his disciples built on the island of Cyprus a church named after the said Father, with many iconographic representations inside, including one of St Epiphanius himself. If he [Epiphanius] had despised the sight of icons, why did his disciples even paint an icon of him? All of you who listen, judge for yourselves and

296C

296D

296E

---

15 Epiphanius' *Anchoratus* ('The Anchor Book'), PG 43:17–236, is a treatise against the Pneumatomachians, with an exposition of the Trinitarian and other doctrines of the Church. The book was written in 374 and was received enthusiastically by the various local churches. The *Panarion* was written later to enhance the results of the *Anchoratus*, by providing an extensive list and refutation of all heresies, past and contemporary ones.

separate the truth from falsehood. These treatises are not of this
Father but of Manichaean influence. May we, then, depart from
them, for they are full of bitter gall. The Manichaeans, and those
who introduced the teaching of confusion [with regard to the
natures of Christ], never accepted the sight of icons, because
they believed that God the Word did not truly become a man
in flesh, but only seemingly so, and in conjecture.

That is why, having hallucinations, and understanding one
thing instead of another, they say also the following:

GREGORY THE BISHOP read: 297A
Similarly, also, Gregory the Theologian in his Epics says:

> *An injury it is to put faith in colours*
> *and not in the heart.*
> *For what is in colours is easily washed away,*
> *while what is in the depths of the mind –*
> *this is, indeed, pleasing to me.*

EPIPHANIUS THE DEACON read:
Having taken it once again in a distorted way, they produce   297B
another saying from Gregory the Theologian. What the Father
has delivered as:

> It is an injury to put faith in colours
> not in the hearts;
> colours, flowing, wash away,[16]
> but the depth is what I love,

these falsifiers put this way:

> An injury it is to put faith in colours
> and not in the heart.
> For what is in colours is easily washed away,
> while what is in the depths of the mind –
> this is, indeed, pleasing to me.

16 Gregory of Nazianzus, *Moral Epics*, No. 31, PG 37:912.

Having violated the traditions of the Church, they plugged their ears, shut their eyes, and had no desire to think rightly.   297C *For they heard, indeed, but they did not understand; and they saw, indeed, but they did not perceive.*[17] Blinded in the heart, they twisted the teachings and the traditions of the Fathers according to their own desires. St Gregory the Theologian, in the sayings from his metric writings, which they have produced, speaking explicitly, makes a moral statement, giving instructions for our life, that we should abstain from what is temporal and worldly, and derives from carnal desires, and we should pursue a spiritual life which leads up to what is heavenly; also that we should not put faith in this world, nor rely upon things which are temporal and do   297D not last – which he called 'colours' – but rather should pursue what is spiritual and truthful, that which the heart confirms and which remains forever. Our life is ebbing, and living here is a sojourn. As colour or ink fades fast away, even if it is retouched by the painter, so does this present life, as the same Father says. Our affairs are run in a cyclic way which at different times and in different ways, in one day or, at times, in one hour, brings changes. Thus everything human disappears like a shadow and   297E man's entire power disintegrates faster than a bubble. For *every man is grass, and all the glory of man as the flower of grass.*[18] However, to have spiritual deeds to show is something that is unshaken, and its reward among the lasting things. Therefore, if the state- ment had been directed against icons, he would have said clearly: 'It is an injury to put faith in colours and not in God.' But he decreed: 'and not in the hearts'; which means that we must labour for those things which are firm, certain, and belong to the Kingdom of heaven; and not for the things of this world which, being transitory and thus deteriorating rapidly, are unreliable.

Again, allegorizing badly and interpreting everything to suit   300A their own thinking, they bring forward as testimonies statements of those great masters of the mysteries,[19] saying:

17 Cf Is. 6:9; Matt. 13:14.
18 Cf Is. 40:6.
19 In Greek *mystipōlos*, literally, he who solemnizes mysteries. It seems to us that the qualification given here to Basil the Great and John Chrysostom does not refer to their sacerdotal function as bishops but rather to their excellence in and mastering of theology. The Christian East understood theology to be a mystery, as it pertains to man's involvement in the mystery *par excellence* of God. The Orthodox Church

GREGORY THE BISHOP read:
John Chrysostom also teaches as follows:

We enjoy the presence of the saints through writings, thus having the icons not of their bodies but of their souls. For, what has been said by them are icons of their souls. The study of writings inspired by God, St Basil said, is a most effective way of discovering what is proper. For in them one can find the deposits of the deeds as well as the biographies of blessed men, handed down like animate icons of the conduct according to God, placed in front for the imitation of the works which are in accordance with the will of God.[20]   300B

EPIPHANIUS THE DEACON read:
In no way has any man of right thinking understood, or will understand, that these statements were made as refutations of the venerable icons. For it is manifest to everyone that, when   300C
we hear of the bravery of the saints and of their endurance, we bless the firmness and the stamina of their souls. Also, when we struggle with the holy Scriptures, or read the lives of holy men, or look at iconographic paintings, we are reminded of the works which are according to the will of God. For as Basil the Great said in the encomium to the Forty Saints: 'That which speech presents through hearing, painting – even though silent – does show through imitation.'[21]

John Chrysostom, also, in his discourse *That the Law-giver of both the Old and New Testament, is one. Also on the vestments of the priest*, which starts with the words: 'Prophets proclaim in advance   300D
the gospel of the Kingdom of Christ,' says later on:

I have also loved the painting on melted wax[22] for reasons of piety. For I saw on an icon an angel pursuing hordes of barbarians and barbarian

removed theology from the realm of scholastic-philosophical enterprises to a whole way of life. The Eastern Church reserved the title 'Theologian' for three men: John, the author of the fourth gospel and the theologian of the Logos, Gregory of Nazianzus, and Symeon 'the New Theologian,' the singer of union with God. Cf also Lossky, *The Mystical Theology*, pp 7–22. Cf also above, 248B, n 3.

20 Cf John Chrysostom, *Epistle to St. Gregory on his solitary life*. On John Chrysostom (ca 344–397) see Quasten, *Patrology*, III, 424–482.

21 For reference cf above, 277C, n 23.

22 The reference here is to the encaustic iconography made on a surface of melting wax upon which the paints are applied and consolidated as the wax hardens.

races being traded. Thus I saw what David said truthfully: *O Lord in thy city thou wilt despise their image.*[23]

It has been shown, therefore, that being outside of the divine congregation, they have distorted what the holy Fathers have rightly stated.

However, they still cleave to wickedness; and, in order to refute   300E
iconographic representations, they present what our holy Father Athanasius said against the idols, saying:

GREGORY THE BISHOP read:
Moreover, Athanasius also, the splendour of Alexandria, said:

How is it possible not to pity those who worship creatures? For they who see, pray to those who cannot see, and they who hear, to those who cannot hear.[24]

For a creature will never be saved by another creature.

EPIPHANIUS THE DEACON read: 301A
Alas, what madness! Having discovered a new way of blaspheming, they have deviated from the truth. For, while the divine Father made this statement against idols, they accuse the Christians, saying that after having known the truth, confessed the faith sincerely, and been regenerated by God, they worship creatures – along with the one God of all. They also charge that   301B
the Christians worship idols. O Lord, spare your people, and do not allow any one to be carried away by their blasphemy. For all of us who are called with your name confess that You have delivered us from the deception and the error of idols. After we came to know You, we, who were deemed worthy of divine regeneration, in no way deviated in offering the divine adoration that belongs to You to any creature under the sky but You, our only Saviour; and we sing: *O Lord, we know not any other beside Thee: we name thy name.*[25] You are witness to this, as well as the

---

23 Ps. 72(73):20. John Chrysostom, *That the law-giver of both, the Old and the New Testament, is one. Also on the vestments of the priest; and on repentance*, PG 56:407.

24 Cf Athanasius of Alexandria, *Against the Heathen*, PG, 25:29A. Only the second part of the quotation gives the actual words of Athanasius. On Athanasius (ca 295–373) see Quasten, *Patrology*, III, 20–79.

25 Is. 26:13.

host of angels, and the divine congregation of the Apostles, proph- 301C
ets, martyrs, and holy Fathers. And in order that all our senses
be reminded, so that we may be lifted up towards your majesty,
we have, as a way of glorifying You, the figure of the holy cross,
the narrative of the gospel, and iconographic representations,
as well as many other consecrated utensils which we kiss, because
they have been made in, and devoted to, your name.

However, *those who have gathered treasures with a lying tongue have
pursued vanity*.[26] That is why all their idle talk has vanished. As
darkness disappears the moment the light shines out, so is the
lie of their tongue cut off by the sword of the Spirit at the ap- 301D
pearance of the truth. Yet, with the remnants of what has already
been mutilated, they continue, saying:

GREGORY THE BISHOP read:
Similarly, Amphilochius of Iconium says the following:

*we should not endeavour to depict on boards with colours the carnal faces of
the saints; we do not need these. What we need, instead, is to imitate their conduct
through virtue.*[27]

EPIPHANIUS THE DEACON read: 301E
A characteristic of heretics is to present statements in a fragmented form. However, even if one searches carefully, he will
nowhere find the intention of the Father to prohibit the reproduction of venerable icons. Rather, the Father says this in praising
the bravery and the firmness of the spiritual disposition of the
saints, and in preferring the toil of virtues. He does so in order
to lead us to imitate their conduct. For we do not praise the
saints, nor do we represent them in painting, because we like 304A
their flesh. Rather, in our desire to imitate their virtues, we retell
their life-stories in books and we depict them in iconographies,
even though they have little need to be praised by us in narratives
or to be depicted in icons. Yet, as we have said, we do this for
our own benefit. For it is not only the sufferings of the saints
that are instructive for our salvation, but also this very writing

26 Cf Prov. 21:6.
27 Amphilochius of Iconium, PG, 39:36–129. On Amphilochius (ca 340–394) see Quasten,
   Patrology, III, 296–300.

of their sufferings, shown also in iconographic representations, as well as their annual memorial. This is the meaning of the entire character of the discourse. What the Father said was not in order to refute the venerable icons; nor did he attempt to 304B undermine them in any way. And although he says that 'we should not endeavour to depict on boards with colours the carnal faces of the saints,' he said this with the aim of [focusing on] their virtue. For he continues: 'What we need, instead, is to imitate their conduct through virtue.' We must endeavour to single out the virtues of virtuous men, to imitate their works and strive after their conduct. However, it is not commendable continuously to build churches to them or to show them forth in icons, while we look down upon their virtues. No one would praise a man if he saw him on the one hand rejecting the virtues of the saints while on the other hand dedicating icons to them day after day, 304C or building many churches, or making holy utensils, without decorating the temple of himself with virtues inspired by God. For God said to those who have this disposition, through Isaiah the prophet: *Though ye bring fine flour, it is vain. Also When ye stretch forth your hands, I will turn away mine eyes from you; and though ye make many supplications, I will not hearken to you. But what should you do? Wash you, be clean; remove your iniquities from your souls before mine eyes; cease from your iniquities; learn to do well; diligently seek judgment, deliver him that is suffering wrong, plead for the orphan, 304D and obtain justice for the widow.*[28]

When we achieve this, then the things which we offer – holy churches, or holy utensils, or even venerable icons – are acceptable to God. Thus, in order to remember the saints, it is fitting for us to single out their virtues and, in so far as possible, to imitate them faithfully. For 'This is what an encomium to martyrs is: that those who are gathered together supplicate to attain virtue,' as Basil the Great said in his ethical discourses.[29] But as it has been said, it is praiseworthy that, along with the virtues, one may build churches, paint icons, and offer holy utensils to God. For the word of truth teaches us that *one ought to do these, without* 304E *neglecting the others.*[30]

---

28 Is. 1:13, 15–17.
29 Basil of Caesarea, *To the holy Forty Martyrs*, Homily 19, PG 31:509A.
30 Cf Matt. 23:23.

One would not be able to attain virtue unless he walked through the courts of the Lord, through reading gave ear to the divine discourses, and through sight led himself to feel the meaning and the message of the gospel, of the narratives of the victories of the martyrs. However, it is dutiful and utterly necessary to do what is virtuous at every time, in every place, every moment and every hour. For it is necessary for us, now and for ever, to live in ourselves the sufferings of Christ, as it is also profitable *to carry His death in our body*,[31] and to do this diligently. This leads to the Kingdom of heaven. However, to   305A inscribe many crosses in a little house while disregarding the commandments of Christ and the imitation of his sufferings makes no sense, because *faith without works is dead*.[32] Thus, the Lord says in the words of the gospel: *Not every one who says to me, 'Lord, Lord,' shall enter the Kingdom of heaven, but he who does the will of my Father who is in heaven*.[33]

Continuing this discussion even further we offer another indication. It is customary for our holy Fathers, who have elucidated for us the redemptive will of God, in teaching us to keep the commandments to exaggerate and to direct the listeners to that commandment which they have set as their target, by   305B declaring this to be a high one, the greatest. So, in holding to this [commandment] steadfastly as a secure anchor, we should not neglect the others. Thus, putting to the side most of them [the Fathers] – for otherwise it [the discourse] would be too lengthy – let us bring into our midst Asterius of Amasea. In an oration which he wrote *On Lazarus and the rich man*, after speaking with an emphasis on feeding the poor and against those who grow richer, he urges the rich to yield fruits of charity, rather than to dress cheerfully and brightly in soft clothes. He interpolates also an admonition to those who live a more pious life to abandon their riches, saying this: 'Do not portray Christ in clothing. With the cost of their expenditure procure rather goods   305C for the poor.' Afterwards, and in his desire to sever the inclination towards riches, he adds: 'For one humiliation – that of assuming

31 Cf 2 Cor. 4:10
32 Cf James 2:17
33 Matt. 7:21.

a body – is sufficient for Him.'[34] In other words, Christ our God does not like the mystery of his dispensation to be shown through a passionate attachment to the world, or through an exhibition of avarice. It is neither pious nor acceptable to Him for us to accumulate material riches and make sinful pretentions, supposedly for the purpose of doing what the gospel says, while, however, we look down upon those who need food and clothing and lack shelter. This is characteristic of avarice, not of piety. Just as light does not coexist with darkness, or righteousness has no share in unlawfulness, so the inclination towards riches and the wearing of soft clothing have nothing in common with the gospel's import and narrative. The latter teaches us emphat- 305D ically the events of the dispensation – something which leads up to salvation. The former are condemned as a cause of punishment, as James the brother of God[35] says: *You rich weep and howl for the miseries that are coming upon you. Your riches have rotted and your garments are moth-eaten. Your gold and silver have rusted and their rust will be evidence against you.*[36] As has been said, therefore, whatever is done out of avarice vanishes with the world. It is 305E possible for us, by spending little, to have food, clothes, and shelter, enough to suffice. For 'Everything that is acquired not for a use but for adornment is a vain glory,' as Basil the divine said.[37] Therefore, let us be content with what we need and from these provide enough for the poor and lend them a helping hand, so that we also may hear the voice of the Lord telling us: *Blessed*

34 Asterius of Amasea, *On Lazarus and the rich man*, PG 40:168B. Asterius, like Amphilochius of Iconium, before he became a bishop (between the years 380 and 390) was a lawyer. He is known for his rhetorical style, which he demonstrates in his sixteen homilies and panegyrics on various martyrs. See Datema, *Asterius of Amasea*. One of these orations, *On the martyrdom of St. Euphemia* – because of its direct reference to Christian art – has been extensively quoted by this Council of Nicea (787) in support of the veneration of icons. On Asterius see Quasten, *Patrology*, III, 300–301.

35 This is a literal translation of the adjective *adelfōtheos*, which usually accompanies the name of James, reported to have been a brother of Jesus (Matt. 13:55). The meaning, however, of the name is 'the brother of Him Who is God.' The component *theo-* in such adjectives as Theotōkos, *adelfōtheos*, *Theomētor*, etc, refers to the divine nature of Christ. Cf also above, 256D, n 27.

36 James 5:1–3.

37 Basil of Caesarea, *Detailed Rules*, PG 31:977C.

are the merciful, for they shall obtain mercy;[38] *and, since you did it*
to one of the least of these my brethren, you did it to me.[39]

Since we have mentioned Asterius, let us prove, by using his
own words, that the tradition of the venerable icons is an early   308A
institution of the catholic Church. Thus he [Asterius], upon seeing
an icon of the passion of Euphemia the martyr, praised it with
the following encomium:

There was a divine woman, an undefiled virgin, who dedicated her
prudence to God. Her name is Euphemia. During a time when a tyrant
was persecuting those who were pious, she preferred most readily the
venture of death. Thus the citizens, as well as those who share with
her in the religion for which she died, having admired the virgin for
being both brave and saintly, placed her coffin in a sepulchre near the
church and they now offer honours to her, and all together hold an   308B
annual celebration. During such celebrations the priests of the mysteries[40]
of God always honour her memory with words, and they diligently
preach to those who come together how she carried through the struggle
of endurance. The painter also, expressing his own piety through art,
has, in so far as he has been able, designed on a canvas the entire
story which he has placed by the sepulchre as a holy spectacle.

This is what is on this piece of art: high on a throne sits a judge
looking at the virgin with a bitter and adverse look. When it wants,
art shows anger even with inanimate material. Surrounding the authorities are many soldiers. Two of them charged with keeping the minutes
are holding writing-tablets and styluses. Each of them, with a hand   308C
raised from the waxen tablet, is looking intently at the accused, with

38 Matt. 5:7.
39 Matt. 25:40.
40 Literally, 'the celebrants of the mysteries,' i.e., the priests. (Cf 1 Cor. 4:1: 'stewards of the
mysteries of God.') The Christian East has always been impressed by and
preoccupied with the reality of God as the ultimate mystery. What in the West were
termed 'sacraments,' the East considered and treated as mysteries, in which human
reason or intelligence does not suffice to explain that inexplicable dispensation in
which the invisible and divine reality joins with the visible and material elements
(water, oil, wine, bread, etc) to procure for a man holiness, continuously and at the
most fundamental junctures of his life. For the East the sacredness of these acts is a
consequence of the dispensation of the presence of the divine reality, which
nevertheless remains for man – the beneficiary – an unfathomable mystery. Cf also
above, 300A, n 19.

his face turned all the way, as if he is demanding that she speak louder, lest by not hearing well he may write wrong things for which he may be held liable. The virgin is standing, wearing a fair gown and an outer garment – which according to the painter signifies philosophy – with a refined appearance, which to me symbolizes the soul decorated with virtues. Two soldiers are escorting her to the ruler, the one pulling her forward and the other following behind her, the disposition of the virgin being a mixture of modesty and firmness. For she is turning her face down towards the ground as if she is blushing at the sight of men. Yet she stands undaunted without losing courage for the battle. 308D

When I saw the drama of the Colchian woman, I praised those painters of the past. When that woman was about to strike with the sword against her children, [the painter made] her face show both mercy and anger. One of the eyes showed anger, while the other disclosed the mother who was merciful and horrified. Now I have transferred admiration for that feeling to this painting. I admire this artist immensely, because he has made a better combination of colours, as he has combined together modesty and bravery – dispositions which are by nature contrary to each other.

As she proceeds towards the imitation,[41] some public executioners, 308E barely dressed in their short shifts, are already beginning with their work. One, seizing and bending her head, turns the face of the virgin so that the other may easily proceed with the punishment. The other one, standing, is pulling out her teeth. It looks as if the instruments of punishment were a hammer and a gimlet.

From this point on, however, I am in tears, and the suffering cuts my speech short. The painter has made the drops of blood so real that you think they are indeed being shed from her lips, and you would like to go away and cry. Then follows the prison. Again the virgin, modest, 309A in her light clothes, is sitting alone stretching both her hands towards

41 The word 'imitation' implies and here stands for the word 'martyrdom.' Martyrdom in the early Church was considered to be the ultimate act by which man manifests his imitation of Christ. 'Christian' is the adjective that signifies not simply the one who believes in Christ but the one who imitates Christ: the one in whose life other men can see the life of Christ re-enacted and perpetuated on earth (cf Ignatius, *Romans*, III, 2). The martyrs and saints were considered to have, through their lives, relived (to the degree of their ability, but faithfully) the life of Christ, in terms of virtue and deeds. Thus the veneration of the saints and martyrs was one aspect of a twofold interest of the Church: on the one hand to maintain the divine life, or the life of holiness, tangible in the life of living men, and on the other hand, through these tangible and human means, to convey her worship to the divine prototype.

the sky and calling God to be an ally in her hardships. While she is praying, there appears over her head the sign which is customary for the Christians to bow to and with which they sign themselves.[42] I take this to symbolize the suffering which she gladly accepted. Soon afterwards the painter set up in another place an intense fire, with a bright red colour, aflame on both sides, thus giving to the flame the shape of a body. In the middle it is she standing, with hands stretched open to the sky, while no distress shows in her face. On the contrary, she is joyful, because she is departing to the incorporeal and blessed life.   309B The painter has stopped his hand at this point; so have I my speech. But it is time for you now, if you wish, to complete the narrative, so that you may comprehend it precisely – lest we stop very short of its meaning.[43]

This is what Asterius said. If we examine what the holy Scripture says, we shall find that what he preached was chosen from it. Thus, when God was giving orders to his servant Moses about the tabernacle, after He prescribed several different works for it, He added: *Thou shalt make ... curtains of fine linen spun, and blue and purple, and scarlet spun with cherubs; thou shalt make them with work of a weaver.*[44] This ordinance teaches us that what is   309C dedicated to God is to be made with great expenditure. Not so, however, with regard to human beings. For it was said to the people: *And thou shalt not put upon thyself a garment woven of two double materials.*[45] The divine Apostle makes the meaning of these words utterly clear with the exhortation: *the women should adorn themselves modestly and sensibly in seemly apparel, not with braided hair or gold or pearls of costly attire but by good deeds, as befits women who profess religion.*[46]

---

42 That is, the sign of the cross.
43 Asterius of Amasea, *On the Martyrdom of St. Euphemia*, PG 40:336A–337C.
44 Exod. 26:1.
45 Cf Lev. 19:19.
46 1 Tim. 2:9. This passage is another example of the questionable rendering which the RSV has produced in English. Two points must be made here. First, Paul speaks about the dressing of women, not their adornment. In Greek *Katastolē* is clearly 'the dress' (and especially 'a modest dress'), 'the clothing,' 'the attire.' Second, the expression 'who professes religion' is inaccurate and confusing. *Theosēbia* means devotion, respect, reverence, or fear towards God. The passage, therefore, should be translated: 'The women should wear modest attire ... as befits women who [claim that they] have reverence for God.'

Thus we, who offer our worship in spirit and truth to God alone, knowing these things, shall continue kissing and embracing everything consecrated and dedicated to Him – whether the   309D divine form of the precious cross, or the holy gospel, or venerable icons, or holy utensils – in the hope that we may receive sanctification from them. We shall also continue paying the veneration of honour to them.[47] For it [the Scripture] says, *worship at his footstool; for he is holy*.[48] This is the reason why Gregory the Theologian, also, in his oration on the birthday feast of Christ, says: 'Honour Bethlehem, and bow to the manger.'[49] For whatever has been dedicated to God is holy, by his descent upon and his association with it. Moreover, as in the case of a saint, holiness is not otherwise honoured, except by our relative adoration.   309E

However they, still breathing falsehood in having stitched together something that is alien to the catholic Church, say:

GREGORY THE BISHOP read:
Consonant with them, Theodotus of Ancara teaches the following on the same subject:

We have received the tradition to revitalize the notions about the saints; not, however, on icons with colours which are material. Rather, we have been taught to refurbish   312A *their virtues and, through what is said about them in writings, as if animate icons, stimulate ourselves towards the same zeal as theirs.*[50]

Let, therefore, those who reinstate such figures, tell us what kind of benefit they may draw from them, or unto what level of spiritual contemplation they are lifted by being reminded of them? Obviously, such notion is vain and an invention of diabolic cunning.

EPIPHANIUS THE DEACON read:
If Theodotus were alive, he would have exclaimed to God, like   312B Susanna: *O Eternal God, Who dost discern what is secret, Who are aware of all things before they come to be, Thou knowest that these men,*

---

47 Cf also above, 281E, 45.
48 Ps. 98(99):5. The verb here is *proskyneïte* ('bow down in respect,' or 'venerate,' rather than 'worship,'), from which the noun *proskȳnesis* derives. Cf also above, 281E, n 45.
49 Gregory of Nazianzus, *On Theophany, that is the Nativity of the Savior*, Oration 38, PG 36:329A–332A.
50 Theodotus of Ancara, PG 77:1313–1432.

who are the authors of this novelty corruptive of the souls, and who have envied the elders of the confusion of Babel, *have borne false witness against me.*[51] However, in their desire to prove themselves able and prominent, they bawl out empty talk. The reed-pen of their writing has proven false and they are clearly found to be forgers of the truth. For many people who have looked and searched with us for the said quotation in the discourses of Theodotus – if, indeed such a thing was ever written – found 312C nothing whatsoever anywhere. For he himself stated nothing of this sort. It is obvious that this is not Theodotus' statement. Its wording is full of bitterness and agitation; and the daring chatter that the icons are an invention of diabolic cunning is something from an unrestrained tongue and defiled lips. This is characteristic of the accusers of the Christians and one of their own fabrications, rather than of Theodotus. If, as they claim, they produced this testimony from his works, they ought to have stated explicitly the discourse from which this passage was taken. However, knowing that this is a fabrication, they let the falsehood rest in silence. Having turned to his discourses – we mean the discourses which he wrote to Lausus, *Against Nestorius,* in six 312D volumes, the *Interpretation of the Creed*[52] of the holy Fathers of Nicea, the orations *To the Nativity of the Lord, To Epiphany,*[53] *To Elijah and the widow, To saints Peter and John, To the lame man sitting by the royal door, To those who received the talents,* and *To the two blind men,* – we say that we have found nowhere the passage which they have brought forward. Not even, when this false gathering of theirs took place as a mob court, was this passage taken from any book of the Father of Ancara and included in 312E their false writing. Rather, it ran through [the council] like a plague by means of a pseudo-message,[54] which the simplest ones

51 Susanna (Daniel 13):42. The translation is from the RSV.
52 Literally, symbol.
53 Literally, the Feast of Lights, i.e., the commemoration of the Baptism of Jesus and of the epiphany of the Trinity.
54 *(pseudo) pittākion:* literally, a tablet where only a short message can be written. The meaning of this passage is, therefore, that this quotation, uncritically attributed to Theodotus, circulated rapidly during the council by word of mouth and ultimately found its way to the decree of the Synod of 754 without verification.
According to the testimony of two participants in the second council of Nicea, who had also taken part in the iconoclastic Council of 754, Gregory of Neocaesarea and

accepted. However, those who have been prudent and who have believed in the truth, have always considered this to be false.

Furthermore, they present as leader of their pestilent heresy him who was a defender of Arius and an ally of Eusebius of Nicomedeia, of Theognes of Nicea, and of Maris of Chalcedon, and who distinguished himself among the opponents of the holy Council of Nicea, saying this:

GREGORY THE BISHOP read: 313A
Similarly, Eusebius of Pamphilus says to Augusta Constantia, who had requested that an icon of Christ be sent to her:

Since you have written referring also to a certain icon of Christ that you wanted us to send you, which icon of Christ do you mean? ... that which is true and unchangeable and which bears the characteristics of his nature, or that which He assumed for us, the figure, that is, that He took in the form of a servant? ... But in so far as the form of God is concerned, I do not myself think that 313B you would ask for that, once you have been instructed by Him; because neither has one known the Father, except the Son, nor will any one ever know even the Son Himself, except the Father alone,[55] *who gave birth to Him.*

And afterwards:

But, certainly, you are asking for an icon of the form of the servant and that of a bit of flesh,[56] *which He put on for us. Yet, we have been taught that even that has been mingled with the glory of the divinity, and that which is* mortal has been swallowed up by life.[57]

And shortly after:

Who, then, would he be able to draw with dead and inanimate colours, or in 313C *sketches, the glittering and sparkling scintillations which are so very precious*

Theodotus of Amorium, no books against the icons were read during the council, except short extracts (*pittākia*): Mansi, 13:37B, 173D,E. Also during the Council of 754 an extract from Nilus' *Letter to Olympiodorus, the sub-prefect* was read as having iconoclastic connotations. The same letter, however, was read during the Council of 787, in its full form ... as a testimony in favour of the icons! Mansi, 13:36A–D.

55 Cf Matt. 11:27.
56 The word here is *sarkīon*, a diminutive form of *sarx* (flesh).
57 Cf 2 Cor. 5:4.

*and glorious? The divine Apostles on the mountain could not even endure to
look at Him, and they fell on their faces confessing that they could not bear
the sight.*[58] *If, therefore, his incarnate form became so powerful when it was
transformed into the divinity which was dwelling in it, what more needs to be
said about Him, who, after He took off mortality and washed away corruptibility,
transformed the figure which was in the form of a servant to that of the glory
of the Lord and God – being victorious over death, and ascending into heaven,
and sitting on the royal throne at the right side of the Father, and taking rest*   313D
*in the unnamed and unspeakable bosom of the Father? It is this [divine glory]
that the heavenly powers, when He was ascending and being restored, acclaimed,
saying:* Lift up your gates, ye princes; and be ye lifted up, ye everlasting
doors; and the King of glory shall come in.[59]

EPIPHANIUS THE DEACON read:
To them would apply the word which God pronounced through
Jeremiah the prophet, scolding the Jewish people: *They have
forsaken me, the fountain of the water of life, and hewn out for themselves*   313E
broken cisterns, which will not be able to hold water.[60] The chosen
men among the falsifiers, having left the teaching of the accepted
Fathers and having envied those who have been banished with
the shovel of divine judgment from the threshing floor of the
Lord – I mean from the catholic Church – bring them [the banished
ones] together in order to consolidate their own heresy. For who
of the faithful in the Church and of those who have knowledge   316A
of the true doctrines does not know that Eusebius of Pamphilus,
having given himself up to a base mind, became one in belief
and mind with those who adhered to the teaching of Arius?
For, in all his historical books, he called the Son and Word of
God a creature, subservient and second in adoration. Thus, if
any one makes the claim for him that he signed with the council,
let it be. However, as all his writings and letters indicate, he

---

58 Cf Matt. 17:6.
59 Ps. 22(23):9. Eusebius of Caesarea, *Letter to Constantia the Queen*, PG 20:1545A–1548A. The
Acts of the Seventh Ecumenical Council and Nicephorus of Constantinople, who
have copied this portion, are the only sources of this otherwise missing letter. The
letter was addressed to Constantia, the sister of the Emperor Constantine and wife of
Licinius. That is why Constantia is called 'Queen' or 'Augusta.' On Eusebius of
Caesarea (ca 263–340) see Quasten, *Patrology*, III, 309–345, esp p 345.
60 Jer. 2:13.

honoured the truth *with his lips, but his heart was far from it.*[61]
If he was confused and changed [his mind] in different ways
at different times, according to the times and the circumstances,
one time praising those who held the same opinion as Arius,   316B
and another time pretending the truth, [then] he is proven to
be, according to James the brother of God,[62] a *double-minded man,*
unstable in all his ways, who must not suppose that he will receive anything
from the Lord.[63] For if he had believed with his heart in the pursuit
of righteousness, he also would have confessed the word of truth
with his body in the pursuit of salvation,[64] as he certainly would
have asked forgiveness for his writings by rectifying them, and
would have made an apology for his letters. However, in no
way did he do so. He remained an 'Arab,' without a change
in the colour of his skin. Thus, in interpreting the passage *I said*   316C
to the Lord, 'Thou art my Lord,'[65] having gone astray from the true
knowledge, he says this:

According to the laws of nature the father of every son is also his lord.
For this reason, He who gave birth to the only-begotten Son of God,
would be his God, as well as God, Lord, and Father.[66]

Moreover, in the letter to St Alexander, the teacher of Athanasius the Great – which begins with the words 'I came upon
these writings with the greatest eagerness and diligence ...' –
blaspheming most explicitly, he [Eusebius] says the following
about Arius and his followers as he criticizes their writings for
saying that the Son was made from non-existence like anyone
else:

They produced a document which they presented to you [O Alexander].   316D
In this, they were making an exposition of their faith, which they
confessed with the following words: 'The God of the Law, of the prophets,
and of the New Testament gave birth to an only-begotten Son before

---

61 Cf Is. 29:13; Matt. 15:8.
62 Cf above, 305D, n 35.
63 Cf James 1:8.
64 Cf Rom. 10:10.
65 Ps. 15(16):2.
66 Eusebius of Caesarea, *Commentary in Ps. 15*, PG 23:153–160.

all ages, through Whom He made the ages and everything else. He gave birth to Him not seemingly, but truly, giving Him a hypostasis with a will of his own; unchangeable and incorruptible, a perfect creature of God, although not like one of the creatures.' Now, if these words of theirs [the followers of Arius] are authentic, they certainly reflect on you. In this they confess that the Son of God, Who is before all ages, and through Whom He made the ages, is unchangeable and a perfect creature of God, although not like one of the creatures. However, 316E your letter criticizes them for saying that the Son was made like one of the creatures, though they do not say so, but rather clearly specify that He is not like one of the creatures. Be keen, therefore, not to give them any more cause immediately to start seizing and distorting whatever they wish. Again, you held them liable for saying that He Who Is gave birth to a being. I wonder whether one can say this otherwise. For if He Who Is is one, it is obvious that everything that exists after Him was made by Him. However, if He is not the only one, but He 317A is also Son, how, then, did He give birth to the being? In that case there would be two beings.[67]

This is what Eusebius wrote to Alexander, the memorable one.

However, there are also other letters to the same holy man which are attributed to Eusebius, in which one could find various blasphemies claimed by the followers of Arius. He most evidently blasphemes in a letter sent to Euphrasion the bishop. This begins with the words: 'In everything I confess my gratitude to my Lord ...,' and later on it reads:

for we say that the Son does not co-exist with the Father, but that the Father is before the Son. However, this is something that the Son Himself, Who knows everything better than anybody else, knowing that He is different from the Father, minor and subordinate, teaches us in 317B a most pious way, saying: The Father who sent me is greater than me.[68]

---

67 The Acts of the Seventh Ecumenical Council are the only source of the present portion of this otherwise missing letter of Eusebius. In this letter Eusebius quotes the creed which Arius submitted to the Council of Nicomedia in defence of his teaching. On this letter see Quasten, *Patrology*, III, 345.
68 Cf John 14:28. Cf also the previous note.

And after a while: 'the Son is also God Himself, although not a true God.' Therefore, from these writings of his it is proven that he has the same opinion as Arius and his followers.

The inventors of Arius' madness, along with this heresy of apostasy, maintain that there is one nature in the hypostatic union. They are also of the opinion that our Lord, at his redemptive dispensation, assumed a flesh without a soul, saying that his divinity was in place of will and the emotions of the soul. They say so in order, according to Gregory the Theologian,[69] to ascribe suffering to the divinity. It is obvious, therefore, that those who ascribe the passion to the divinity are Theopaschites,[70] and those who share in this heresy do not allow themselves to accept icons, as neither Severus the impious one did, nor Peter Gnapheus, Philoxenus of Hieropolis, or any of their many-headed and yet headless Hydra. Therefore Eusebius, being a member of this gang – as it has been shown from his epistles and from his historical writings – rejects, as a Theopaschite, the icon of Christ. It is for this reason that he writes to Constantia, the wife of Licinius, that no icon is ever found in his possession. In that same letter he also says: 'His incarnate form changed into the divine nature.'[71] However, none of our holy Fathers thought or taught so, nor is this the truth. Let us hear what Athanasius, the demolisher of Arius' madness, says in his dogmatic letter to Eupsychius, presbyter of Caesarea, as well as what Cyril says in the first Letter to Sukensus, bishop of Diocaesarea, and also in his discourse against the Synousiasts. For both of them, having lived in the same city on earth as they do now in the celestial one and inspired by the same Spirit, speak in harmony with each other. Thus, Athanasius, in the above-mentioned letter to Eupsychius – which begins with the words 'On those matters on which you expressed your opinion to us, most Reverend ...' – subsequently says:

317C

317D

317E

Common is the produce from sheep. Thus, this harvest from the back of the sheep, that is, the wool, is available to everyone to use. However, when it is dipped into the dye of the sea, it is called purple. Once

69 Gregory of Nazianzus, *First Letter to Cledonius*, PG 37:116-193.
70 Cf above, 253B, n 21.
71 Cf above, 313C.

it takes up this name it becomes something which is fitting to be used exclusively by kings. Although this is wool, yet it is not. In so far as the nature is concerned, it is what it used to be. This is not so, however, with regard to its use, for it [the purple] transcends the common character, because of the dignity of him who uses it. So is it with the flesh of the common nature which was assumed. Since it became a vestment 320A of a King, it became worthy of the same honour of Him Who used it, even though the [created] nature itself did not become so. Thus He is called Lord of glory - and rightly so - even as a man. And while it was that nature of his which was accepting the passion, the insult was conveyed to Him Who made use of the flesh as a vestment. In the same manner as he who tears a purple robe is liable to punishment as if he had assaulted the king himself - even though the king himself did not suffer anything, and only the damage of the robe is reflected on him - so do we say that the suffering of the flesh, in spite of the impassibility of the Logos, has come upon Him through the insult.[72] It is for this reason that Paul teaches that the Lord Christ, even as 320B a human, is Son of God. Even before him the archangel Gabriel, giving the good tidings to Mary of the extraordinary birth, said: '*Hail, O favoured one, the Lord is with you; behold, you will conceive in your womb and bear a son and they shall call his name Jesus. He will be great, and will be called the Son of the Most High.*'[73] Thus, He is called Jesus, Son of God, not because the flesh changed into the divine nature, but because, by its union with God the Word, it received the homonymous dignity.[74]

Cyril also, in the above-mentioned letter to Sukensus - which begins with the words: 'I came across the reminding note which was sent by Your Holiness ...' - further on says the following: 320D

Even after the resurrection there was the same body which had suffered, although with no longer the human weaknesses in itself. Thus we say that it is no longer susceptible to hunger, fatigue, or anything of this sort, but that from then on is incorruptible. Not only that, but that it is a life-giving body; for it is a body of life, that is, of the only-begotten One. It also became splendid with a glory which is most appropriate to God, and it is understood to be God's body. Thus, should one call

72 Cf above, 253B, n 21.
73 Luke 1:18, 31-32.
74 Athanasius of Alexandria, *Letter to Eupsychius*, PG 26:1245-1248.

this body divine – as if he was neglecting the human body of the man – he would not be thinking improperly. This, I think, is what Paul, the wisest one, meant in saying that *even though we once knew Christ according to the flesh, yet we no longer know him this way.*[75] Everything human is from God.[76] However, a body which is made of earth cannot undergo a change into the nature of divinity; it is incapable of that. In such a case we would qualify divinity as that which is born, and also takes something more upon itself, which is not characteristic of its nature. It is as absurd to say that the body changed into the nature of divinity, as it is to say that the Logos changed into the nature of flesh, for He is inconvertible and unchangeable; so is the flesh. For this is not something that any creature can achieve, that is, changing its nature into the essence of divinity; and the flesh is a creature. Therefore we say that the body of Christ is divine, because it is God's body, one which has been made splendid with an unspeakable glory, one which is incorruptible, holy, and life-giving, although we do not say that it was transformed into the nature of divinity. Neither did any of the holy Fathers consider or say this, nor are we disposed to do so.[77]   320E

Similarly, in the discourse against the Synousiasts – which begins with the words: 'The blessed discourse of the doctrines of truth has been toiled through completely ...' – he further on says:

If, therefore, by changing his flesh to the divine nature He ceased being the Son of man, it would then be clear to everyone that we also lost the adoption, since we have no longer the One Who, when He came to us, became the first-born among many brothers.[78]

And shortly after:

Have we, then, slipped away unexpectedly from the glory granted to us? By no means. We shall not, driven to untested thinking by the   321A

---

75 2 Cor. 5:7.
76 This sentence reads differently in Migne's edition: 'Being, as I said, God's own body, it has superseded everything human': PG 77:236C. Cf also above, 256D, n 27.
77 Cyril of Alexandria, *To Sukensus, the most blessed one, bishop of the Diocaesareans. First Letter on Faith*, Epistle 45, PG 77:236B–D.
78 Cf Rom. 8:29.

silliness and the superficial inventions of certain men, think otherwise than we ought to think. But rather, accepting the holy and divinely inspired Scripture as the rule of the right and undistorted faith, we say that when the only-begotten Word of God became the first-born among us, He did not cease to be and be called – along with the name 'true God' – the Son of man. Thus He is viewed not as having transformed the consistency of the flesh, which was united with Him without change or confusion, to the nature of divinity. Rather, one should naturally think that He made it all splendid with his own nature and He filled it with the dignities proper to God.

This is how He will appear some day to those throughout the earth   321B
when He returns from heaven. Thus, having completed the greatest mystery of the incarnate dispensation, He returned to heaven; something which those who saw the happening put down as a testimony. For, as it is written *a cloud took him up.* Then an angel addressed the ones who were astonished: *'Men of Galilee, why do you stand looking into heaven? This Jesus, who was taken up from you into heaven, will come in the same way as you saw him go into heaven.'*[79] Did, then, those to whom this word was addressed see the Word returning to the Father without flesh? Or did He get rid of the likeness to us? Or, was He not in a tangible and   321C
visible body, but was He rather transformed into an intangible and invisible nature? Who would dare say that? Also, if He will return in the same way as He ascended, is it not true to say that He will come back again in a body, and not as a naked and fleshless Word?

And shortly after:

Notice, therefore, that showing to them in advance how the descent from heaven would be at the end of the ages, He transfigured Himself. However, the act of the transfiguration, says the wonderful evangelist, took place not by putting aside the figure, that is, not by shaking off the human form. Rather, this had to do only with the glory. For he   321D
says that his face shone and sparkled with a brightness which was as bright as the rays of the sun.[80]

---

79 Acts 1:9, 11.
80 Cf Matt. 17:1–5.

And shortly after:

Paul also, the all-wise one, has written with regard to Christ that He *will transform the body of our lowliness to conform with the body of his glory.*[81] Therefore, how do they say that He changed his flesh to the nature of the Logos? Would, then, the bodies of the saints also be transferred by means of a change to the nature of divinity, in order that they may conform with the body of his glory? Is this not nonsense, full of ultimate ignorance? If, as they claim, the flesh was completely changed to the nature of divinity, what kind of a body did the Logos make use of,   321E since He is God? For divinity is something incorporeal and it is true that *no one has ever seen God.*[82]

Again, the same wonderful Father, as in the same discourse, as if he is addressing Eusebius himself, says with the greatest emphasis the following:

According to what they say there is another word to be introduced to this matter. Thus Paul, the wonderful one, is found to have written: *Even though we once knew Christ according to the flesh, yet we no longer know him this way.*[83] They say, therefore, that if He is not known according   324A to the flesh, it is necessary to say that He changed the flesh into the nature of the Logos Himself, so that He may be known as God. But I think that one would say to them at once: Therefore when, speaking about us and saying, *those who are in the flesh cannot please God; but you are not in the flesh, you are in the Spirit,*[84] does he [Paul] know us to be without flesh and blood? Then he addresses these words to spirits without bodies! Is it not pedantic to think and speak this way? Therefore, in reference to us, he calls 'flesh' the extraordinary passions which are not without blemish. However, in reference to Christ, Who is the Saviour of us all, Who is all pure and has no experience of wrongdoing - *for*

---

81 Phil. 3:21. This is my translation. The RSV has rendered this passage as follows: *He will change our lowly body to be like the glorious body.* The expression 'glorious body' is less definite than 'the body of his glory' which points to the body of the transfiguration and of the resurrection. The expression also 'like his ... body' is less definite than the adjective *sӯmmorphon*, which suggests not simply likeness but identity.
82 John 1:18.
83 2 Cor. 5:16.
84 Rom. 8:8–9.

He committed no sin[85] – the expression 'according to the flesh' must be understood in a different way. For He is not 'in flesh,' that is, He is no longer under the shortcomings of the flesh.[86]

Therefore, we know clearly from the Fathers, speaking under 324B the inspiration of God, that the defenders of this quarrel did not draw from the fountains of Israel in order that their drinking might result for them in eternal life.[87] Instead, they gave themselves to drinking from fountains which are wicked and sterile. Having followed somebody else, they are led to cliffs and ravines. If they had been nourished within the Church, they ought to have presented Basil the Great, who says that 'the honour of the icon is conveyed to the prototype';[88] or Gregory of Nyssa, who says: 'I saw an icon of the passion and I was not able to 324C pass by the sight without tears, because the art was conveying the story vividly';[89] or John, who says that he loves the painting on melted wax which is full of piety; or others from the same group and their fellow-teachers.

Afterwards, without ever rectifying the distorted issues, but rather proliferating evil with additions, they said further:

GREGORY THE BISHOP read:
Therefore, having collected the biblical and patristic testimonies, we have 324D *put together in this present Definition of ours only a few of them out of many, so that this may not become too long. For, although there are many more, we wittingly left out an infinite number of them.*

Having been constituted firmly by these blessed Scriptures inspired by God, and by the Fathers, and having fixed our feet with certainty on the stone of worshipping in spirit and in truth, we all, who have been vested with the office of the priesthood, having reached one opinion, we DECREE unanimously, in the name of the holy and supersubstantial

85 Is. 53:9; 1 Peter 2:22.
86 Cyril of Alexandria, *Ex libra contra synousiastas* (*adversus eos qui naturas confundunt*). With the exception of these quotations, this work is available only in a Latin translation (PG 76:1427–1438), consisting of fragments from the said work of Cyril, '*ex Apologia Joannis Caesariensis pro concilio Chalcedonensis quae in codice Syriaco Vaticano superest.*' Mai, *Bibliotheca nova Patrum*, II, 445; quoted in PG 76:1427, n 1.
87 Cf John 4:14.
88 Basil of Caesarea, *On the Holy Spirit*, PG 32:149C.
89 Gregory of Nyssa, Sermon 8, PG 44:1292–1301.

Trinity, the principle of life, that every icon, made of any matter and 324E
of any kind of gaudiness of colours by painters, is objectionable, alien,
and repugnant to the Church of the Christians;

EPIPHANIUS THE DEACON read:
Not bearing to bow their neck to the tradition of the Church,
having become too blind to choose what is profitable or to grasp
the truth, and having denounced the pious tradition, the ones
ever-babbling of this novelty, not wanting to be watered by the 325A
torrent of delight so that it might become within them a *spring*
of water welling up to eternal life,[90] but rather, having drunk from
dry cisterns, are now sprouting ill-smelling stems, which bear
fruits of a gall of bitterness. Adding also falsehood upon falsehood,
they decree: 'Although there are many other testimonies, we left
them out wittingly.' Thus – as has already been shown – with
regard to the statements which they presented previously from
the accepted Fathers in *seeking to establish their own righteousness,*[91]
they understood them in a distorted way. As for the statements
which are from the adversaries, these do not have their source
in the holy Spirit. Thence, David the blessed one, singing under
the inspiration of the Spirit, says to them: *Everyone has spoken* 325B
vanity to his neighbour; their lips are deceitful in their heart, and they
have spoken evil in their heart;[92] while Isaiah, the outspoken one,
responds, saying that those who sit in council are wicked,
deliberating unlawfulness, for *they have no understanding to perceive,*
because they have been blinded so that they should not see with their
eyes.[93] Having left behind sound definitions and laws, they make
a show of piety with words. They also attempt to make a few
statements of piety in order that, on the basis of what right faith
there is in them, they may not be disbelieved with regard to
the rest, saying: 'In the name of the holy and supersubstantial
Trinity, the principle of life.' However, in their desire to pervert
the mind, they produce statements and definitions from their

90 John 4:14.
91 Cf Rom. 10:3.
92 Ps. 11(12):2. The English translation of Bagster's edition reads as follows: 'Their lips are
   deceitful, they have spoken with a double heart.'
93 Cf Is. 44:18.

own minds, putting forth the impiety boldly; not even taking 325C
into consideration God's judgment, and without understanding
the Lord's assertion which says forcefully: *But whoever causes one
of these little ones who believe in me to stumble, it would be better for
him to have a great millstone fastened around his neck and to be drowned
in the depth of the sea.*[94]

Afterwards, like swine who have trodden on pearls – I mean
the traditions of the Church – they chattered that 'every icon
made of any matter is objectionable and repugnant to the Church
of the Christians,' thus having decreed not under the guidance
of the Lord, and made articles not under the inspiration of the
Spirit. Instead, they attacked the flock of Christ like wolves.[95] 325D
However, the brightness of the truth and the sparkling of the
light remain firm and unshaken.

For who does not know that when an icon is dishonoured
the insult applies to the person who is depicted on the icon?
The truth knows this to be so and the nature of things teaches
so. The Fathers also agree with this: for example, Basil, who says:
'The honour of the icon is conveyed to the prototype'; Athanasius,
who says: 'He who bows to the icon bows to the King in it';
and Chrysostom, who in a similar way says: "Do you not know
that if you insult an icon of a king, you refer the insult to the 325E
dignity of the prototype?" These Fathers clearly followed what
is natural. However, they [the iconoclasts] are up against both,
the Church and the truth. Not only are they full of blasphemy,
but their word also is loaded with madness and ignorance. They
ought rather to have promulgated that teaching which has been
held by everyone, not the one which is controversial; as they
ought also to have supported and cherished for themselves as
important the ancient tradition which all the believers have kept
and confessed, after the tradition of the Apostles and Fathers.
They ought not to have brought in an innovation or a reduction
of a practice, which has prevailed among us out of piety. For 328A
what has been handed down to the catholic Church is subject
to neither addition nor reduction. He who causes an addition

94 Matt. 18:6. The verb *scandalīzein* has been translated in the RSV as 'to cause to sin,' which
has a much more definite and final meaning than the verb 'to tempt,' or 'to cause to
stumble,' both of which are closer to the original.
95 Cf Acts 20:29.

or a reduction is bound to the greatest punishment. For it [the Scripture] says: *Cursed is he that removes his father's landmarks.*[96] However, they had no intention of knowing the truth. They will hear, therefore, the words of wisdom: *He that gathers treasures with a lying tongue pursues vanity to the snares of death.*[97]

---

96 Cf Deut. 27:17.
97 Prov. 21:6.

SIXTH VOLUME

EPIPHANIUS THE DEACON read: 328B
Would they had taken into consideration the words which the
Lord addressed to Peter, the supreme one among the Apostles:
*You are Peter, and on this rock I will build my church, and the powers
of death shall not prevail against it.*[1] However, having estranged
themselves from harmony and from this edifice, they babble
things worthy of laughter, decreeing the following:

GREGORY THE BISHOP read:
No man should ever attempt to occupy himself with such an impious 328C
*and unholy endeavour. He who from now on attempts to make an icon,
or to venerate one, or to set one up in a church or in a private home,
or to hide one, if [he be] bishop, presbyter, or deacon, let him be unfrocked;
if monk or layman, let him be anathematized and subjected to the royal
laws,*[2] *as an opponent of the commandments of God and an enemy of
the doctrines of the Fathers.*

EPIPHANIUS THE DEACON read: 328D
Having accused the entire Church, and not being content even
with this, nor yet being satiated with impiety, they furthermore
define, unlawfully and in spite of such a practice, against the
making of icons. But who of those who think and live in piety
will obey them? Icons are so manifestly shown in the churches,
as they have been shown in them from the time of the proclamation of the gospel to the present; and 'that which excels
in antiquity, is worthy of respect.'[3] For what else does the divine
Apostle urge the Corinthians when he writes: *hold the traditions* 328E

---

1 Matt. 16:18. This paragraph reads as an interpolation into the texts of the Refutation. The
subsequent paragraph is more in the spirit and style of all previous introductions to
new volumes of the Refutation. The reference to Matt. 16:18 is unwarranted and
makes no sense in this context. Why should the iconoclasts have taken into consideration these words of Jesus? It might be that this introductory statement betrays a
Latin intervention, possibly of Anastasius the Librarian (cf introduction, p 37, n 166),
aimed at confirming and supporting the rising claims of supremacy of the bishop of
Rome.
2 That is, the state laws.
3 Basil of Caesarea; cf also above, 252B.

which you have received?[4] He also writes to Timothy and Titus: *avoid the godless chatter.*[5]

Therefore all of us Christians, having been born within the holy catholic Church, and in obedience to the divine Apostle, hold the traditions which we have received, establish ourselves in them, and disavow the new vain talking. We also accept everything that at different times seemed good to our memorable Fathers *to build upon the foundation of the Apostles and prophets.*[6] But we despise, as hateful and adverse, everything that the shameful and impious heresies have chattered, including the newly fabricated heresy of the accusers of the Christians, which   329A
we despise strongly as an unguarded babbling hated by God.

However, since their impiety grew so much, not only did they sharpen their tongue to utter evil, but by having said that he who does not obey should be subject to the royal laws, they directed the hand of those in power to make charges and strike. Thus, as a result of this pronouncement the world suffered many afflictions of every kind. Intensive cruelty was excercised against the opposing bishops on the part of those in power and their superiors. What language is able to narrate these tragedies? Where   329B
and how shall I begin describing every one of these? Agitation and fear, persecutions, the confinement of the monks in every city, their flogging and imprisonment for many years with their legs tied up in chains, the destruction of holy utensils, the burning of books, the turning of holy churches to places of common utility, and the profane alteration of chaste monasteries to worldly hovels. Thus those pious men who used to live in them, after their belongings had been seized, took up the lands of the barbarians, considering – in the manner of the Apostle – that it is better to reside among gentiles than to live together in a profane way with men of the same race, obeying the injunction of the divine Apostle *not even to eat with such ones.*[7] What is worst of all is that   329C
this impiety of desecrating undefiled monasteries unlawfully continues even today by some men. In place of holy hymns and a voice of joy in the tents of the righteous ones, there is the

4 Sic. Cf 2 Thess. 2:15, 3:6.
5 1 Tim. 6:20.
6 Eph. 2:20.
7 Cf 1 Cor. 5:11.

singing of harlots and of Satan; and in place of successive kneelings, there is sinuous dancing. In addition to these, one should mention the hazards, the turmoil, the restlessness and the shock; the punishments, the plucking out of eyes, the mutilation of noses, the cutting off of tongues; the dishonourable persecutions, that is the exiles of reverent men who are scattered all over the world; the burning of the faces of saintly men, the burning of their beards; the lawless and forced marriage of virgins after their engagement[8] to Christ; and – worst of all – the murders.   329D These are the fruits of those who quarrel against the truth. They constitute, clearly, a madness, not a true judgment. God has looked upon and delivered his Church from all these sufferings afflicting her. Glory be to Him. Amen.

Being overlooked even by their own lawless deliberation, they are refuted by the truth, when they say:

GREGORY THE BISHOP read:
We also decree this: than no man whatsoever who presides over a church   329E *or a pious institution may, thinking that this error of the icons has been diminished, put forth his hands to bring alterations to holy utensils[9] which are dedicated to God, because these are* enzoda, *that is, they have carved figures on them,*

EPIPHANIUS THE DEACON read:
It is mouths of men who do not fear the Lord that have vomited   332A these words forth. For which one of those whose mind is fixed in the fear of God would dare to call what is dedicated to God by a name used for idols? Not even the most ignorant and uninstructed would be oblivious to the great and redemptive mystery which God the Word, having come and lived among us in flesh, accomplished, delivering us from the error of idols. For 'carved figures'[10] is the usual term of pious men for describing the idols of the gentiles.

---

8 This is the closest translation of the word *sȳntaxis* [with Christ], which means 'taking sides with,' 'alignment,' 'incorporation into the order of.' The expression implies the monastic vocation.

9 Here the utensils used during the liturgy for the preparation and serving of the holy communion, (i.e., the chalice, the paten, the asterisk, the lance, and the spoon) are implied.

10 *ēnzoda.*

Indeed, this stuttering is by those who speak from earth, and the pronouncements are of their belly,[11] which, being filled with dirty food, sends odorous evaporations to the mind, making them senseless and delirious, worthy of ridicule. For this reason they say further:

332B

GREGORY THE BISHOP read:
or on the altar-cloths[12] *or other veils, or on anything else that is designated for the divine service, lest these become desecrated.*

EPIPHANIUS THE DEACON read:
While they defame the holy Church of God and decree that she is wrong in accepting iconographic representations – calling them 'shameful things,' 'idols,' 'carved figures' – now, as if forgetting their own wicked decision, they reckon that these should stay in the Church, having been dedicated to God. But if these are dedicated to God, how can they be shameful, inventions of diabolical cunning? Obviously this is a Caiaphas-like decision. For he committed Christ to death out of malice, while unaware that he spoke the truth in declaring that He is the Saviour of humankind.[13] So it has happened to them, who have become like Caiaphas. While out of malice they calumniate the sight of the holy icons as 'error,' 'carved figures,' 'shameful things,' and an 'invention of diabolic cunning,' yet, being unwittingly criticized by the truth, they are forced to confess these as holy, and as objects dedicated to God. They fall into the snares of their own quarrrels.

332C

332D

Thus, deceiving those who follow them, they add the following:

GREGORY THE BISHOP read:
Should any one, however, strengthened by God, wish to alter such utensils or vestments, let him not attempt to do so without the consent and knowledge of the most holy and blessed Ecumenical Patriarch, and without permission of our most pious and Christ-loving kings, lest the devil may, under this excuse, profane[14] *the churches of God. Also let not any of the rulers*

332E

---

11 Cf also above, 240E, n 45.
12 These include the covers of the altar and of the prōthesis (the auxiliary table in the sanctuary), including the covers of the utensils used in the liturgy.
13 Cf John 11:50–52.
14 Literally, humiliate.

*or any one of their subordinates, that is any of the laity, under the same
pretext [attempt to] lay hands on the holy churches and take hold of
them, as things of this sort have taken place in the past by men who
have behaved in a disorderly manner.*

EPIPHANIUS THE DEACON read: 333A
Who would not laugh, or rather weep, at this law? For, on the
basis of these empty statements, many – obviously using the
excuse of these words – dared to put the hands of the giant
with a hundred hands[15] onto the utensils of the priests. Wickedness is something into which one slips easily. Thus, even if one
overlooks those 'most blessed bishops,' as they call them – but
actually 'defrauded' ones, as is the truth – who appropriated
the gold and the silver of holy dedicatory gifts and the icons   333B
in the shrines,[16] these are the ones who did the same thing. They
converted this[17] into public places, baths, and theatres. Because
of their judgment everything holy was desecrated. Yet they say
with pride:

GREGORY THE BISHOP read:
*Be this as it may, and confirmed by the grace of God, we deemed it proper
to articulate in this catholic and God-pleasing writing of ours some
fundamental definitions. For we think that we speak in the spirit of the*   333C
Apostles and, furthermore, we believe that we have the spirit of
Christ.[18] *In the same way as those before us believed and, thus, spoke
out what they had defined in a conciliar manner, so do we also believe,*
and so we speak.[19]

*Thus, after the definitions of the Fathers which we state first, we define
what has seemed good to us, which follows and agrees with these.*

EPIPHANIUS THE DEACON read:
Having said previously many frivolous things of all kinds, and
having declared expressly their own wickedness in many ways,   333D
they now introduce themselves indirectly as equals to the

15 From the mythical Aegaeon in *Iliad*, 1:403.
16 Literally, in the museums.
17 That is, the gold and the silver.
18 Cf 1 Cor. 7:40.
19 Cf 2 Cor. 4:13.

teachers of the Church. They also make false pretensions to have their cursed decrees accounted together with the sacred pronouncements of the former, in their desire to mingle falsehood with truth, mixing, that is, poison with honey.

However, those who are guided by the divine Spirit are able to distinguish what is better from that which is worse, thus accepting everything that has been defined in piety by the holy Fathers, while discarding everything that has been spoken distortedly by these latter. For these speakers of falsehood confess to having a knowledge of God, although they deviate from the 333E
path which leads to the royal way,[20] having tarnished the words of our pure faith with the rust of wickedness, and although they border on the same lack of discipline as the heresiarchs of the past. Those [heresiarchs], too, were in agreement with the catholic Church on most matters. Having digressed, however, on one or two things, they were anathematized. It is with those that they [the iconoclasts] share, even though they pronounce the following:

GREGORY THE BISHOP read:

If anyone does not confess, in accordance with the traditions of the Apostles and Fathers, that in the Father, in the Son, and in the Holy Spirit there 336A
is one and the same Godhead, as well as [one and the same] nature and essence, will and energy, power and lordship, sovereignty and authority, glorified in three hypostases, that is persons, let him be anathema.

If anyone does not confess that the one of the holy Trinity, that is our Lord Jesus Christ, is from the Father according to the divinity before the ages, and that the same one in the last days descended from heaven for our salvation and became flesh by the holy Spirit and the virgin Mary, and that He was born of her in a manner which is beyond any human comprehension, let him be anathema.

If anyone does not confess that Emmanuel is in truth God and, thus, 336B
that the holy Virgin is Theotokos[21] – for she gave birth according to the flesh to the Word of God who became flesh – let him be anathema.[22]

20 Cf above, 208A, n 12.
21 The simple translation of 'Theotōkos' as 'mother of God' is perhaps, and justifiably so, confusing. The term means 'the one who gave birth to Him Who is God.' The best definition of the term 'Theotōkos' is the phrase of Cyril of Alexandria in this statement: 'the one who gave birth according to the flesh (*sarkekōs*) to the Word of God Who became flesh.' Cf also above, 256D, n 27, and 305D, n 35.
22 This and the next two anathemas are the first, second, and eleventh anathemas of the

If anyone does not confess that the Word of God the Father was united hypostatically with the flesh and that with his own flesh He is one Christ, that is, that the same one is together God and man, let him be anathema.

If anyone does not confess that the flesh of the Lord is life-giving and that it is the flesh of the very Word of God the Father, but [he rather confesses] that this is of someone else, other than Him, attached to Him according to the dignity – that is that [the Lord] has simply the divinity dwelling in Him – but not that the flesh of the Lord is itself life-giving, as we said, for it became His, that is, of the Word, who can breathe life into all things, let him be anathema.   336C

If anyone does not acknowledge two natures in one Christ, our true God, and two natural wills and two natural energies, in communion [with each other] and inseparable [from each other], without change, without division, without confusion, according to the teaching of the holy Fathers, let him be anathema.

If anyone does not confess that our Lord Jesus Christ sits in council with God the Father along with that which He assumed,[23] *that is, along with his flesh which was animated by an intellectual and rational soul, and that He will return again in the same way, with the glory of his Father, to judge the living and the dead – being no longer flesh, nor incorporeal either,*[24] *but with a more Godlike body described with words which only He knows, so that He may even be seen by those who pierced* 336D *Him, and yet remain God beyond the density of substance*[25] *– let him be anathema.*

EPIPHANIUS THE DEACON read:
Up to this point, they express the right faith, being in agreement with the promulgations of the holy Fathers. Or rather, having appropriated to themselves the teachings of the Fathers, they bestow the honour upon themselves. However, in what follows they vomit the bitter doctrines of their venomous tongue, which [doctrines] are like a viper, full of deadly poison:

twelve which Cyril of Alexandria appended to his third letter to Nestorius (430): PG 77:105–122. On Cyril of Alexandria (d 444) see Quasten, *Patrology*, III, 116–142.

23 *to prōslemma*: cf above, 217A, n 1.

24 Literally, not without a body either. Notice here the distinction made between 'flesh' and 'body.' The constant reference to a 'body' aims at safeguarding against any notion of abstraction, unreality, impersonality, or docetism – in contrast, however, to *sarx*, which is the material substance.

25 We translate as 'density of substance' what the Greek word *pachētes* means to convey, literally, 'thickness,' 'fatness,' 'thick consistency.'

GREGORY THE BISHOP read: 336E

If anyone endeavours, through material colours, to understand the divine
impress of God the Word according to his incarnation, and not to offer
adoration to Him – Who is beyond the brightness of the sun and is
seated at the right side of God in the highest on a throne of glory –
with his spiritual eyes and with all his heart, let him be anathema.

EPIPHANIUS THE DEACON read: 337A

This imaginary declaration proves them to be strange allegorizers.
For, while the Apostle proclaimed that the Son is the impress
of God the Father because of the identity in the essence, they,
having reversed this and understood it to apply to the flesh which
was assumed by God the Word, discharge a new declaration
from a senseless mind, and say: 'If anyone endeavours, through
material colours, to perceive the divine impress of God the Word 337B
according to His incarnation.'

That the flesh which God the Word assumed is of a different
essence from the nature of God the Word, is something that we
all know well, because we have been instructed so by the truth
and by the holy Apostles, who were the first leaders of the Church,
and by our divine Fathers. Thus, as we have said, Paul the divine
Apostle, who saw things which cannot be told,[26] in his desire
to proclaim the consubstantiality of God the Word and Son to
God the Father, found nothing that would be both familiar and
in accordance with this, except the proclamation that the Son
is 'an impress of the hypostasis of the Father.'[27] 337C

Thenceforth, they fall into notions which constitute a blasphemy. Having also given themselves up to a base mind,[28] they
say even further:

GREGORY THE BISHOP read:

If anyone endeavours to circumscribe with material colours in icons, in
an anthropomorphic way, the uncircumscribable essence and hypostasis

---

26 Cf 2 Cor. 12:4.
27 Cf Heb. 1:3. I find the rendering of this significant passage in the RSV ('He reflects the
   glory of God and bears the very stamp of his nature') to lack proper insight into the
   original: 'He is the reflection of his glory and the impress (literally, "character") of his
   hypostasis.'
28 Literally, to an untested thinking.

of God the Word, because of the incarnation, and not to predicate[29] *Him*   337D
*as God – being not less uncircumscribable, even after the incarnation
– let him be anathema.*

EPIPHANIUS THE DEACON read:
They make these statements because on crucial matters of Church
traditions they have become sick beyond curing and because,
having been corrupted in their minds, they have contracted once
again the pestilent disease. Thus they inflict the shamefulness
of deception upon the right thinking. Furthermore, they deceive
their own minds by confusing the flesh which was assumed by
the divine Word, and which was circumscribed, with his own
uncircumscribable nature. For this is what their statement, 'being
not less uncircumscribable even after the incarnation,' clearly   337E
means.

How did the ones wise in vanities ever invent this empty
talk? For it is thoroughly blasphemous to say that the Lord of
all, Jesus Christ, our true God, is undescribable after the incarnation, especially since He Himself said to the disciples: *Lazarus
our friend has fallen asleep ... and for your sake I am glad that I was
not there.*[30] Is, therefore, the statement 'I was not there' not
characteristic of circumscription? By all means. Let us also –
leaving aside what the gospel says about Him before the passion
– discuss what it says about Him after the resurrection. The fact   340A
that He made Himself apparent to the women shows that He
was not uncircumscribable at all. Also his appearance to the two
disciples is a characteristic of circumscription. The fact that He
entered while the doors were closed and that He was touched
by Thomas is what else but circumscription? It is also a fact
that the disciples walked to Galilee and there they saw Him
and bowed down before Him. As for the fact that while the
disciples were watching He was taken up to heaven and an angel
standing by said to them, *Men, why do you stand looking into heaven?
This Jesus, who was taken up from you into heaven, will come in the
same way as you saw him go into heaven,*[31] is it not also characteristic
of circumscription? All these [cases] certainly are!   340B

29 The verb here is *theologeīn*. Cf also above, 300A, n 19.
30 Cf John 11:11, 15.
31 Cf Acts 1:11.

Moreover, this is what all our God-fearing Fathers teach explicitly, as is evident to those who think right; that is, in so far as He is God and the Word of God the Father, He is invisible, uncircumscribable, incomprehensible, and present in every place of his sovereignty. However, in so far as He assumed man's nature, He is visible and circumscribable – for he Himself said to the disciples that He was not there – as well as comprehensible, as Thomas confirmed for us.

Thus, those who introduce the deceptive insanity of the accusers of the Christians, through one blasphemy, fall together into many iniquities. For, making again false accusations, they say:

GREGORY THE BISHOP read: 340C

If anyone attempts to paint in an icon the undivided hypostatic union of the nature of God the Word along with that of the flesh – which two resulted in one, which is unconfused and undivided – calling this 'Christ,' while the name Christ implies God and man, and as a result of this one proclaims absurdly a confusion of the two natures, let him be anathema.

EPIPHANIUS THE DEACON read: 340D

Notice how the shamefulness of deception is inflicted upon right thinking. This is because for them to conceive that the making of icons contradicts the undivided and unconfused hypostatic union in Christ, as introducing a confusion of the two natures, is false and wicked. However, *the truth of God is not fettered*.[32] For the name 'Christ' implies two natures, the one being visible and the other invisible. Thus this Christ, while visible to men by means of the curtain,[33] that is his flesh, made the divine nature

---

32 Cf 2 Tim. 2:9.

33 The Greek here is *katapētasma*. Matt. 27:51 uses the word to refer to the curtain of the Temple that divided the holy of holies from the rest of the sanctuary. The metaphor of the flesh of Christ as the 'curtain of the Temple' is obvious: Christ in flesh is the means through which man encounters existentially, and gains a glimpse of, the divine.

In an Orthodox church the *katapētasma* of the old Temple has been replaced by the *iconostāsion*. Cf also above, 276D, n 20.

On the *iconostāsion* the icons of Christ, of Theotokos, of John the Baptist, and of holy persons face the congregation. The icons are painted against a golden background,

– even though this remained concealed – manifest through signs.[34] 340E
Therefore it is in this form, seen by men, that the holy Church
of God depicts Christ, according to the tradition of the holy
Apostles and Fathers. She does not divide Christ, as they
frivolously accuse her of doing. For, as we have said many times,
what the icon shares with the prototype is only the name, not
what defines the prototype. The icon lacks a soul – something
impossible to describe, for it is invisible. Thus, if it is impossible
for one to depict a soul – even though soul is created – how
much more is it impossible for one to consider depicting, in a
perceptible way, the incomprehensible and unfathomable divin- 341A
ity of the only-begotten Son? – unless one is totally out of his
mind.

Thus their toil has returned upon their own heads. The
anathema which they promulgated idly remains with them
forever. However, they say again:

GREGORY THE BISHOP read:
*If anyone sets aside the flesh which was united with the hypostasis of
God the Word, thinking of it as mere flesh, and consequently, endeavours
to describe it in an icon, let him be anathema.*

symbolic of the glory and the incorruptibility of the Kingdom. In this symbolic
although most tangible way the *iconostāsion* depicts the curtain-flesh of Christ. The
icon-screen distinguishes, without separating, the holy of holies from the nave while
at the same time marking the boundary-line where the human and the divine meet
each other, as the congregation comes forward to receive communion. The
iconostāsion was never meant to be an impenetrable wall. It is more a perforated
screen that allows a partial, mystical view of the elements, the symbols, and the
movements of the celebrants, in anticipation of the fullness of the experience in the
communion. The eucharistic service in the Orthodox Church is a re-enactment of the
history of the divine dispensation, an experience of the Transfiguration and a paschal
meal.

34 *Semeīa* (signs) is a New Testament word which, along with the often conjoined word
tērata (marvels), refers to what has uncritically been translated and understood as
'miracles.' Both these words are primarily words which imply a pointer towards, or
an indicator of, something ultimately more significant than the pointer itself. Indeed,
the entire gospel narrative is actually an exercise in pointing, through the 'signs' and
the 'marvels' of Jesus, to an ultimate culmination in the resurrection, which is the
'miracle' *par excellence*. The gospel narrative makes infinitely greater sense, and reveals
the essence of Christianity, if it is read ... backwards, in light of the resurrection!

EPIPHANIUS THE DEACON read: 341B

This is what St Gregory, the one who is surnamed after Theology, says: "Whenever the natures are distinguished from one another in our thoughts, the names are also distinguished."[35] Most of the Fathers also had this notion, for this is what seems to be the truth.

However they, having been separated from the truth as well as from the traditions of the Fathers, say: 'If any one sets aside the flesh which was united with the hypostasis of God the Word in thinking ...'[36] Thus even in this respect they are found not 341C agreeing with what the holy Fathers have stated. Rather, repeating the same kind of things, they most clearly fight against the truth and accuse the catholic Church of having the same belief as Nestorius.

Then, saying what is in accordance [only] with their own [thinking], they add:

GREGORY THE BISHOP read:

If anyone divides the one Christ into two hypostases, placing in one part the Word of God and in the other the Son of the virgin Mary, and if he does not confess that there is one and the same Christ, but rather that there was only a nominal union between them, and if he consequently 341D *describes in an icon the Son of the Virgin, as if this had a hypostasis of his own, let him be anathema.*

---

35 Cf above, 248c, 257c.
36 There seems to be a misunderstanding here of the inconoclasts by their opponents. This becomes evident when one compares the iconoclastic statement with the way in which the defenders of the icons repeated it. They extended the main phrase to include the words *en epinoïa* (in one's thinking), which in the iconoclastic definition are part of a parenthetical sentence ('thinking of it as mere flesh'). The thrust of the iconoclastic position at this point is that one cannot think of the flesh of Christ lightly, as mere flesh, because this flesh was united with the hypostasis of God the Word; therefore, it is a unique and perhaps different flesh. The defenders of the icons understood this to mean that one cannot divide the flesh conceptually (in one's thinking) from the divine nature. The point of the iconoclasts is not whether or not the flesh of Christ can be divided in one's thinking but whether this flesh is not mere flesh, like any other, but the flesh of the incarnate Logos – a spiritualized conception of the flesh of Christ, which certainly betrays a docetic or a Monophysite tendency.

EPIPHANIUS THE DEACON read:
Repeating in cycles the same kinds of things, they make so many pronouncements that what they chatter will be almost beyond numbering. Thus, having discovered Nestorius' impious opinion, they inflict it upon the painting of icons, stitching together certain strange and peculiar petty words. But, having refuted these words in many ways, we now deem it necessary to commit them to silence.

341E

Once again they utter the following:

GREGORY THE BISHOP read:
If anyone depicts in an icon the flesh which was deified by the union with the divine Logos, let him be anathema, because he separates the flesh from the divinity that assumed and deified it, and as a consequence he renders it undeified.

EPIPHANIUS THE DEACON read:

344A

Even though the catholic Church depicts Christ in human form, she does not separate this from the divinity united with it. Rather, she believes that this is deified, as she confesses it to be one with God,[37] according to Gregory the Great, the Theologian, and according to the truth. Not, as they have said, speaking like barbarians with no knowledge or training, that the flesh of the Lord is as a consequence [of the icon] rendered undeified. For, just as when one paints a man, one does not render him without

344B

a soul, but he remains one who has a soul and the icon is called his because of his resemblance, so it is when we make an icon of the Lord. We confess the Lord's flesh to be deified, and we know the icon to be nothing else but an icon, signifying the imitation of the prototype. It is from this that the icon has taken also the name of the prototype, which is the only thing that it has in common with the prototype. That is why it is venerable and holy. However, if the icon is of a cursed man, or of a demon, then it is profane and defiled; for so is the prototype.

Thus, having toiled in empty works, they collect fruitlessness in their hands. They also receive anathema from the truth from which they will not be free, as long as they say the following:

37 Cf Gregory of Nazianzus, Oration 23, PG 35:1160C.

GREGORY THE BISHOP read: 344C

If anyone attempts to reform with material colours God the Word, who
though he was in the form of God took upon his own hypostasis
the form of a servant, and became like us[38] *in every respect, without*
sin, for being supposedly a mere man, and if one separates Him from
the inseparable and unchangeable divinity – this way introducing a fourth
person in the holy Trinity, the principle of life – let him be anathema.

EPIPHANIUS THE DEACON read: 344D

What folly and madness! They have no shame in putting together
this anathema. Instead, like worms which feed themselves by
wallowing in mire, they, entangled in the same old discussion,
cannot satisfy themselves enough as they attempt to curse the
sanctified Church of God, being themselves worthy of cursing.
For *those who bless her,* says the Scripture, *are blessed, and those*
who curse her are accursed.[39]

As for the matter that, because of the reproduction with colours,   344E
one may imply that Christ the Saviour is a mere man, or that
one may separate Him from divinity and introduce a fourth
person, who would not burst into a loud laughter, or rather lament
at this blasphemy? For by making an icon of Christ in his human
form one does not express the belief that this is a fourth person,
but rather confesses that God the Word became man truly, not
in conjecture. It is Nestorius, the deranged one, about whom
it has been said that he introduced a fourth person, because
he blasphemously thought of two natures in Christ as two
hypostases. However, the holy Church of God, which confesses   345A
rightly that there is one hypostasis of Christ in two natures,
has been instructed by God to represent Him in icons, in order
for her to remember his redemptive dispensation.

Then, in their desire to show that they are trustworthy and
that they state something true, they say the following:

GREGORY THE BISHOP read:

If anyone does not acknowledge that the ever-Virgin Mary is indeed and
truly Theotokos,[40] *and that she is exalted above any creature, visible and*   345B

38 Cf Phil. 2:6–7.
39 Gen. 27:29.
40 Cf above, 336B, n 21.

invisible, and if he does not entreat her intercession with sincere faith, as having audience[41] *with our God to Whom she gave birth, let him be anathema.*

EPIPHANIUS THE DEACON read:
The catholic Church, being founded and established on these precepts, does not need to heed those of a different mind from the tradition of the Church which is inspired by God. For the Lord also, even when He was proclaimed by demons, drove them away.[42] Also, when Paul the divine Apostle and his cotravellers   345C
were witnessed to by demons as men of God the most high proclaiming the way of salvation,[43] they sent them away. So is it with these. Even though they pronounce something that is true, they are expelled by the holy catholic Church of God.

However, like dogs who return to their own vomit,[44] and like swine who bathe themselves by wallowing in mire, they again grumble the following:

GREGORY THE BISHOP read:
*If anyone endeavours to reinstate the effigies of the saints in inanimate and speechless icons made of material colours, which bring no benefit – for the idea [of the icon] is vain and an invention of diabolic cunning   345D
– and does not rather reproduce in himself their virtues through what has been written about them in books, like animate icons, consequently to incite in himself the zeal to become like them, as our Fathers inspired by God have said, let him be anathema.*

EPIPHANIUS THE DEACON read:
Our divine Fathers have neither taught nor proclaimed anything of this sort. Rather, it is these falsifiers who have appropriated   345E

---

41 Greek *parhresia*. The word means, literally, outspokenness, frankness, and freedom of speech. In this use it implies the uninhibited condition in which the Theotokos and the saints are able to be in the act of 'conversing' with Christ. The intercession of Mary and the saints does not stand between the direct communication which exists between every man and God. For the believer entreating the intercession of Mary and of men of holiness is rather a manifestation of the 'communion of saints' and an act of striving after holiness.
42 Cf Mark 5:7.
43 Cf Acts 16:17.
44 Cf 2 Peter 2:22.

their name for themselves. This frivolous talk is their own, for in what comes next they call themselves the Seventh Council.[45] However, a certain wise man has said: *Let thy neighbour, and not thine own mouth, praise thee; a stranger, and not thine own lips.*[46] Although they were neither taught nor praised by anyone, they procure praise for themselves, and they want to be called by men 'rabbis,'[47] assuming themselves to be Fathers of the catholic Church. Yet they falsely accuse her of abandoning Christ our God and of becoming attached to idolatry, even though He Him- 348A self said to her through Isaiah the prophet, *I will make thee a perpetual gladness, a joy of many generations;*[48] and through Ecclesiastes, *Thou art all fair, my companion, all fair; there is no spot in thee.*[49]

Let us consider, therefore, the foolishness of their boasting to be the teachers of those whom they accuse of idolatry. If they are Fathers of idolaters, let them answer to this: are they teachers of a part of the Church which has fallen to idolatry, or of the whole Church? If they are Fathers of a part of the Church, they ought to have looked upon the catholic Church in her entirety, been justified by her, and collected the fruits of truth from her. This is how our Fathers used to rectify what happened to be 348B wrong and bring together what was broken. But while the catholic Church enjoys this tradition, they, having broken away from her, have thought to reprove her in her entirety as being wrong. To speak [against them] is terrible, but even to remain silent is condemnable. For, according to them, the right confession of Christ has gone, and everything else has been utterly destroyed. But let us have no share in such words and dismiss them as if they have never been spoken, or as having been spoken superficially.

Either way, therefore, they will be rejected, because the painting of venerable icons is something that has been handed down to the catholic Church from earliest times, it has been reproduced inside her venerable churches, and it is the holy Fathers who have taught and accepted it, as did the entire com- 348C

---

45 Below, 349E.
46 Prov. 27:2.
47 Cf Matt. 23:7.
48 Is. 60:15.
49 Cf Song 4:7.

munity of Christians. However, they not only departed from all these, but – worst, most awful, of all – their cry of anathema has spread about like something from Sodom and Gomorrah. Consequently their sin is great indeed. Who will be able to bear the utmost fury of this madness and the ugliness of these satirical noises? Would they had known the truth! For, it is perfectly clear to everyone who wants to think in piety that, as by reading in books narratives about saints we are reminded of their zeal, so it is with inconographic representations. Looking at their sufferings, we come to remember their bravery and their life in- 348D spired by God.

Afterwards, expressing once more a right opinion, they say the following:

GREGORY THE BISHOP read:
If anyone does not confess that all the saints – those from the beginning to the present time, those from before the Law, and those who lived during the Law, as well as those who by grace have been pleasing to God – 348E *are honourable in his sight in soul and in body, and if he does not entreat their prayers as having audience,*[50] *according to the tradition of the Church, to intercede for the sake of the world, let him be anathema.*

EPIPHANIUS THE DEACON read:
As soon as they said 'tradition of the Church,' they ought also to have declared: 'If anyone does not accept iconographic representations, let him be anathema.' For this is, indeed, an early tradition of the catholic Church, well known to us for the purpose of bringing to mind the prototypes. However, having refused to be initiated into this tradition, out of shamelessness and to 349A their own destruction, they even say to the catholic Church: 'We do not want to know your ways.' Thus they have also rejected the presentation of supplications welcomed by God, which they have belittled[51] with this very treatise of theirs; and this is something that everybody knows. It is customary for heretics, when they see piety standing high and they are deviating from the way of truth, to fall into many different errors. For truth is all of one kind, while falsehood is complex. Thus the Arians,

50 Cf above, 345B, n 41.
51 Literally, they have made them smooth, or flat.

in addition to their irreverent blasphemy that God the Word   349B
was a creature, said idly that He became a man without a soul.
Eutyches also, the unfortunate one,[52] by holding that there was
one nature in the dispensation of the Lord, blasphemed, saying
that He assumed a flesh which was a more divine-like one, and
not one which was of the same substance with our nature.
Similarly, therefore, the leaders of this present heresy, having
envied those heretics and having not been contented in one
novelty – having no satiety for wickedness – have pronounced
another heresy related to this last one.

Then, hypocritically, pretending to be pious, they make pronouncements which are consistent with the Fathers, thinking
of themselves as equal to them:

GREGORY THE BISHOP read: 349C
*If anyone does not acknowledge the resurrection of the dead, the judgment,
and the retribution of each one's worth according to the just measures
of God, and if he does not confess that there is no end either to the
punishment or to the heavenly Kingdom, which is the constant delight
in God – for, according to the divine Apostle,* the kingdom of heaven
is not food and drink, but righteousness and peace and joy in
the Holy Spirit[53] – *let him be anathema.*

EPIPHANIUS THE DEACON read: 349D
This is an aphorism by the leaders of our true faith, that is, of
the holy Apostles and of the divine Fathers. This is a confession
of the catholic Church, and not of those who indulge in heresy.

However, the following is characteristically theirs, as it is full
of ignorance and of an undisciplined disposition, as they buzz:

GREGORY THE BISHOP read:
If anyone does not accept our present holy and Ecumenical Seventh Council,   349E
*but defames it in any way, and does not adopt with certainty what has
been defined by it, which according to the teaching of the Scripture is
inspired by God, let him be anathema by the Father and the Son and
the Holy Spirit, as well as by the holy Seven Ecumenical Councils.*

52 Cf above, 236C, n 37.
53 Cf Rom. 14:17.

EPIPHANIUS THE DEACON read:

Falling away from truth is a blindness of the mind and of sense 352A
as well. This pronouncement of theirs, in addition to construing
impiety, is full of ignorance and insanity. They are wise, but only
in what constitutes ignorance. For while they call themselves
'the Seventh Council,' they apply their anathema as if it were
from seven other councils, saying: 'let him be anathema by the
holy and Ecumenical Seven Councils.' They are ridiculed for
ignorance as much as they are lamented for impiety. For, having
abandoned the truth and deviated from the well-paved and royal
way, they have led themselves to ditches, ravines, and cliffs; for
whom the word of Proverbs says: *They have caused the axles of*
their own husbandry to go astray: ... and they gather barreness with 352B
their hands.[54]

For this reason those who love truth and seek righteousness
will thrust the pointed arrows and the stretched bows into the
hearts of those who have launched them against the Church.
These same ones, assuming to themselves David, who sings under
the inspiration of the Spirit, say: The authors of this new
wickedness *have opened a pit, and dug it up, and they have fallen*
into the ditch which they have made. Their trouble has returned on their
own head, and their unrighteousness shall come down on their own crown;[55]
for they call the bitter sweet, and the sweet bitter. They, furthermore, make the light darkness, and the darkness light, saying:

GREGORY THE BISHOP read: 352C

Having, therefore, declared these things with all precision and diligence,
we DECREE that no other faith should be professed, that is, no one should
write about, or compose, or believe, or teach otherwise. If anyone attempts
to state, or to introduce, or to teach, or to promulgate a different confession
to those who wish to return to the knowledge of truth from whichever
heresy or innovation, that is, if any one attempts to introduce an inverted 352D
teaching for the purpose of reversing what has been defined by us, if
they are bishops or clergymen, let the bishops be deposed from the episcopate
and the clerics from the clergy; and if monks or laymen, let them be
anathematized.

54 Cf Prov. 9:12.
55 Cf Ps. 7:15–16.

EPIPHANIUS THE DEACON read:

Having been fed[56] in ignorance, they have stolen these words from our divine Fathers, and they have uttered them as if they were their own. Thus, their word is vain and inefficient, unworthy of an answer.

GREGORY THE BISHOP read: 352E

The most divine kings, Constantine and Leo, said: 'Let the holy and Ecumenical Council say whether the Definition just read has been pronounced with the consent of all the most venerable bishops.' The holy council exclaimed: 'This is what we all believe. We all have the same opinion. We all have signed after we have reached consensus and are satisfied [with it]. We all believe in the orthodox way. When we worship 353A *God who is spirit, we all offer our veneration in spirit. This is the faith of the Apostles; this is the faith of the Fathers; this is the faith of the orthodox. This is how all of them offered their veneration when they worshipped God. Long live the kings! Grant them, O Lord, a life of piety. May the memory of Leo and Constantine be eternal! You are the peace of the world. May your faith protect you. You honour Christ and He will protect you. You have confirmed the orthodox faith. Grant them, O Lord, a life of piety. Let envy be away from their reign. May God protect your sovereignty. May God pacify your reign. Your life is the* 353B *life of the orthodox. O Heavenly King, protect the ones [kings] on earth. It is through you that the Church in the entire world has been pacified. You are the splendour of orthodoxy. O Lord, protect those who are the splendour of the world. May the memory of Constantine and Leo be eternal. Long live the new Constantine, the most pious king! O Lord, protect him, who is of orthodox descent. Grant him, O Lord, a life of piety. Let envy be away from his reign. Long live the most pious Queen. May God protect her, who is pious and orthodox. Let envy be away from your reign. May God protect your sovereignty. May God pacify your reign. You have distinguished the unconfused nature of the dispensation of Christ. You have proclaimed the undivided character of the two natures of Christ more firmly. You have confirmed the doctrines of the Six Holy and Ecumenical Councils. You have abolished every idolatry. You have triumphed over the teachers of this error. You have reprobated those of contrary opinion.'*

56 Literally, grazed.

EPIPHANIUS THE DEACON read:

Having addressed the kings as is the custom, and having been burnt in their heart by the frenzy of falsehood, they speak out 353D with the cunning of the devil himself, saying: 'You have abolished every idolatry.' Would that our ears had been deaf to these words which are corruptive of the soul; for the word of Proverbs says, *give no heed to a prostitute.*[57] In their desire to ruin the redemptive word of the dispensation they have delved into every exaggeration of blasphemy. What can be said about this lamentable rage, except what has been said by the holy Spirit through David the divine one? *The poison of an asp is under their lips; their throat is an open sepulchre; and with their tongues they use deceit.*[58]

Thus, being condemned by Christ our God, Who has delivered 353E us from the error of idols, they have failed in their deliberations. For it is He Who, by having consented to become a perfect man for the sake of our salvation, has abolished every idolatry; for He said through the prophet: Behold, there will come days *that I will utterly destroy the names of the idols from off the land, and there shall be no longer any remembrance of them.*[59] It is obvious that the prophecy refers to Him and not, as they have said, to the power of kings. It is characteristic of apostasy to ascribe this grace and gift to other beings. However, the Christians, having taken it from Isaiah the most outspoken one, say loudly: *Not an ambassador,* 356A *nor a messenger, but the Lord himself saved us.*[60]

However, if, as they say, it was the council of bishops and presbyters and the power of kings which delivered us from the error of the idols, then the human race has been deceived about the truth, since one person has saved it but someone else is boasting that he did. For, while it was Christ our God Who delivered us from the error and the deception of the idols, they boast that they are the ones who have accomplished the redemption. What an arrogance and madness! Having departed from the truth, they have become blind in both thinking and intellect. Also, having immersed themselves completely in their own conjectures and fantasies, they have been wandering about in

57 Cf Prov. 5:3. The Septuagint version has 'to a worthless woman.'
58 Cf Ps. 13(14):3.
59 Cf Zech. 13:2.
60 Cf Is. 63:9.

flattery. Having disregarded the praise which is fitting to and   356B
proper for kings, they have addressed the kings with what,
instead, refers to Christ our God. They ought rather to have
praised the braveries of them, their victories over the enemies,
the defeat of the barbarians – which many of them have depicted
on icons and on wall paintings for the purpose of remembering
the narrative, this way urging the spectators to exert themselves
in desire and zeal – their keeping safe their subjects, their council
meetings, their trophies of victories, their social gatherings, the
civil ordinations, and the reconstruction of cities. These are deeds
which for a king are worthy of praise, deeds which invite every
citizen to be of good will.

However, with tongues still pointed, and breathing anger and   356C
slander, they think that, being themselves in darkness, they will
shoot dead those of a straight heart, by saying the following:

GREGORY THE BISHOP read:
You have dissolved the opinions of Germanus, George, and Mansur,[61]
those of ill faith.

To Germanus, the double-minded and worshipper of wood, anathema.

To George, who is of the same opinion as he, and a falsifier of the
teaching of the Fathers, anathema.

To Mansur, the one with a vile-sounding name and of Saracen opin-   356D
ions, anathema.

To the worshipper of icons and writer of falsities, Mansur, anathema.

To the insulter of Christ and conspirator against the Kingdom, Mansur,
anathema.

61 Germanus I, Patriarch of Constantinople (715–730), George, Patriarch of Constantia of
Cyprus, and John of Damascus were among the leading theologians of icons before
the iconoclastic Council of 754. Noticeable here are the vehemence and the specificity
of the anathemas promulgated against John of Damascus. He is referred to by his
Arabic name rather than by the ecclesiastical one by which he was known and under
which he wrote; a name which, according to Theophanes, Emperor Constantine V
(741–775), the main opponent of the Damascene, perverted to Manzer (*sic* Mamzer),
meaning in Hebrew 'bastard.' In the same spirit John of Damascus is cursed for
having Saracen opinions and being a conspirator against the Byzantine state. These
accusations refer rather to John of Damascus' Arab descent and to the fact that his
predecessors and he himself had held official positions in the Umayyad
administration after the fall of Damascus to the Muslims (635). On John of Damascus'
background and his relation to Islam see Sahas, *John of Damascus on Islam, the 'heresy of*
the Ishmaelites.'

To the teacher of impiety and misinterpreter of the Holy Scripture, Mansur, anathema.
The Trinity has deposed all three.

EPIPHANIUS THE DEACON read:
In response to these, let us recite the saying of the prophet: *Thou hadst a whore's face, thou didst become shameless toward all.*[62] Whores, taking pride in their own disgrace and in their shameful works, are used to mocking those who have lived a decent life, for godliness is an abomination to sinners. So it is with them. Having deceitful lips, *they spoke iniquity against the righteous ones with pride and scorn.*[63] However, *the Lord hid them in the secret of His presence. He covered them from the vexation of them; and He delivered them from the contradiction of their tongues;*[64] for they shone in the world like stars, having had a word of life.

356E

Thus Germanus was nursed in the holy writings and, like Samuel, was dedicated to God since infancy. He is comparable to the divine Fathers, so that one ought to follow his discourses. The writings of this Germanus are celebrated in the entire world; for *the high praises of God are in his throat and two-edged swords in his hands,*[65] drawn against those who disobey the tradition of the Church.

357A

George, a native of Cyprus, having lived a life according to the gospel and having imitated Christ our God, Who gave us his dispensation as an example, did not quarrel, nor did he ever shout. *When he was reviled, he did not revile in return; when he suffered, he did not threaten;*[66] to him who struck him on his cheek, he offered the other also;[67] with him who forced him to go one mile, he went two.[68] *He bore the yoke in his youth,* considering that it is good, according to the prophet, *to sit alone, and be silent.*[69]

357B

John, insultingly called by them 'Mansur,' abandoned everything and, emulating Matthew the evangelist, followed Christ,

62 Jer. 3:3.
63 Cf Ps. 30(31):18.
64 Cf Ps. 30(31):20.
65 Cf Ps. 149:6.
66 1 Peter 2:23.
67 Cf Luke 6:29.
68 Cf Matt. 5:41.
69 Cf Lament. 3:27–28.

because *he considered abuse suffered for Christ greater wealth than the treasures of Arabia*.[70] He also *chose to share ill-treatment with the people of God than to enjoy the fleeting pleasures of sin*.[71] Thus, after he took up his own cross as well as that of Christ, and followed Him, he sounded his trumpet from the East in favour of Christ and 357C of those who are Christ's;[72] for he could not bear the novelty which had been fostered in a foreign land, the unlawful machinations and the raging madness against the holy catholic Church of God. And when he had triumphed over this novelty, he ensured by means of exortations and admonitions that no one would be carried along with those who work lawlessness. In so doing he sought to have that ancient practice and the state of peace prevail in the churches; that peace which the Lord, saying *My peace I give to you; my peace I leave with you*,[73] granted to his disciples so that they would be distinguished as those who are called after his name.

What, then, is this rousing and moreover horrible and even 357D unbearable accusation against these venerable men, worthy of the faith, who have been so much distinguished in the catholic Church? Indeed, these miserable ones were utterly ignorant when, with tongues stripped entirely of all grace, they called Germanus, the celebrant of the mystical sacrifice and the priest of God,[74] 'double-minded' and a 'worshipper of wood.' So did they call George and Mansur. Never has anyone inflicted such a blasphemy against his fellow-believers. Such accusations have rather been made in many ways against the Christians by Jews, Hagarenes, and other infidels, referring to the holy form of the cross, to venerable icons, and to sacred objects dedicated to God. 357E Never did, however, a Christian level such a charge at someone else of the same faith. Now, just as it is a hindrance to look

---

70 Cf Heb. 11:26.
71 Heb. 11:25. The reference here is to the luxurious life and prestige of John of Damascus while he was living in the court of the Caliph. The passage alludes also to the growing jealousy and the anti-Christian sentiment on the part of potential Muslim officials, which led eventually to the expulsion of all Christians, including John of Damascus, from public office, and to their replacement by Muslims.
72 The allusion here is to the ardent defence of the icons by John of Damascus, from the monastery of St Sabbas in Palestine.
73 John 14:27.
74 Cf also above, 300A, n 19.

at the sun, so the righteous person is a hindrance to the unjust. Thus, having fled from the truth and driven themselves out of the practice of the Church, they have given themselves up to false accusations and to insults. They accomplish nothing more, other than accusing Christians and the priests of God of having abandoned the living and true God and worshipping icons; thus, they have become men who throw words around, slanderers, babbling without discretion and speaking evil. Who of those who fear the Lord and who laugh at them will not burst into a great 360A laughter; or rather, will not lament bitterly and be overtaken by a sense of deep darkness at this impiety of theirs?

They, as *inventors of evil*,[75] according to the divine Apostle, have been left to scrutinize scrutinies and to claim that they are strengthened by their own babbling. However, we, through the grace of God having put together sufficient arguments for a complete refutation of the vain syllogisms of their false knowledge, and having treated this error of their empty[76] wickedness as one of the old heresies, have cut it off with the sword of the Spirit.

Let us now instruct the minds of those who listen. Indeed, everything is *evident to those that understand, and right to those that* 360B *find knowledge*,[77] as seems good to the author of the Proverbs, and to truth.

Thus, the holy catholic Church of God, using many different means, attracts those who are born within her to repentance and to the knowledge of how to keep the commandments of God. She hastens to guide all our senses to the glory of the God of all, as she works out a rectification through both hearing and sight, by displaying to the gaze of those who come forward what has taken place. Thus, when she takes someone away from greediness and avarice, she presents him with an icon of Matthew, who from a tax collector became an Apostle, abandoning the madness of avarice and following Christ;[78] or of Zacchaeus climb- 360C ing a sycamore because he wanted to see Christ, and making a commitment to Him to give half of his goods to the poor and,

75 Rom. 1:30.
76 Or 'new,' according to another reading.
77 Prov. 8:9.
78 Cf Matt. 9:9–13.

if he had defrauded anyone of anything, to return four times as much.[79] In this way, the continuous looking at pictorial drawings serves to preserve one's conversion and keeps one constantly mindful of it, so that one may not return to one's own vomit. Again, she catches someone else who is suffering from a passion to commit adultery and she brings before him the icon of chaste Joseph who, having despised adultery and having won over it through chastity,[80] preserved the image which is after the image of God, in which share only those who love chastity. Again, for someone else she holds up blessed Susanna, 360D decorated with chastity and extending her arms as she invokes help from heaven, with Daniel presiding like a judge, delivering her from the hands of the lawless elders.[81] Thus, the remembrance of the pictorial drawing becomes instrumental in preserving the life of chastity. She catches the one who has spent his life in luxury and who is dressed in soft clothes, spending what he ought to be giving to the poor for such clothing, and him who has embraced the well-bred life. She shows him Elijah, dressed in sheepskin and satisfied with only whatever food is necessary; or John, dressed in a garment of camel's hair, being fed with locusts and wild honey,[82] pointing with his finger towards Christ and prefiguring Him as the One Who is to take away the sin 360E of the world.[83] In addition to these, she shows Basil the Great, and a crowd of ascetics and monks with emaciated bodies. And so that we may not prolong the speech, we have mentioned only a few cases, leaving the rest for the listeners to search out.

Thus we have the entire story of the gospel depicted in icons, leading us to the remembrance of God and filling us with joy. When these [icons] are before our eyes, the hearts of those who fear the Lord rejoice; faces bloom; the disheartened soul turns cheerful, singing along with David, the forefather of Him Who 361A is God: *I remembered God and rejoiced.*[84] Therefore, through the icons we are continually reminded of God. For sometimes there is no

79 Cf Luke 19:1–8.
80 Cf Gen. 39:6–20.
81 Cf Susanna (Daniel 13).
82 Cf Matt. 3:4.
83 Cf John 1:29.
84 Ps. 76(77):3.

reading chanted in the venerable churches,[85] while the reproductions of icons, being established in them, tell us either at
daybreak or at noon the story, as they also proclaim to us the
truth of the things which have been accomplished.

Therefore, let us accept the tradition of the Church. Let us
honour its practice. Let us not scrutinize a practice which is pious
and lawful. Let us not become too meddlesome with ancient
statutes. For everything that is instituted for the purpose of
bringing God to mind is acceptable to Him. However, those who   361B
are outside this tradition – in which all those who have been
authentically adopted as sons within the catholic Church have
a share – are illegitimate children, not sons. Therefore, let us
accept the dedication of venerable icons in the Church as
something good and proper, knowing that through them one
is led spiritually to the remembrance of the prototypes, that one
kisses and embraces them because they are precious, and that
one offers a veneration which is due to them. One kisses something out of love or veneration. Both are the same, although
some understand veneration to be worship – which is something
else, as has been shown in many ways. But let him who comes   361C
forward be worthy to offer the veneration. If he is not worthy,
let him first cleanse himself and then proceed to the venerable
iconographic representation. Let there be no Satanic objection
about the veneration of icons, nor any hesitation with the wicked
excuse that if one proceeds to the icon and kisses it one has
offered to it the worship which is in spirit. Far from it. These
are things which those who fight against God and imitate the
serpent take pains to bring up. It was the serpent who, after
he approached the woman, whispered lies to her: *Wherefore God
said, of every tree which is in the garden thou mayest freely eat, but
of the tree which is in the middle of the garden ye shall not eat.*[86] In   361D
the same way they deceive effeminate hearts, saying that he
who bows to the icon of the Lord or of our immaculate Lady,
who is truly Theotokos, or of the holy angels, or of any of the
saints, offers to the icon worship which is to be in spirit.

Therefore, let us not be deceived by their word; this is an

85 The entire liturgy, and every other service in the Orthodox Church, is chanted,
    including the readings from the New Testament.
86 Cf Gen. 3:2; 2:16–17.

admonition of the devil. Gregory the Theologian refutes this myth, urging us all: 'Honour Bethlehem, and bow to the manger.'[87] With him the ever-memorable Maximus, who is praised by all churches, who once when discussing matters of the Church with some men, to confirm what they had said, ordered that the divine form of the precious cross, the holy gospel, and a venerable icon be brought into their midst. Then he, together with them, kissed them. He also who is named after immortality,[88] in his letter to Marcellinus which he put as a preface to the book on the interpretation of the Psalms, speaks to us emphatically, saying the following: 'When one takes up the book of Psalms, he goes through the prophesies about the Saviour, which one usually admires and venerates in the other Scriptures.'[89] Do you see? The divine Father urges us to venerate the prophesies about the Saviour. If it is pious to venerate them, how much more is it necessary for us to venerate what is the fulfilment of the prophetic reflection which we see on an icon? Thus, the prophecy says: *Behold, a virgin shall conceive in the womb, and shall bring forth a son.*[90] Therefore, when we see this prophecy on an icon, that is, the Virgin holding in her arms Him to Whom she gave birth, how can we bear not to bow and kiss it? Who is so uninstructed in his thinking that he would not attempt to offer such an embrace?

361E

364A

Therefore, let us make ourselves worthy to offer the veneration, so that we may not, by proceeding unworthily, suffer the punishment of Uzzah. When he touched the ark, he died instantly because he had approached it without being worthy.[91] Incidentally, that ark was decorated with a variety of figures, and was made of wood, as are the icons. As to those who say that it is sufficient to have the reproduction of icons as a means of remembering, without kissing them – thus accepting the one and rejecting the other – they seem to be half-wicked and falsely truthful, confessing the truth in one thing while being wicked in the other. What insanity!

364B

---

87 Cf also above, 309D.
88 That is, Athanasius (= the immortal one).
89 Cf Athanasius of Alexandria, *To Marcellinus on the Interpretation of the Psalms*, PG 27:12–45.
90 Is. 7:14.
91 Cf 2 Kings 6:6–7.

Now let us become advocates of those who once cursed orthodoxy and the truth. Let us plead for the forgiveness of their sin of violating the traditions of the Church. Above all, let us preserve the commandments, through what has been ordained   364C
to us. Let us move on, with our ear turned to the word of the prophet, which says: *Has it not been told thee, O man, what is good? or what does the Lord require of thee, but to do justice, and love mercy, and be ready to walk with the Lord thy God?*[92] Let us also calm our anger; bridle the tongue to avoid falsehood, indecent words, and insult; discipline the eye; moderate the stomach; devote ourselves to chanting and prayer. Let us give thanks to God for everything that He has granted to us. Let us not use our mouth to swear,   364D
but rather listen to the word of the Lord, which says, *but I say unto you, Do not swear at all.*[93] Let us tread under the foot the glory which stays here on earth. Let us invite what is for us the greatest of all goods, that is, mercy and love conjoined with the fear of God; for, without the fear of God, love is untested. It was Jehosh'aphat who was making friends with Ahab when he heard: *Dost thou act friendly towards a sinner, or help one hated of the Lord?*[94] Let us from now on do everything with the fear of God, beseeching the intercessory prayers of our immaculate Lady Mary, who is by nature Theotokos and ever-virgin, of the holy angels and of all the saints, embracing also their venerable relics, so that we may share in their sanctity. *In this way we may be equipped with every good work*[95] in Jesus Christ our Lord; to Whom belongs glory, power, and worship, along with the Father and the Holy Spirit, now and for ever, and unto the ages of ages.   364E
Amen.

---

92 Mic. 6:8.
93 Matt. 5:34.
94 Cf 2 Chron. 19:2.
95 Cf Heb. 13:21.

Definition of the Holy Great and Ecumenical Council, the Second in Nicea

The holy, great, and Ecumenical Council – convened by the grace of God and by the sanction of our pious kings, those lovers of Christ, Constantine and his mother Irene, for a second time in the magnificent capital of the Nicaeans of the province of the Bithynians, and in the holy church of God which is named after Wisdom – having followed the tradition of the catholic Church, has DEFINED the following:

Christ our God, Who granted to us the light of His knowledge and Who delivered us from the darkness of the insanity of the idols, after He betrothed His holy catholic Church, which is *without spot or wrinkle*,[1] commanded that she may be so preserved. He also gave assurances to his holy disciples, saying: *I am with you* *always, to the close of the age.*[2] He gave this commandment not only to his disciples but also to us who through them have believed in his name.

However, some men, paying no regard to this gift, and encouraged by the deceitful enemy, deviated from right thinking and, after opposing the tradition of the catholic Church, erred in the perception of truth. As the word of the Proverbs says, *they caused the axles of their own husbandry to go astray and ... they gathered barreness with their hands;*[3] for even though they are called priests – without being so – they dared to discredit the decency which dedicated items have, [a decency] proper to God. It is

1 Eph. 5:27.
2 Matt. 28:20.
3 Cf Prov. 9:12.

for them that God cries out through the words of the prophecy: *Many shepherds have destroyed my vineyard and they defiled my portion.*[4] For, having followed men of impiety who put faith in their own minds, they have accused the holy Church, which has been joined to Christ the God, and they have made no distinction between the holy and the profane, calling the icon of the Lord and those of his saints with the same name as the wooden symbols of the idols of Satan.

For this reason God the sovereign One, not bearing to see his people destroyed by such a pestilence, through his good will brought us, the leaders of the priesthood, together from all parts, 376C through the divine zeal and inspiration of Constantine and Irene, our most faithful Kings, so that the divine tradition of the catholic Church may regain its authority by a common vote. Having, therefore, sought most diligently and conferred with each other, and having set as our goal the truth, we neither delete nor add anything, but preserve undiminished everything that is of the catholic Church. Adhering also to the six holy Ecumenical Councils, first that which convened in the magnificent capital of the Nicaeans, and also that which convened after this in the Royal City guarded by God,

WE BELIEVE in one God, Father almighty, maker of heaven and earth and of all things, visible and invisible.

And in one Lord Jesus Christ, the only-begotten Son of God, begotten 376D of the Father before all ages; light of light, true God from a true God, begotten not made, being of one substance with the Father, through Whom all things were made; Who for us men and our salvation came down from heaven and was incarnated by the holy Spirit and the virgin Mary and became man: He was crucified for us under Pontius Pilate; He suffered and was buried, and He rose on the third day according to the Scriptures; and He ascended into heaven, where He sits on the right hand of the Father; and He shall come again with glory to judge the living and the dead, whose Kingdom shall have no end. 376E

And in the holy Spirit, the Lord, the Giver of life,[5] who proceeds

---

4 Jer. 12:10.
5 The syntax of the Greek original suggests a slightly different translation of this article: 'And in the Spirit, Who is holy, sovereign, and life-giving.'

from the Father, who together with the Father and the Son is worshipped and glorified; who spoke through the prophets.

And in one, holy, catholic and apostolic Church.

I acknowledge one baptism for the remission of sins;

I look for the resurrection of the dead, and the life of the age to come. Amen.

However, we despise and anathematize Arius and those of the same opinion with him who share in his insane misbelief; as well as Macedonius and his adherents, who have rightly been 377A called 'Offenders of the Spirit.'[6] We acknowledge our Lady, the holy Mary, to be properly and truly Theotokos, for having given birth, as far as the flesh is concerned, to Christ our God Who is one of the holy Trinity, as it has been taught before by the Council in Ephesus, which expelled from the Church Nestorius, the impious one, and his adherents for introducing a duality of persons. In addition to these we acknowledge the two natures of Him Who for us became incarnate from the immaculate Theotokos and ever-virgin Mary, knowing Him to be perfect God and perfect man, as the Council in Chalcedon declared, which expelled from the holy court Eutyches and Dioscorus, who had 377B taught blasphemies. With them we subject [to anathema] Severus, Peter, and those in the same line who are interwoven with them, who have repeatedly pronounced blasphemies. Along with them we anathematize the myths of Origen, Evagrius, and Didymus, as the Fifth Council did, which convened in Constantinople. Afterwards we, too, proclaim the two wills and energies in Christ, according to the quality of each nature, just as the Sixth Council in Constantinople pronounced, when it renounced Sergius, Honorius, Cyrus, Pyrrus, and Macarius, who did not like piety, as well as the ones of the same mind with them.

In summary, we preserve all the traditions of the Church, which for our sake have been decreed in written or unwritten form, 377C without introducing an innovation. One of these traditions is the making of iconographic representations – being in accordance with the narrative of the proclamation of the gospel – for the purpose of ascertaining the incarnation of God the Word, which was real, not imaginary, and for being of an equal benefit to

6 Pneumatomāchians; cf also above, 233C, n 34.

us as the gospel narrative. For those which point mutually to each other undoubtedly mutually signify each other.

Be this as it may, and continuing along the royal pathway, following both the teaching of our holy Fathers which is inspired by God and the tradition of the catholic Church – for we know that this tradition is of the holy Spirit dwelling in her – in absolute   377D
precision and harmony with the spirit, WE DECLARE that, next to the sign of the precious and life-giving cross, venerable and holy icons – made of colours, pebbles, or any other material that is fit – may be set in the holy churches of God, on holy utensils and vestments, on walls and boards, in houses and in streets. These may be icons of our Lord and God the Saviour Jesus Christ, or of our pure Lady the holy Theotokos, or of honourable angels, or of any saint or holy man. For the more these are kept in view through their iconographic representation, the more those who look at them are lifted up to remember and have an earnest desire for the prototypes. Also [we declare] that one may render to them the veneration of honour: not the true worship of our   377E
faith, which is due only to the divine nature, but the same kind of veneration as is offered to the form of the precious and life-giving cross, to the holy gospels, and to the other holy dedicated items. Also [we declare] that one may honour these by bringing to them incense and light, as was the pious custom of the early [Christians]; for 'the honour to the icon is conveyed to the prototype.'[7] Thus, he who venerates the icon venerates the hypostasis of the person depicted on it. In this way the teaching of our holy Fathers – that is, the tradition of the catholic Church,   380A
which has accepted the gospel from one end of the earth to the other – is strengthened. Thus, we faithfully follow Paul, who spoke in Christ, as well as the entire divine assembly of the Apostles and holy Fathers, *holding the traditions which we have received*.[8] Using the words of the prophet we repeat loudly to the Church the hymns of victory: *Rejoice, O daughter of Zion: cry aloud, O daughter of Jerusalem; rejoice and delight thyself with all thine heart. The Lord has taken away from thee the iniquities of thine opponents, he has ransomed thee from the land of thine enemies: the Lord, the King*

7 Basil of Caesarea, *On the Holy Spirit*, PG 32:149C.
8 Cf 2 Thes. 2:15, 3:6.

is in the midst of thee: thou shalt not see evil any more, and peace will be unto thee for ever.[9]

Hence those who take the liberty of thinking or teaching otherwise, or – like the accursed heretics – of violating the traditions of the Church and inventing some sort of novelty, or of rejecting some of the things which have been dedicated to the Church – that is the gospel, or the form of the cross, or an iconographic representation, or a holy relic of a martyr – or of contriving crookedly and cunningly to upset any of the legitimate traditions of the catholic Church, or of using the holy treasures or the venerable monasteries as a common place, if they are bishops or clergymen, WE DIRECT that they be unfrocked; if monks or laymen of the society, that they be excommunicated. 380B

I, Peter, unworthy protopresbyter of the throne of the holy Apostle Peter, being in the place of Pope Hadrian of the senior Rome and having so defined, have signed. 380C

I, Peter, unworthy presbyter and abbot [of the monastery] of our holy Father Sabbas, being in the place of Pope Hadrian of the senior Rome and having so defined, have signed.

I, Tarasius, by the grace of God bishop of Constantinople, the new Rome, following the doctrines of the Fathers and the tradition of the catholic Church, having so defined, have signed.

I, John, by the grace of God presbyter and patriarchal secretary, attending for the three apostolic thrones of Alexandria, Antioch, and Jerusalem, following the doctrines of the Fathers and the tradition of the catholic Church, having so defined, have signed. 380D

I, Thomas, by the grace of God presbyter and abbot of the monastery of our holy Father Arsenius in Egypt, upper Babylon, attending for the three apostolic thrones of Alexandria, Antioch, and Jerusalem, following the doctrines of the Fathers and the tradition of the catholic Church, having so defined, have signed.

9 Cf Zeph. 3:14–15.

I, Agapius, unworthy bishop of Caesarea, following the doctrines of the 380E
Fathers and the tradition of the catholic Church, having so defined,
have signed.

I, John, unworthy bishop of Ephesus, following the doctrines of the
Fathers and the tradition of the catholic Church, having so defined,
have signed.

I, Constantine, by the grace of God bishop of the island of the Cypriots,
following the doctrines of the Fathers and the tradition of the catholic
Church, having so defined, have signed.

[The 301 participants who signed the Definition all made this
same declaration. The names of the subsequent signatories are
listed here in the order in which their declarations appeared at
the end of the Definition.]

Leo of Heraklea [Thrace]
Basil of Ankara
Nicholas of Kyzikos
Euthymius of Sardis
Peter of Nicomedia
Elias of Crete
Hypatius of Nicea
Staurakius of Chalcedon
Leo presbyter, in the place of the
    bishop of Sidites
Daniel of Amasea
Constantine of Gangra
Epiphanius deacon from Catanae
    [Sicily], in the place of Thomas
    of Sardinia
Nicephorus of Dyrrachion
Anastasius of Nicopolis
Nicetas of Claudiopolis
Gregory of Neocaesarea
Gregory of Pisinous
Theodore of Myra [Lycia]
Theophylactus deacon, represent-
ing the see of Stauropolis, that
is, Karia
Eustathius of Laodicea
Michael of Synadon
Leo of Ikonion
George of Antioch, Pisidia
Constans of Perga
George presbyter, representing
    the see of Mokisos
Christopher of Trapezous
Leo of Rhodes
Emmanuel of Hadrianopolis
Basil of Sylaion
Theodore of Seleucea
Nicholas of Hierapolis
Constans of Rhegion
Cyril monk, in the place of Nice-
    tas of Gothia
Stephen of Sougdaon
Theodore of Catanae
John of Tauromeneon
Galaton [or Plato?] presbyter, in

the place of Stephen of
Syracuse
Gaudiosus of Messina
Theodore of Panormon
Stephen of Bibonon
Constans of Leontina
Theodore of Taurus
Christopher of Saint Kyriake
Basil of Liparitae island
Theotimus of Croton
Constans of Karina
Theophanes of Lilyvaion
John of Treokaleos
Theodore of Tropaion
Sergius of Nicotera
Theophylactus of Euchaita
Maurianus of Pompeiopolis
Theodore of Bizia
Anthony monk, in the place of
the see of Smyrna
Eustathius of Apamea
Peter of Germia
John of Arcadiopolis
Sisinnius of Pariun
Epiphanius of Melitene
Nicetas of Proiconessos
Constans of Sebastiopolis
John presbyter, representing the
see of Colonia
Eustratius of Methymne
Leo of Kios
Gregory presbyter, representing
the see of Nicopolis
John of Asprou
Theophylactus of Kypselae
Theodore of Heracliopolis
Eustathius of Kotradon
Kyriakus of Drizyparon
Leo of Mesembria
Gregory of Derkon

John of Nysos
George of the Imperial Thermae
Soterichus of Kiskisson
George [or Gregory?] of
Kamoulianon
Damianus of Mitylene
Constans of Mastauron
George of Vrioulon
Theodosius of Nyssa
Theophylactus of Tralle
Olvianus of Elaia
Pardus of Pitane
Leo of Algizon
Theognis presbyter, representing
[the see of] Sion
Stratonicus of Cyme
Basil of Atrammyteion
Theophylactus of Hypepon
Theophanes of Caloe
Leo of Phocea
Basil of Pergamos
Gregory of Palaiopolis
John of Assos
Basil of Magnesia
Marinus of Atandrus
Licastus of Bareta
Constans, representative [of the
see] of Agae
Nicephorus, representative [of
the see] of Gargara
Nicodemus of Euazon
Savvas of Aneon
Nicephorus of Arcadiopiolis
Cosmas of Myrina
John of the Salountiane church
Ursus of the Avaritians church
Laurentius of the Apsartians
church
Eustathius of Solon
Spyridon of Cythra

Theodore of Kition
George of Trimithous
Alexander of Amathous
John of Nicea [Thrace]
John of Rhedesos
Melchisedek of Kalliopolis
Leonides of Koilon
John of Panion
Theophylactus of Charitopolis
John of Lithoprosopon
Sisinnius of Chalkis
Sisinnius of Tzouroulou
Benjamin of Lizicon
Constans presbyter, representing
    [the see of] Hexamilion
Constans of Metron
Gregory of Theodoropolis
Constans of Juliopolis
Theophilus of Anastasiopolis
Leo of Mizoua
Synesius of Kina
Peter of Aspone
Anthimus of Verinopolis
Lycastus of Philadelphia
Stephen of Silandon
Theophanes of Mionia
Michael of Kerasai
John of Setai
John of Dalde
John of Tavala
Theopistus of Hermocapelon
Nicholas of Aureliopolis
Anastasius of Tripolis
Zacharias of Hierocaesarea
Michael of Tralae
Gregory of Gordos
Leo of Tracoula
Eustathius of Hyrcanis
Joseph of Attaleia
Leontius of Poemaninos

Nectarius [or Nicetas?] of Ilaion
Basil of Adranoutherae
Symeon of Oca
Theodore of Germa
Theodotos of Palaion
Theodore of Abydos
Strategius of Dardanos
Michael of Melitopolis
Sisinnius of Adrania
Theophylactus of Apollonias
Constans of Caesarea Bithynia
George of Basilinopolis
Cyrion of Lophos
Leo of Arista
Nymphos of Hadrianou
Theodore of Prousa
Basil presbyter, representing [the
    see of] Dascylion
David of Helenopolis
Anastasius of Knossos
Sisinnius of Chersonesos
Epiphanius of Eleutherna
Meliton of Cydonia
Photinus of Kantanos
Leo of Phoenicion
John of Arcadia
Leo of Kissamos
Theodore of Subritae
Epiphanius of Lampe
John of Limbos
Gabriel of Aigina
Peter of Monemvasia
Anthony of Troezena
Leo of Porthmos
Philetos of Oreos
Nectarius of Meloa
Neophytus of Gordoservae
Gregory presbyter, representing
    [the see of] Cephalenia
Phillip of Kerkyra

Leo of Zacynthos
John of Gemon
Constans of Sasimon
Leo of Aspondos
Leo of Amisos
Hercalius of Junopolis
Theophanes of Soron
Nectarius [or Nicetas?] of
  Hadrianae
Constans of Crateia
Theophilus of Prousias
Michael of Tios
Theodore of Comanon
John of Kerasous
Constans of Polemonion
Nectarius [or Nicetas?] of Rizaion
Nicephorus of Claneon
Leontius of Trocnadon
Theodore of Pinnaron
George of Nissa
Stephen of Kamnos
Constans of Tlae
Constans of Kandibon
Leontios of Korydalon
Peter deacon, representing the
  see of Oricandos
Nicodemus of Sidyma
John deacon, representing [the
  see of] Phaselis
Stephen of Araxos
George of Hyniandos
Leo of Limyra
Stauracius of Zenopolis
Constans of Kombon
Gregory of Cibyra
Basil of Tabon
Dorotheus of Neapolis
Constans of Alabandon
Gregory of Heracleia
David of Iassos

Gregory of Mylassa
Sergius of Bragylion
John of Mindos
Stauracius of Stadeia
Gregory of Stratonicea
Nicetas presbyter, elected of
  Ceramos
Maurianus of Acmonea
Leo of Aleon
Zacharias of Trapezopolis
Leo of Eumenia
Philip of Tranopolis
Dositheus of Chonae
George of Pelton
George of Appia (Phrygia)
John of Souvlion
Pantoleon of Galatia
Michael of Chaerotopon
Gregory of Timenoutheron
George of Mindaeion
Nicetas of Nacoleia
Constans of Kattianeion
Leo of Docimion
Constans of Eucarpia
Michael of Hieropolis
Damianus of Kinavaron
Gregory presbyter, representing
  [the see of] Polybyton
Theophylactus presbyter, repres-
  enting the see of Hypsos
Nicholas of Phyteia
Stephen presbyter, representing
  the see of Ostros
Constans of Ambladon
Epiphanius of Pelta
Michael of Pappae
Sisinnius of Philomelion
John of Tymbriadae
Stephen of Orymnon
Nicephorus of Phoglon

Marinus of Magydae
Leo of Didon
Stephen of Parnassos
Theophilus of Chios
Sergius of Leros
Heraclius of Samos
Galation of Milos
Constans of Andros
Eustathius of Tinos
Kallistos of Eudociadae
Theodore of Kremnon
Constans of Lagnon
Constans of Andriane
John of Kodroulon
Eustratius of Develtou
Euthymius of Sozopolis
Theodore of Bulgarophygon
George of Ploutinopolis

Sisinnius of Gariela
Rubem of Scopelos
Basil of Perbereos
Michael of Pamphylos
Manzon of Pracanon
Eustathius of Celendereos
Sisinnius of Mousvadon
Eustathius of Lamos
Leo of Sibilon
Stephen of Philadelphia
Zacharias of Kardavounda
Stephen of Synaous
Constans of Ankara
Theodore of Kados
John of Azanous
Theophylactus of Mosynyon
John of Praenetou

APPENDIX

Appendix

The biblical, patristic, and other sources used by the Seventh Ecumenical Council in support of the icons are listed here in the way in which they were identified and in the order in which they were read, in excerpts, during the fourth and fifth sessions.

I / BIBLICAL TEXTS

Exodus 25:16–21
Numbers 7:88–89
Ezekiel 41:1, 16–20
Hebrews 9:1–5

II / PATRISTIC AND OTHER LITERATURE

1 John Chrysostom, excerpts from the 'Encomium to Meletius'
2 John Chrysostom, 'That the Law-giver of both, Old and New Testament, is one'
3 Gregory of Nyssa, 'On the divinity of the Son and of the Spirit, and on Abraham'
4 Cyril of Alexandria, 'Letters to Acacius, bishop of Skythopolis'
5 Gregory of Nazianzus, 'Epics'
6 Antipater of Bostra, 'Oration on the woman in haemorrhage'
7 Asterius of Amasea, 'On Euphemia the martyr'
8 'Martyrdom of Anastasius the Persian'
9 'Miracles of Anastasius the martyr'
10 Athanasius of Alexandria, 'On the miraculous icon of our Lord Jesus Christ'
11 Nilus, 'Letter to Heliodorus silentarius'
12 Nilus, 'Letter to Olympiodorus'

13 Maximus the Confessor, from the discussion between him and Theodosius of Caesarea of Bithynia

14 From the Canons of the Sixth Ecumenical Council

15 Leontius of Neapolis of Cyprus, from the Fifth Oration of the 'Apology on behalf of the Christians against the Jews'

16 Anastasius of Theopolis, 'Letter to a certain scholastic'

17 Anastasius of Theopolis, 'Discourse to Symeon, bishop of Bostra on the Sabbath'

18 Sophronius of Jerusalem, 'Encomium to Saints Cyrus and John'

19 Sophronius, 'Leimonarion'

20 'Miracles of Cosmas and Damian'

21 John Chrysostom, 'On the Washing of the Feet'

22 Athanasius of Alexandria, 'Fourth Oration against the Arians'

23 Basil of Caesarea, 'On the Holy Spirit'

24 Basil of Caesarea, 'Against the Sabellians, Arius and the Anhomians'

25 Basil of Caesarea, 'Letter to Julian the Apostate'

26 Theodoretus of Cyrus, 'Life of Symeon the Stylite'

27 'Life of Symeon the Stylite'

28 Basil of Caesarea, 'On Barlaam, the Blessed Martyr'

29 Photinus, 'Life of John, the Fasting One'

30 'Life of Saint Mary the Egyptian'

31 'Martyrdom of Saint Procopius'

32 'Life of our Holy Father Theodore, Archimandrite of Sekeans'

33 Gregory, Pope of Rome, 'Letter to Germanus, Patriarch of Constantinople'

34 Germanus of Constantinople, 'Letter to John of Synadon'

35 Germanus of Constantinople, 'Letter to Bishop Constantine of Nacoleia'

36 Germanus of Constantinople, 'Letter to Bishop Thomas of Claudiopolis'

37 Cyril of Jerusalem, 'Second catechesis'

38 Symeon the Stylite, 'Fifth Letter to Justin the Young'

39 John, bishop of Salonica, 'Oration'

40 'Disputation of a Jew and a Christian'

41 'Itineraries of the Holy Apostles'

42 Eusebius of Caesarea, 'To Euphration'

43 Antipater Bishop of Bostra, 'Refutation of Eusebius' apology in favour of Origen'

44 Theodore the Reader, 'Ecclesiastical History'

45 John Diacrenomenos, 'Ecclesiastical History'

46 'Life of St Sabbas'

47 'Petition to the Council of Constantinople against Severus and the Acephaloi by the monks of the Church of Antioch'

48 John, bishop of Gavala, 'On the Life of Severus the heresiarch'
49 Constantine the deacon, 'To all the holy martyrs'
50 Evagrius, 'Ecclesiastical History.' Fourth Discourse
51 'Leimonarion'

SELECT BIBLIOGRAPHY

BIBLICAL REFERENCES

PATRISTIC REFERENCES

INDEX

Select Bibliography

Ahmad, Aziz. *Islamic Modernism in India & Pakistan 1857-1964*. London, Oxford University Press, (1967), 1970

Ahrweiler, Hélène. 'The Geography of the Iconoclast World.' In *Iconoclasm*, Ninth Spring Symposium of Byzantine Studies. Birmingham, Centre for Byzantine Studies, University of Birmingham, 1977. Pp 21-27

Alexander, Paul J. 'An Ascetic Sect of Iconoclasts in Seventh Century Armenia.' In *Late Classical and Mediaeval Studies in Honour of Albert Mathias Friend, Jr.*, ed Kurt Weitzmann. Princeton, Princeton University Press, 1955. Pp 151-160

- 'The Iconoclastic Council of St. Sophia (815) and Its Definition (*Horos*).' *Dumbarton Oaks Papers* 7 (1953) 35-57

- *The Patriarch Nicephorus of Constantinople. Ecclesiastical Policy and Image Worship in the Byzantine Empire.* Oxford, Clarendon Press, 1958

Ali, Ameer. *The Spirit of Islam: A History of the Evolution and Ideals of Islam with a Life of the Prophet.* London, Christophers, (1961), 1967

Anastos, Milton V. 'The Argument for Iconoclasm as Presented by the Iconoclastic Council of 754.' In *Late Classical and Mediaeval Studies in Honour of Albert Mathias Friend, Jr.*, ed Kurt Weitzmann. Princeton, Princeton University Press, (1955). Pp 177-188

- 'The Ethical Theory of Images Formulated by the Iconoclasts in 754 & 815.' *Dumbarton Oaks Papers* 8 (1954) 153-160

- 'Iconoclasm and Imperial Rule 717-842.' In *The Cambridge Mediaeval History*. Cambridge, Cambridge University Press, 1966. IV, 61-104

- 'Leo III's Edict against the Images in the Year 726-27 and Italo-Byzantine Relations between 726 and 730.' *Byzantinische Forschungen* 3 (1968) 5-41

Bank, Alisa V. *Byzantine Art in the Collections of Soviet Museums.* New York, Abrams, 1978

Barnard, Leslie W. 'Byzantium and Islam. The Interaction of Two Worlds in the Iconoclastic Era.' *Byzantinoslavica* 36 (1975) 25-37
– 'The Emperor Cult and the Origins of the Iconoclastic Controversy.' *Byzantion* 43 (1973) 13-29.
– *The Graeco-Roman and Oriental Background of the Iconoclastic Controversy.* Leiden, Brill, 1974
– 'The Theology of Images.' In *Iconoclasm*, Ninth Spring Symposium of Byzantine Studies. Birmingham, Centre for Byzantine Studies, University of Birmingham, 1977. Pp 7-13
Baynes, Norman H. 'The Icons before Iconoclasm.' In his *Byzantine Studies and other Essays*. London, Althon Press, 1955. Pp 226-239
Becker, Carl H. *Von Werden und Wesen der islamischen Welt, Islamstudien*. Leipzig, Verlag Quelle & Meyer, 1924. Vol I
Beckwith, John. *Early Christian and Byzantine Art.* Harmondsworth, Penguin, 1979
Belting, Hans. 'An Image and Its Function in the Liturgy: The Man of Sorrows in Byzantium.' *Dumbarton Oaks Papers* 34-35 (1980-1981) 1-16
– , Cyril Mango, and Doula Mouriki. *The Mosaics and Frescoes of St. Mary Pammakaristos (Fethiye Camii) at Istanbul*. Washington, Dumbarton Oaks Centre for Byzantine Studies, 1978
Benz, Erst. *The Eastern Orthodox Church. Its Thought and Life*. Garden City, NY, Doubleday, (1957), 1963
Brehier, Louis. *La Querelle des images, VIIIᵉ-IXᵉ siècles*. Paris, 1904
– 'La Querelle des images jusqu'au Concile iconoclaste de 754.' In *Histoire de l'Église depuis les origines, jusqu'a nos jours*, ed A. Fliche and V. Martin. (Paris), Bloud & Gay, 1938. v, 431-470
Bria, Ion. 'L'Espoir du Grand Synode orthodoxe.' *Revue théologique de Louvain* 8 (1977) 51-54
Brown, P. 'A Dark Age Crisis: Aspects of the Iconoclastic Controversy.' *The English Historical Review* 88 (1973) 1-34
Byzantine Art. A European Art. Ninth Exhibition held under the auspices of the Council of Europe. Zappeion Exhibition Hall. Athens, 1964
Campenhausen, Hans von. 'The Theological Problem of Images in the Early Church.' In his *Tradition and Life in the Church*. Philadelphia, Fortress Press, 1968. Pp 171-200
Cavarnos, Constantine. *Orthodox Iconography*. Belmont, Mass., Institute for Byzantine and Modern Greek Studies, 1977
Cresswell, K.A.C. 'The Lawfulness of Painting in Early Islam.' *Arts Islamica* 11-12 (1946) 159-166
Cutler, Anthony. *Transfigurations. Studies in the Dynamics of Byzantine Iconography.*

University Park and London, Pennsylvania State University Press, 1975

Datema, C., ed. *Asterius of Amasea. Homilies I-XIV. Text, introduction, and notes.* Leiden, Brill, 1970

De Boor, Carolus. *See* Theophanes the Confessor

Diehl, Charles. 'Leo III and His Isaurian Dynasty (717-802).' In *The Cambridge Mediaeval History.* Cambridge, Cambridge University Press, (1923), 1927. IV, 1-26

Duschesne, L. *Le Liber pontificalis. Texte, Introduction et Commentaire.* 3 vols. Paris, Ernst Thorin, 1886-1957

Dvornik, Francis. 'The Patriarch Photius and Iconoclasm.' *Dumbarton Oaks Papers* 7 (1953) 69-97

Evdokimoff, Paul. *L'Art de l'icône. Théologie de beauté.* (Paris), Desclée de Brouwer, (1970)

Farès, Bishr. *Philosophie et Jurisprudence illustrés par les Arabes. La Querelle des images en Islam.* Damas, Institut Français de Damas, 1957

Finney, Paul. 'Antecedents of Byzantine Iconoclasm: Christian Evidence before Constantine.' In *The Image and the World. Confrontations in Judaism, Christianity and Islam*, ed Joseph Gutmann. Missoula, Mo., Scholars Press, 1977. Pp 27-47

- 'Gnosticism and the Origins of Early Christian Art.' Paper presented at the meeting of the North American Patristic Society, 1978

Florovsky, Georges. 'The Iconoclastic Controversy.' In his *Christianity and Culture*, vol II of his *Collected Works.* Belmont, Mass., Nordland Publishing Company, 1974. II, 101-119

Forsyth, George H., and K. Weitzmann. *The Monastery of Saint Catherine at Mount Sinai. The Church and Fortress of Justinian.* Ann Arbor, University of Michigan Press, 1973

French, R.M. *The Eastern Orthodox Church.* London, Hutchinson's University Library, 1951

Frey, J.B. 'La Question des images chez les Juifs à la lumière des récentes découvertes.' *Biblica* 15 (1934) 265-300

Galavaris, G. *The Icon in the Life of the Church. Doctrine, Liturgy, Devotion.* Leiden, Brill, 1981

- *The Illustrations of the Liturgical Homilies of Gregory Nazianzenus.* Princeton, Princeton University Press, 1969

- *The Illustrations of the Prefaces in Byzantine Gospels.* Vienna, Verlag der Osterreichischen Akademie der Wissenschaften, 1979

Geischer, H.J. *Der byzantinische Bilderstreit. Texte zur Kirchen und Theologiegeschichte.* Guterloh, 1968. Vol IX

Gerhard, H.P. *The World of Icons.* London, Murray, 1971

Gero, Stephen. *Byzantine Iconoclasm during the Reign of Leo III, with Particular*

Attention to the Oriental Sources. Louvain, Secretariat du Corpus SCO, 1973
- *Byzantine Iconoclasm during the Reign of Constantine V, with Particular Attention to the Oriental Sources.* Louvain, Secretariat du Corpus SCO, 1977
- 'The Eucharistic Doctrine of the Byzantine Iconoclasts and Its Sources.' *Byzantinische Zeitschrift* 68 (1975) 4–22
- 'Notes on Byzantine Iconoclasm in the 8th c.' *Byzantion* 44 (1974) 23–42
Gouillard, Jean. 'Aux origines de l'Iconoclasme: Le Témoignage de Grégoire II?' *Travaux et Mémoirs* 3 (1968) 243–307
- 'Le Synodikon de l'Orthodoxie: Édition et commentaire.' *Travaux et Mémoires* 2 (1967) 1–316
Grabar, André. *L'Art du Moyen Age en Occident: Influences byzantines et orientales.* London, Variorum Reprints, 1980
- *L'Art paléochrétien et l'art byzantin: Receuil d'études 1967–1977.* London, Variorum Reprints, 1979
- *Byzantine Painting.* New York, Rizzoli International Publications, 1979
- *Byzantium. Byzantine Art in the Middle Ages.* London, Methuen, 1966
- *Byzantium. From the Death of Theodosius to the Rise of Islam.* (London), Thames and Hudson, 1966
- *Christian Iconography. A Study of Its Origins.* London, Routledge & Kegan Paul, 1969
- *Early Christian Art. From the Rise of Christianity to the Death of Theodosius.* New York, Odyssey Press, 1968
- *L'Iconoclasme byzantin. Dossier archéologique.* Paris, Collège de France, 1957
- *Martyrium: Recherches sur le culte des reliques et l'art chrétien antique.* London, Variorum Reprints, 1972
- *Les Voies de la création en iconographie chrétienne.* Paris, Flammarion, 1979
Grabar, Oleg. 'Islam and Iconoclasm.' In *Iconoclasm*, Ninth Spring Symposium of Byzantine Studies. Birmingham, Centre for Byzantine Studies, University of Birmingham, 1977. Pp 45–52
Grumel, V. *La Chronologie.* Paris, Presses Universitaires, 1958
Grunebaum, Gustaf E. von. 'Byzantine Iconoclasm and the Influence of the Islamic Environment.' *History of Religions* 2 (1962) 1–10
Guillaume, Alfred. *The Life of Muhammad* (a translation of Ishâq's *Sîrat Rasûl Allâh*). Oxford, Oxford University Press, 1968
- *The Traditions of Islam. An Introduction to the Study of the Hadith Literature.* Beirut, Khayats, 1966
Gutmann, Joseph. 'Deuteronomy: Religious Reformation or Iconoclastic Revolution?' In *The Image and the Word. Confrontations in Judaism, Christianity and Islam*, ed Joseph Gutmann. Missoula, Mo., Scholars Press, 1977. Pp 5–25

- , ed. *No Graven Images. Studies in Art and the Hebrew Bible.* New York, KTAV, (1971), 1972

Haddad, Robert M. 'Iconoclasts and Mut^cazila. The Politics of Anthropomorphism.' *The Greek Orthodox Theological Review* 27 (1982) 287–305

Haldon, J.F. 'Some Remarks on the Background to the Iconoclastic Controversy.' *Byzantinoslavica* 38 (1977) 161–184

Head, C. 'Who Was the Real Leo the Isaurian?' *Byzantion* 41 (1971) 105–108

Hefele, Karl Joseph. *A History of the Councils of the Church, from the Original Documents.* Trans from the German by H.N. Oxenham. Vols II–V: New York, AMS Press, (repr from the 1883–1896 edition), 1972. Vol I (from the 2nd ed, 1894), repr under the title *A History of the Christian Councils*

Henderson, Isabel. 'The Published Works of David Talbot Rice.' In *Studies in Memory of David Talbot Rice*, ed Giles Robertson and George Henderson. Edinburgh, Edinburgh University Press, 1975. Pp 317–325

Hennephof, Herman, ed. *Textus byzantinos ad iconomachiam pertinentes. In usum academicum.* Leiden, Brill, 1969

Hetherington, Paul. *The Painter's Manual of Dionysios of Fourna.* London, Sagittarius Press, 1974

Hodgson, Marshall G.S. 'Islam and Image.' *History of Religions* 3 (1963–1964) 220–260

Holl, Karl. 'Die Schriften des Epiphanius gegen die Bilderverehrung.' *Gesammelte Aufsätze zur Kirchengeschichte.* Tübingen, (1928). II, 356–363

Huber, Paul. *Image et message. Miniatures byzantines de l'Ancient de du Nouveau Testament.* Zurich, Editions Atlantis, 1975

Huskinson, J.M. *Concordia apostolorum: Christian Propaganda at Rome in the Fourth and Fifth Centuries: A Study in Early Christian Iconography and Iconology.* Oxford, BAR, 1982

Iconoclasm. Papers given at the Ninth Spring Symposium of Byzantine Studies, University of Birmingham, March 1975. Birmingham, Centre for Byzantine Studies, University of Birmingham, 1977

Jeffery, Arthur. 'Ghevond's Text of the Correspondence between ^cUmar I and Leo III.' *The Harvard Theological Review* 37 (1944) 269–332

Jenkins, Romilly. *Byzantium. The Imperial Centuries AD 610–1071.* London, Weidenfeld and Nicolson, 1966

John of Damascus. *St John Damascene. Barlaam and Ioasaph.* Loeb Classical Library. Cambridge, Mass., Harvard University Press, (1914), 1962

- See also Kotter

Kaegi, Walter. 'The Byzantine Armies and Iconoclasm.' *Byzantinoslavica* 27 (1966) 48–70

Kalokyris, Constantine D. *The Essence of Orthodox Iconography.* Brookline, Mass.,

Holy Cross Orthodox Press, 1971

Karmiris, Ioannis. *Ta dogmatikâ kai symbolikâ mnemeîa tes Orthodôxou Katholikês Ekklesîas.* Athens, 1960. Vol I

Kirschbaum, Engelbert von. *Lexikon der christlichen Ikonographie.* Rome, Herder, 1968

Kitzinger, Ernst. *The Art of Byzantium and the Mediaeval West: Selected Studies,* ed W. Eugene Kleinbauer. Bloomington, Indiana University Press, 1976

- *Byzantine Art in the Making. Main Lines of Stylistic Development in Mediterranean Art. 3rd–7th Century.* Cambridge, Mass., Harvard University Press, 1977
- 'The Cult of Images in the Age before Iconoclasm.' *Dumbarton Oaks Papers* 8 (1954) 85–150
- 'On Some Icons of the Seventh Century.' In *Late Classical and Mediaeval Studies in Honour of Albert Mathias Friend Jr.,* ed Kurt Weitzmann. Princeton, Princeton University Press, 1955. Pp 132–150

Kontoglou, Fotis. *Ekphrasis tes Orthodôxou eikonographîas.* 2 vols. 2nd ed. Athens, Astir, 1979

Kotter, P. Bonifatius, ed. *Die Schriften des Johannes von Damaskos.* 4 vols. Berlin, Walter de Gruyter, 1969–1981

Kraeling, Carl H. *Excavations at Dura-Europos. Final Report.* New Haven, Yale University Press, 1956. Vol VIII, Part I

Labrecque-Pervouchine, Nathalie. *L'Iconostase. Une évolution historique en Russie.* Montréal, Editions Bellarmin, 1982

Ladner, Gerhart B. 'The Concept of the Image in the Greek Fathers and the Byzantine Iconoclastic Controversy.' *Dumbarton Oaks Papers* 7 (1953) 3–34
- 'Origin and Significance of the Byzantine Iconoclastic Controversy.' *Mediaeval Studies* 2 (1940) 127–149

Lossky, Vladimir. *The Mystical Theology of the Eastern Church.* Cambridge and London, James Clark, 1968

McHugh, Michael P. 'The Demonology of Saint Ambrose in Light of the Tradition.' *Wiener Studien* 12 (1978) 205–231

Maguire, Henry. *Art and Eloquence in Byzantium.* Princeton, Princeton University Press, 1981
- 'The Iconography of Symeon with the Christ Child in Byzantine Art.' *Dumbarton Oaks Papers* 34–35 (1980–1981) 261–269

Mango, Cyril. *The Art of the Byzantine Empire, 312–1483. Sources and Documents.* In the series Sources and Documents in the History of Art, ed H.W. Janson. Englewood Cliffs, NJ, Prentice-Hall, 1972
- 'Historical Introduction.' In *Iconoclasm.* Ninth Spring Symposium of Byzantine Studies. Birmingham, Centre for Byzantine Studies, University of Birmingham, 1977. Pp 1–6

Mansi, Giovanni Domenico. *Sacrorum Conciliorum nova et amplissima collectio.* Florentiae, Expensis Antonii Zatta, 1859–1898

Martin, Edward J. *A History of the Iconoclastic Controversy.* London, SPCK (1930)

The Masterpieces of Byzantine Art. Sponsored by The Edinburgh Festival Society in association with The Royal Scottish Museum and the Victoria & Albert Museum. London, 1958

Meyendorff, John. *Byzantine Theology. Historical Trends and Doctrinal Themes.* New York, Fordham University Press, 1974

Müller, Rudolf. 'The Theological Significance of a Critical Attitude in Hagiography.' *The Ecumenical Review* 14 (1962) 279–282

Munitz, J.A. 'Synoptic Greek Accounts of the Seventh Council.' *Revue des études byzantines* 32 (1974) 147–186

Nellas, Panayiotis. 'Theologie de l'Image: Essai d'anthropologie orthodoxe.' *Contacts* 25 (1973) 259–286

Nelson, Robert S. *The Iconography of Preface and Miniature in the Byzantine Gospel Book.* New York, New York University Press, 1980

Nersessian, Sirarpie der. 'Une Apologie des images du septième siècle.' *Byzantion* 17 (1944–1945) 58–87

– 'Image Worship in Armenia and Its Opponents.' *Armenian Quarterly* 1 (1946) 67–81

Nicodemos Hagioretes. *Pedalion.* Athens, Astir, 1957

Novgorod Icons. 12th–17th Century. Oxford, Phaidon / Leningrad, Aurora Art Publishers, 1980

Onasch, Konrad. *Russian Icons.* Oxford, Phaidon, 1977

Orthodox Centre of Ecumenical Patriarchate. *Towards the Great Council. Introductory Reports of the Interorthodox Commission in Preparation for the Next Great and Holy Council of the Orthodox Church.* London, SPCK, 1972

Ostrogorsky, Georges. 'Les Debuts de la querelle des images.' In *Melanges Charles Diehl*, 2 vols. Paris, Leroux, 1930

– *History of the Byzantine State.* Oxford, Blackwell, 1956

– *Studien zur Geschichte des byzantinischen Bilderstreites.* Amsterdam, Hakkert, 1964

Ouspensky, Leonid. *Theology of the Icon.* Crestwood, NY, St. Vladimir's Seminary Press, 1978

– , and Vladimir Lossky. *The Meaning of Icons.* Boston, Boston Book Art Shop, (1969)

Panagopoulos, John. 'The Orthodox Church Prepares for the Council.' *One in Christ* 13 (1977) 229–237

Papageorgiou, Athanasius. *Icons of Cyprus.* New York, Cowles Bock Co., 1970

Pelikan, Jaroslav. *The Spirit of Eastern Christendom (600–1700).* Vol II of *The Christian Tradition. A History of the Development of Doctrine.* Chicago, University of Chicago Press, 1974

Quasten, Johannes. *Patrology*. 3 vols. Utrecht / Antwerp, Spectrum Publishers, 1966

Rice, David Talbot. *The Appreciation of Byzantine Art*. London, Oxford University Press, 1972

– *Art of the Byzantine Era*. London, Thames and Hudson, 1963

– *Byzantine Art*. Harmondsworth, Penguin, (1935), 1962

– *Byzantine Painting. The Last Phase*. New York, Dial Press, 1968

– and Tamara Talbot Rice. *Icons and Their Dating*. London, Thames and Hudson, 1974

Rice, Tamara Talbot. *Russian Icons*. London, Spring Books, 1963

Sahas, Daniel J. *Epiphanius' Panarion*. Pittsburgh, Pittsburgh Theological Seminary, 1972

– *John of Damascus on Islam, the 'heresy of the Ishmaelites.'* Leiden, Brill, 1972

Schiller, Gertrug. *Iconography of Christian Art*, trans. Janet Seligman. 2 vols. Greenwich, Conn. New York Graphic Society, 1972

Schilling, Sylvester Paul. *Contemporary Continental Theologians*. Nashville, Abingdon Press, 1966

Schmemann, Alexander. *The Historical Road of Eastern Orthodoxy*. New York, Holt, Reinhart and Winston, 1963

Schönborn, Christoph von. *L'Icône du Christ: Fondements théologiques élaborés entre le 1er et le 2e Concile de Nicée (325–787)*. Fribourg, Éditions Universitaires, 1976

Schug-Wille, Christa. *Art of the Byzantine World*. New York, Abrams, 1969

Scouteris, Constantine. 'Never as Gods: Icons and their Veneration.' *Sobornost* 6 (1984) 6–18

– 'Paradosis: the Orthodox Understanding of Tradition.' *Sobornost* 4 (1982) 30–37

A Select Library of the Nicene and Post-Nicene Fathers of the Christian Church. 2nd series. Trans Philip Schaff and Henry Wace. Grand Rapids, Mich, Eerdmans, 1890–1900

Sendler, E. *L'Icône: Image de l'invisible*. Paris, de Brouwer, 1981

The Septuagint Version of the Old Testament, with an English Translation. Grand Rapids, Mich, Zondervan Publishing House, (1970), 1972

Sherrard, Philip. 'The Art of the Icon.' In *Sacrament and Image. Essays in the Christian Understanding of Man*, ed A.M. Allchin. London, The Fellowship of St. Alban and St. Sergius, 1967. Pp 57–67

– 'The Sacrament.' In *The Orthodox Ethos*, ed A.J. Philippou. Oxford, Holywell Press, 1964. Pp 133–139

Soloukhin, Vladimir. *Searching for Icons in Russia*. London, Harvill Press, 1971

Spatharakis, Ioannis. *Corpus of Dated Illuminated Greek Manuscripts to the Year 1453.*
Leiden, Brill, 1981

Splendeur de Byzance. Exhibit at the Musées royaux d'Art et d'Histoire. Brussels,
2 October–2 December 1982

Starr, Joshua. *The Jews in the Byzantine Empire, 641–1204.* New York, Birt Franklin,
(1970)

Stefanidis, Vasilios. *Ekklesiastike Historia.* Athens, Astir, 1959

Stuart, John. *Ikons.* London, Faber and Faber, 1975

Taylor, John. *Icon Painting.* Oxford, Phaidon Press, 1979.

Temple Gallery, 'Icons at the Temple Gallery.' 28 April– 26 June 1982.
Catalogue: *Icons: A Search for Inner Meaning* by Richard Temple. London,
Temple Gallery, 1982

– *Masterpieces of Byzantine and Russian Icon Painting. 12th–16th Century. Exhibition
30 April to 29 June 1974.* London, Temple Gallery, 1974

Theophanes the Confessor. *Chronographia,* ed Carolus de Boor, 2 vols.
Hildesheim, Olms, (1883–1885), 1963

Treasures from the Kremlin. Exhibition of Metropolitan Museum of Art, New York.
New York, Abrams, 1979

Trempelas, Panagiotes N. *Hai treîs leitourgîae: kata tous en Athênais Kôdikas.*
Athens, Verlag der byzantinisch-neugriechischen Iahrbücher, 1935

Trubetskoi, Eugene N. *Icons. Theology in Color.* Crestwood, NY, St. Vladimir's
Seminary Press, 1973

Underwood, Paul A. 'The Deisis Mosaic in the Kahrie Cami at Instanbul.' In
Late Classical and Mediaeval Studies in Honour of Albert Mathias Friend, Jr., ed Kurt
Weitzmann. Princeton, Princeton University Press, 1955. Pp 254–256

– 'First Preliminary Report on the Restoration of the Frescoes in the Kariye
Camii at Instanbul by the Byzantine Institute, 1952–1954.' *Dumbarton Oaks
Papers* 9–10 (1955–1956) 255–288

– *The Kariye Djami.* 3 vols. New York, Pantheon Books, 1966

Vasiliev, A.A. *History of the Byzantine Empire 324–1453.* 2 vols. Madison and
Milwaukee, University of Wisconsin Press, 1964

– 'The Iconoclastic Edict of the Caliph Yazid II, A.D. 721.' *Dumbarton Oaks Papers*
9–10 (1955–1956) 25–47

– 'Sur l'année du rétablissement de l'Orthodoxie.' In his *Byzance et les Arabes.*
Bruxelles, Institute de Philologie et d'Histoire Orientales, 1959. I, 418–421

Walter, Christopher A.A. *Art and Ritual of the Byzantine Church.* London,
Variorum Publications, 1982

– 'Liturgy and Illustration of Gregory of Nazianzen's Homilies.' *Revue des études
byzantines* 29 (1971) 183–212

- *Studies in Byzantine Iconography*. London, Variorum Reprints, 1977
Ware, Kallistos. "The Theology of the Icon. A Short Anthology.' *Eastern Churches Review* 8 (1976) 3-10
- 'The Value of the Material Creation.' *Sobornost* 6 (1971) 154-165
Weitzmann, Kurt. *Byzantine Liturgical Psalters and Gospels*. London, Variorum Reprints, 1980
- *The Icon. Holy Images Sixth to Fourteenth Century*. London, Chatto & Windus, 1978
- *Icons from South Eastern Europe and Sinai*. London, Thames and Hudson, 1968
- *The Monastery of St. Catherine at Mount Sinai. The Icons from the Sixth to the Tenth Century*. Princeton, Princeton University Press, 1976
- , ed. *Late Classical and Mediaeval Studies in Honour of Albert Mathias Friend, Jr.* Princeton, Princeton University Press, 1955
- , Manolis Chatzidakis, and Svetozar Radojcic. *Icons*. New York, Publishers of Art Books, n.d.
- , William C. Loerke, Ernst Kitzinger, and Hugo Buchthal. *The Place of Book Illumination in Byzantine Art*. Princeton, The Art Museum and Princeton University Press, 1975
- , et al. *The Icon*. New York, Knopf, 1982

Biblical References

References to the translator's introduction and footnotes cite the page and note numbers in this book. References to the translated texts cite the Mansi numbers, which appear in the margins opposite the text.

GENESIS
1:26 / 213E
2:16-17 / 361C
3:2 / 277E, 361C
8:21 / 276C
27:29 / 344D
39:6-20 / 360C

EXODUS
20:4-5 / 16, 27 n121
20:34 / 16 n60
25:17-21 / 285A
26:1 / 309B
31:1-6 / 249C
34:17 / 16 n60

LEVITICUS
19:4 / 16 n60
19:19 / 309C
26:1 / 16 n60

NUMBERS
24:9 / 252E
25:7 / 205E

DEUTERONOMY
4:15-19 / 16 n60
5:8-9 / 16 n60, 284C, 285A

6:13 / 285B
27:15 / 16 n60
27:17 / 328A
32:17 / 9 n27, 276C

1 KINGS
17, 18, 19 / 224D

2 KINGS
6:6-7 / 364A
13 / 17 n62
15, 16, 17 / 240D
18:26 / 221D
18:4 / 28 n122

2 CHRONICLES
7:4 / 276C
19:2 / 364D

JOB
6:6 / 245B
38:36 / 249B

PSALMS
7:15-16 / 352B
9:6 / 228D
11(12):2 / 325B
11(12):3 / 228D

11(12):12 / 221A
13(14):3 / 353D
15(16):2 / 316C
18(19):4 / 209A, 273E
22(23):9 / 313D
25(26):5 / 292B
26(27):12 / 273E
30(31):18 / 356E
30(31):20 / 356E
47(48):8 / 221A
49(50):16-18 / 213C
49(50):21 / 208B
63(64):4 / 228A
72(73):20 / 300D
76(77):3 / 361A
88(89):33-34 / 288A
98(99):5 / 309D
105(106):36 / 9 n27
118(119):130 / 205D
144(145):13 / 216E
145(146):10 / 216E
149:6 / 357A

PROVERBS
5:3 / 353D
6:2 / 208B, 264E, 284E
8:7 / 209E
8:9 / 360A-B

Patristic References

References to the translator's introduction and footnotes cite the page and note numbers in this book. References to the translated texts cite the Mansi numbers, which appear in the margins opposite the text.

Index

References to the translator's introduction and footnotes cite the page and note numbers in this book. References to the translated texts cite the Mansi numbers, which appear in the margins opposite the text.

TORONTO MEDIEVAL TEXTS AND TRANSLATIONS

General Editor: Brian Merrilees

1 *The Argentaye Tract* edited by Alan Manning
2 *The Court of Sapience* edited by E. Ruth Harvey
3 *Le Turpin français, dit le Turpin I* édité par Ronald N. Walpole
4 *Icon and Logos: Sources in Eighth-Century Iconoclasm* translated by Daniel J. Sahas